Foreword

Sleek, futuristic and deadly – the General Dynamics F-16 Fighting Falcon was born from the crucible of the air war over Vietnam and the need for cheaper, simpler and more manoeuvrable fighter aircraft with which to combat the many thousands of Soviet bloc-supplied aircraft operated by the enemies of what was seen as the 'free world'.

Even by today's standards, an early production F-16 from the late 1970s looks thoroughly modern – though the design is now more than 40 years old. It has a seamless, blown canopy giving an unrivalled 360-degree view from the cockpit, a blended fuselage and wing joint which usefully holds a lot of fuel, a wide-mouthed air inlet feeding air into the single, powerful turbofan engine, a multi-mode radar which can switch from air-to-air and air-to-ground modes at the flick of a switch and a deadly air-to-air missile on each wingtip.

Back in the early 1970s this was the pinnacle of modern design, integrating the need for a high thrust-to-weight ratio, unrivalled manoeuvrability – thanks to its relaxed static stability and fly-by-wire system with computer control – and all for an affordable price.

I remember the first time I saw the shape of the F-16 – in flight at an air show in the early 1980s – and the performance of the machine, lightly-loaded for a display routine was truly breath-taking. Talking to the pilot afterwards and seeing his smile made me realise this was indeed a pilot's aeroplane, all in the mould of single-seat fighters of old.

With more than 4500 sold to air forces across the world and with an enviable combat record, it has set the standard for performance, value for money and flexibility. That flexibility has seen the F-16 develop away from its lightweight fighter concept roots into a potent, multi-role machine, which can carry weaponry, sensors and advanced electronics that would have been unthinkable back in the late 1960s when the machine was first on the drawing board.

That original design has matured. Right up until the F-16C of the 1990s, the basic design has stayed true to the original, but since then, each lump and bump on the Block 50, 60 and now 70 series of Falcon has offered improved sensors or range while more powerful engines have largely kept performance intact.

Sure, today's F-16 Viper is light years away from the simple, lightweight point-defence fighter envisaged by the Lightweight Fighter Mafia, but it has evolved and matured into the finest and most exported fourth-generation combat aircraft around the world and many would argue the latest variants offer a real-world capability and value-for-money that makes it a wiser choice than its logical successor – the Lockheed Martin F-35 Lightning II.

It would be fair to say that the Lockheed Martin F-16 is now in the twilight years of its development – but not its operational deployment. With new models such as the Block 60 Desert Falcon, F-16 Viper Block 70, QF-16 target drones and rumours of possible new models and UCAV versions of the redoubtable machine, it could well be that the F-16 will continue to roll off the production line at Fort Worth for a little while longer, and yet it will stay in service for perhaps a further 30 years or more, maybe beating the service record of the legendary F-4 Phantom II.

Whatever the future holds for the Lockheed Martin F-16 Fighting Falcon, it has already entered the annals of aviation history, but the beauty is that this versatile machine doubtless has many more pages yet to write. The Viper story is far from over just yet.

Bertie Simmonds

Contents

AUTHOR: Bertie Simmonds
DESIGN: atg-media.com
PUBLISHER: Steve O'Hara
PUBLISHING DIRECTOR: Dan Savage
REPROGRAPHICS: Jonathan Schofield and Paul Fincham
MARKETING MANAGER: Charlotte Park
COMMERCIAL DIRECTOR: Nigel Hole

PUBLISHED BY: Mortons Media Group Ltd, Media Centre, Morton Way, Horncastle, Lincolnshire LN9 6JR.
Tel: 01507 529529

ACKNOWLEDGEMENTS & BIBLIOGRAPHY:
- Modern Combat Aircraft (16) F-16 Fighting Falcon (Bill Gunston)
- Fighters Over Israel (Lon Nordeen)
- World Airpower Journal (various)
- Great Combat Aircraft Lockheed Martin F-16 Volumes 1 and 2 (Frederic Lert)
- Osprey Combat Aircraft 61 F-16 Fighting Falcon Units of Operation Iraqi Freedom (Steve Davies and Doug Dildy)
- Air War on the Edge (Bill Norton) and Ben Dunnell and Tyler Rogoway for quotes in chapter four.

WEBSITES:
www.codeonemagazine.com,
www.f-16.net

DOCUMENTARIES: Raid on the Reactor

PHOTOGRAPHY:
USAF/DOD, Squadron Prints/Berry Vissers for the profiles, Andrew Timmerman, Amit Agronov, Ivan Voukadinov, Milan Mandic, Lindsey Hendersen, Holly Simmonds. Mike Badrocke for cutaways.

PRINTED BY: William Gibbons and Sons, Wolverhampton

ISBN: 978-1-911276-37-1

FALCON FACTS

Almost 3000 pilots world-wide have achieved 1000 hours on the F-16.

Maid of all work: a US Navy Phantom from VF-111 delivers its payload.

The Crucible

The Vietnam War marked a big change to the United States of America. Not only to the fabric of society itself, but to the way it would wage any future war and the weapons it would employ. From this crucible was born the Lightweight Fighter Concept.

The United States of America was in a bad way. In the late 1960s it was embroiled in a costly war it couldn't hope to win (at least not the way it was then fighting it) a succession of Presidents had been faced with difficult decisions on the future prosecution of the war in South East Asia, along with how communism would be fought and how to procure the future weapons with which such wars would be fought. Back home there were demonstrations, repercussions and remonstrations. In the air war above Vietnam, things weren't going right.

Rewind 15 or more years and the air war over Korea was a different story. While it could be argued that the MiG-15 had a slight performance advantage over the North American F-86 Sabres that were battling it out from the end of 1950, it seemed that pilot quality and training had made a real difference. The kill ratio was anything between 9:1 and 5.8:1 in favour of the US/UN pilots (depending on what statistics you believe) while against the elite secret Soviet squadrons it was almost equal at around 1.4:1.

The problem in Vietnam was that this ratio had slumped to as little as 1.5:1. It's worth stating that any time you mention statistics, there's going to be an argument and even with the previously accepted Korean War stats, some suggest that the real trade off was as low as 2:1 in the UN's favour, with the Soviets keeping their best pilots in the battle (as the German had during the Second World War) while the UN rotated successful pilots out of the theatre of war instead. But when it came to the stats for the air war over Vietnam, whatever way you looked at it, things weren't good for the USA.

There were a number of reasons for such poor performance initially. For a start, most of the 'Free World's' armed services were trained and equipped for a major worldwide nuclear struggle with the Warsaw Pact forces that would never come. In military aviation terms, the US Air Force and US Navy were equipped with some of the finest and most advanced military hardware the world had ever seen, all to be used strategically for taking on quantity with quality.

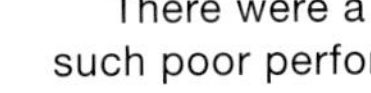

At the cutting edge of this was the F-4 Phantom II, which in various guises served both the USAF and USN. When fully loaded for air combat this leviathan weighed in at 56,000lb (25,000kg) and was armed with four radar-guided AIM-7 Sparrows and four heat-seeking AIM-9B Sidewinders as well as up to three external fuel tanks.

This was a machine designed initially for carrier-borne interception duties, and later developed as a multi-role USAF fighter-bomber. Spearheading the USAF's bomber force was the F-105 Thunderchief. Incredibly fast down low, it was designed as a nuclear bomber with which to face the huge Soviet threat, but now both these types – and others – were facing a war they couldn't possibly win.

The fact that they couldn't win the air war wasn't down to the performance of the machines or their pilots – both of these would prove to be flexible enough to win the battles tactically as the war progressed – instead it was the overall strategy and the hated 'Rules of Engagement' (ROE) that would hamstring the most well-equipped and modern combined air force that the world had yet seen. The notorious ROE often meant that certain targets could not be attacked, or air-to-air targets could not be engaged until a positive identification could be made. Politics ruled tactics and strategy, it seemed, and they were strange bedfellows.

ABOVE: Da Nang Air Force Base during the Vietnam War.

Also in the background were other issues. Fighter pilots who had fought during previous conflicts and were still around during the Vietnam War bemoaned the lack of positive ACM or Air Combat Manoeuvres training. When legendary Second World War ace Colonel Robin Olds came to take command of the 8th Tactical Fighter Wing at the end of 1966, he felt he knew what the problems were. It was as much about tactics as politics. He had long fought against a lack of ACM training, instead claiming that the USAF just wanted pilots to learn how to take off and land safely – while also delivering ordinance.

In a time when long-range missiles offered 100% kill-probability at 20 miles plus, the training syllabus wasn't making dogfighting a priority. Instead, it was the safe employment of the weapons systems that aviators were being trained to carry out. At squadron level, pilots often ignored the rules and would spend some time sneakily dogfighting, but this was between squadron mates flying similar aircraft. By the time Olds was ensconced in the Wolf Pack – as the 8th TFW was known – the big F-4Cs and Ds were up against smaller, lighter, harder-to-see and better manoeuvring machines.

And – of course – the tactics still sucked. Olds – a 12-kill ace – sat down with his pilots and came up with Operation Bolo, an exemplary piece of strategy, where F-4s masqueraded as heavily-laden F-105s, luring up MiG-21s and destroying seven of them. It was an early blip in an otherwise frustrating spell for the USAF in South East Asia.

The United States Navy had remained in the ACM game, but the ROE still hurt them badly. Both services found that blind faith in missiles meant that their chief fighter plane came without a short-range cannon. The argument went that it wasn't needed as fighter planes didn't dogfight anymore. Much has been said of the reasons for neglecting to fit an internal gun to the F-4 family. In both Navy and Air Force guises, for most of that decade the common variants in service F-4B, G, J and N in the Navy and F-4C and Ds in the Air Force didn't have an internal gun, although Air Force kills were made using SUU-16/A cannon pods, carrying the M61 20mm Gatling-type gun, as we will see.

Two aircraft in the Navy and Air Force's inventory were front-line types that did have guns: the Navy's F-8 Crusader family and the USAF's F-105.

Admiral Paul Gillcrist flew everything from the F6F Hellcat of the Second World War to the Grumman F-14 Tomcat. He went on record as saying that the F-8's 6:1 kill ratio in the early part of the Vietnam war came despite some tricky handling characteristics but it seems clear that the relative success of the Crusader compared to the early efforts with the F-4 come from the training differences between the various cadres. With the F-4 specifically using and training with beyond visual range (BVR) AIM-7 Sparrows, it was a question of head-on intercepts, while the Crusaders – armed only with AIM-9B Sidewinders and four 20mm cannons utilised these weapons in their training and therefore were adept at old-school dogfighting tactics.

Comparatively, the F-4 had a 5.4:1 kill ratio for the duration of the Vietnam War, which is much less if you scrutinise just the 1965-68 era where the Crusader shared the struggle, getting a 6:1 kill ratio. In that period F-8s shot down 18 enemy aircraft and three probables compared to 13 by the F-4s in the same period. Although again, in 1965 the first three kills were made by F-4Bs

RIGHT: Anti-radar configured F-4C shows that the Rhino did it all in Nam.

using the often recalcitrant Sparrow, so once more stats can seem to prove anything.

While it can be argued that while the Crusader had the best individual exchange for a US aircraft type of the Vietnam War, it wasn't all down to cannons. Often those temperamental four 20mm Colt Mk 12 cannon (with between 110 and 125 rounds of high explosive and tracer rounds) would jam in turns of more than 3.5g. The low round count also told (compare this to the SUU-16/A or 23 with 1200 rounds) but pilots could choose to fire top or bottom pairs of guns rather than all four at once, which helped save ammo.

> ***Then the MiG exploded and I broke left to avoid the debris. Then I reversed right and saw the MiG in two sections falling towards the ground***

Either way, with the ROE as they were it was quickly realised that a cannon was a good thing to have on an aircraft and it still is, despite the fact that the last recorded air-to-air guns kill was back in 1988. For the Air Force this meant using podded cannon – the SUU family – which replaced the centreline tank on the F-4C and D. The USAF began to use the SUU-16/A on F-4s from May 1967 and the change it brought was almost instant. On May 14 – a day after an F-105 had destroyed a MiG-17 with cannon-fire – aircrew from the 366th TFW destroyed three MiG-17s – two of them with the podded cannon.

Major James Hargrove and 1st Lt Stephen DeMuth heard MiG calls from a formation of F-105s, the lead Thud calling bogies in their 9 o'clock position. Dropping their external fuel tanks, Hargrove and DeMuth tackled one element of the enemy formation with their three and four tackling the second. The combat would take 20 minutes to reach a conclusion, with the F-4s taking on seven MiGs out of the 16-MiG formation.

Hargrove's kill came within five minutes of combat commencing. He had already fired Sidewinders and Sparrows against three other MiG 17s and missed. This was his fourth engagement and he decided to use his SUU-16 gun-pod. In a USAF tactics paper published following the war, he recalled: "The MiG-15 was in a descending turn to the right when we attacked from 20-degrees angle off its tail. I opened fire at around 2000ft from the MiG and continued firing until – at 300ft – flame erupted from the top of the MiG fuselage.

"Then the MiG exploded and I broke left to avoid the debris. Then I reversed right and saw the MiG in two sections falling towards the ground." With other MiGs looking for revenge, Hargrove had to leave the area before he could see his victim hit the ground. Just five minutes later, Captain James Craig Junior, in the third F-4 also downed a MiG with the SUU-16 after missing two MiGs with AIM-7s.

Craig recalled: "Three MiGs were sighted at 9 o'clock low in a left turn. I barrel-rolled to the right and rolled in behind the trailing MiG-17. He tightened up his left turn then reversed hard to the right as I came into guns range. I followed the MiG through his turn reversal, pulled lead then fired a two and a half second burst from my 20mm cannon. Flames erupted from his right wing root and extended past the tailpipe. As I yo-yoed high, the MiG rolled out to wing level in a slight descent and I observed fire coming from the left side of the fuselage.

"I initiated a follow-up attack, but before I could fire he burst into flames

***RIGHT:** Vought's F-8 Crusader was a 'proper' dogfighter and it had guns.*

***BELOW:** The Phantom finally got an internal gun with the F-4E model.*

from the cockpit aft and pitched over and dived vertically into the under-cast. The kills with the gun mode could not have been made with a missile." Later engagements that day were made in similar tactical situations yet the F-4s in those circumstances didn't have cannon, leading to frustration as more than one F-4 had to let a sure-fire cannon kill extend away into Sparrow or Sidewinder parameters.

With the argument over the need for an internal gun settled even before these 1967 combats, development of the F-4E version of the venerable Phantom had begun. This version became available in the late 1960s, in time for service in the Vietnam air war. The US Navy, on the other hand, never developed its own internal cannon-armed F-4. With the development of the F-4E and the use of cannon pods, as well as the M61 being used in the Thunderchief, guns scored an impressive number of kills in Vietnam. The F-4C and D models took down 10 MiGS ➤

ABOVE: **Colonel Robin Olds was an advocate of dogfight training**

BELOW: **For the US Navy, USAF and Marines, the F-4 was the best they had in theatre.**

with podded cannon, the F-4E shot down five enemy aircraft with the internal M61 while the F-105 took down three MiGs (one of which was shared with an F-4D) and even the B-52 bomber shot down two MiGs with its tail barbette of four 0.5in machine guns.

Major Gary Retterbush scored two MiG kills towards the end of the Vietnam air war with the F-4E and his engagement is striking due to the behaviour of his missiles. His first kill was made on September 12, 1972. He recalls: "We were part of a large strike package going into the general area of Hanoi. The strike force was jumped by several MiGs who came from high and behind and dove down through us. Of course they fired missiles as they came. It was a rather chaotic time! During the moves that followed, our flight broke and we split up into two, two-ship elements.

"I was behind a MiG-21 and my back-seater got a good lock on. Conditions were excellent; almost text book. I fired two AIM-7s which did not guide. They simply went ballistic. I continued to close and got a good lock-on for the AIM-9s. I ended up firing three of them but they either did not guide or the proximity fuse did not function. The last missile went right by the cockpit and got the MiG pilot's attention!

"He broke and I followed. I was able to get in position for using the gun and fired a couple of bursts. They impacted on the left wing near the junction with the fuselage. The MiG started to burn almost at once. I was now closing too fast and did a high speed yo-yo which once again put me in position to fire another burst. These impacted in and around the cockpit and the aircraft went into a pitch up. I could see the pilot slumped forward in the cockpit. The aircraft then stalled and snapped down as I went past it. The MiG was observed to continue burning until it impacted the ground in a cloud of smoke."

This showed the usefulness of the internal gun (no need to sacrifice a centreline tank) and the almost shocking failure rate of missiles deployed.

Retterbush would score a further guns kill in the F-4E on October 8, 1972. This was another interesting example of cannon versus missiles. With Red Crown, the call sign for the radar-equipped USS Long Beach cruiser in the Gulf of Tonkin, warning him of a MiG at their 10 o'clock high, Retterbush called on his aircraft to dump their tanks and turn towards the attacker, while ordering the bombers he was escorting to break. He says: "The MiG dove down trying to follow the breaking bombers and I was on his tail but at a very high angle off. I fired two AIM-9s but did not expect them to guide as the angle off was far beyond the limits. They went ballistic.

"I then jettisoned the rest of the missiles including the AIM-7s. I was yelling for Bob, my back-seater to give me a caged sight as the recticle was completely off of the windscreen due to the angle and the Gs. He got it locked and I very quickly did a little Kentucky windage, pulled the pipper way out in front and high and fired a short burst. To my pleasant surprise it impacted the MiG in the fuselage near the left wing and it immediately burst into flames.

"The pilot did not hesitate at all and ejected. Then came an even bigger surprise; he had a beautiful pastel pink parachute! I

ABOVE: ***Vought's A-7D shows the family likeness of the F-8.***

circled him one time and then regrouped the flight for our trip home. Upon checking the ammo after landing, I found I had fired only 96 rounds and that included the 'exciter' burst which was probably about the half."

When looking at the stats comparing gun kills against missile kills, the big difference wasn't always simply down to the aircraft that carried a gun or not, instead it was improving tactics from both Navy and Air Force crews.

Poor missile performance led to the Ault Report, where US Navy Captain Frank Ault – at the command of Admiral Tom Moorer – looked into the performance of the Navy's air-to-air missile systems in the various engagements over Vietnam. The report itself was to look at the quality of the missiles supplied to the Navy, examine in detail how and if they were being operated correctly at squadron level and if the systems actually worked well in the air-to-air-mission. A big part of this was to examine if the pilots and squadrons fully understood how to exploit the capabilities of the aircraft's missile system. One of the major results of the report, which studied the period between 1965 and 1968, was to look at the need for advanced training in fighter versus fighter tactics. This led to the formation of the Navy Fighter Weapons School, known more famously as TOPGUN.

> ***The pilot did not hesitate at all and ejected. Then came an even bigger surprise; he had a beautiful pastel pink parachute!***

The USAF were rapidly coming to their own conclusions. Various 'Project Red Baron' initiatives were instigated from 1966 through to 1974 and – like TOPGUN – the basic finding was 'train like you fight, fight like you train'. This led to the Red Flag series of exercises and the beginning of the Aggressor Squadrons, where experienced, highly-trained pilots in the art of dogfighting would aim to pass on hard-earned lessons to the pilots at squadron level. With both TOPGUN and Red Flag, safe places to practice such missions led to the development of areas such as the Air Combat Manoeuvring Range at Yuma for the Navy/Marines and the Air Combat Manoeuvring Instrumentation range at Nellis. By the time these key decisions had been made about the tactical/training future of US fighter pilots, the successor to the mighty F-4 Phantom had already been designed, using lessons learned over South East Asia.

ENTER THE F-15 EAGLE

The lessons of the Vietnam air-war had to be learned quickly, so in 1965 the USAF began early discussions on a new fighter aircraft. It is beyond the scope of this book to go into the details of the development of the McDonnell-Douglas F-15 Eagle, suffice to say that the original specification called for a lighter-weight machine following on from the lessons learned over South East Asia and a machine that would have a handy "25% superiority over the MiG-21".

Then in 1967 the Soviet Union revealed the new MiG-25 interceptor, a high-speed, high-altitude fighter dedicated to ➤

the stand-off interception of incoming aircraft. With a top speed of Mach 2.8 and apparently armed with long-range missiles and a capable radar, that old American need to have the best equipment began to rear its ugly head. The USAF wouldn't stand for anything smaller, slower and more agile – even if such a machine would be available in the sort of numbers that would go some way to counter the quantitative edge that America faced back in Vietnam and in Europe.

The nascent F-X proposal which would become the F-15 Eagle was changed to take into consideration both the revelation of the MiG-25 and MiG-23. So in 1968 the new requirements were for a single-seat fighter with a maximum take-off weight of 40,000lb (18,000kg) and with a maximum speed of Mach 2.5 and a thrust-to-weight ratio approaching unity at mission weights.

With four companies expressing interest and submitting proposals, by December 1969 McDonnell-Douglas were announced the winners. The resultant aircraft promised to be everything the F-4 was, and wasn't. In no way was the F-15 going to be a tactical strike-fighter with multi-role capability (at least not until the Strike Eagle variant) however it was going to have the added benefit of being able to out-manoeuvre anything in the sky thanks to its large wing and two Pratt & Whitney F100 engines. Other lessons learned from Vietnam saw the inclusion of a 20mm Gatling gun in the starboard wing root and a blown 'bubble canopy'. Like the F-4, it was to become an aviation legend.

With the F-X/F-15 becoming such a large aircraft to tackle the MiG 25, it also meant it could carry a big radar and lots of missiles. The F-15 carried four AIM-7 Sparrow missiles semi-recessed under its belly, like the F-4, it could also carry four AIM-9 Sidewinder missiles and 940 rounds of ammunition for that cannon. In the large nose was carried the most advanced radar of the time – the Hughes APG-63 pulse-doppler 'look-down-shoot-down' unit.

***ABOVE:** In a bid for commonality the F-111 was going to serve both the US Navy and the USAF.*

So, to all intents and purposes, it was a big, powerful, high-performance machine. As the saying went in the Pentagon at the time – 'why have a Volkswagen when you can have a Cadillac?' And the F-15 was truly in the vein of the previous 'Cadillac of the skies' the P-51 Mustang. With such a powerful fighter being built for the USAF, surely there was no room for any other fighter aircraft in the stable; especially with the feeling of standardisation still pervading congress.

A FIGHTER AT ANY COST?

By 1970 the US Government had spent a fortune on fighters and developing them – ironic, considering the background from the 1960s.

When John F Kennedy became president early in the decade, with him came a man with a mission: Robert S McNamara.

***BELOW:** The MiG-17 was one of the F-4s chief adversaries in Vietnam.*

McNamara was to become the longest-serving Secretary of Defence, serving from 1961 until 1968 under both Kennedy and Lyndon Johnson. Coming from the Ford Motor Company, McNamara wanted the best value for his buck and this was going to be the case when it came to defence spending too. In today's world of the Lockheed-Martin F-35 being used for all the US air-arms, McNamara's aim of cutting costs and building one fighter for both the US Air Force and the US Navy seems a logical one, and in September 1961 it was decided that an aircraft would be developed to fulfil both the Air Force's tactical fighter role and the Navy's fleet defence role. This was despite months of wrangling between both forces as to the varied and different needs that made up their requirements. They felt it couldn't be done – but the Government felt otherwise.

The Tactical Fighter Experimental programme then would fulfil two main roles and the winner of the competition was announced at the end of 1962 – it was General Dynamics. The Fort Worth, Texas-based company would undertake the tricky task of making an aircraft suited to the tactical role for the USAF and (with help from carrier-fighter experts Grumman) build a fleet defence fighter for the US Navy.

The aircraft designed and built for these roles was to become the F-111. The idea was that commonality and a longer, larger production run would lead to reduced costs (just as they allegedly should today with the F-35) but here is where things began to unravel.

Basically, the variable-geometry F-111 was too big and too heavy to be a fighter

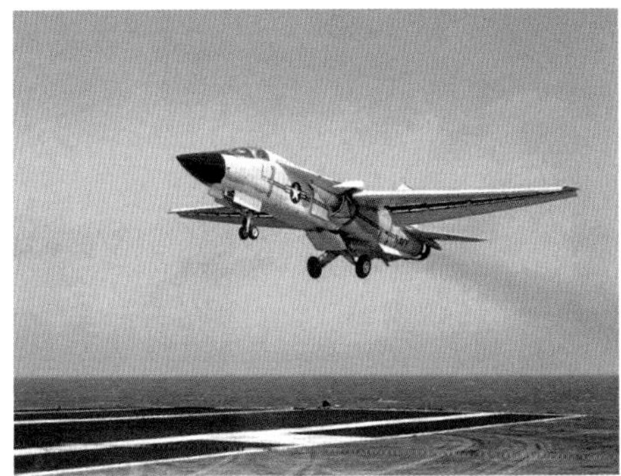

ABOVE: The 'Sea Pig' F-111B during carrier trials.

BELOW: The F-111's avionics and engines would be at the heart of its successor.

– not that this unduly worried those in power. After all, dogfighting was a thing of the past and it was all about carrying a lot of missiles a long way to kill at a distance. Substitute missiles for bombs and you almost have the Air Force's ideal aircraft, but things got steadily worse for the naval F-111B. This version first flew in 1965 and – while it was later shown with the similarly-sized F-14 Tomcat that a machine of this size could become a successful fighter – the F-111's weight and complexity would eventually be its undoing.

Worse was the fact that the aircraft suffered three development crashes and four fatalities. Costs had also tripled, the Pratt & Whitney TF30 powerplants were giving issues, were under-powered and carrier suitability was being described as 'marginal'. Little wonder it was nicknamed the Sea Pig by the men handling the brute on the deck. The final coup de grace on the sorry project came in 1968 during congressional hearings into the troubled TFX. When asked by Senator John C Stennis whether a more powerful engine would turn around the F-111B's fortunes, Admiral Tom Connolly responded by saying: "Mr Chairman, all the thrust in Chistendom wouldn't make a fighter out of that aircraft."

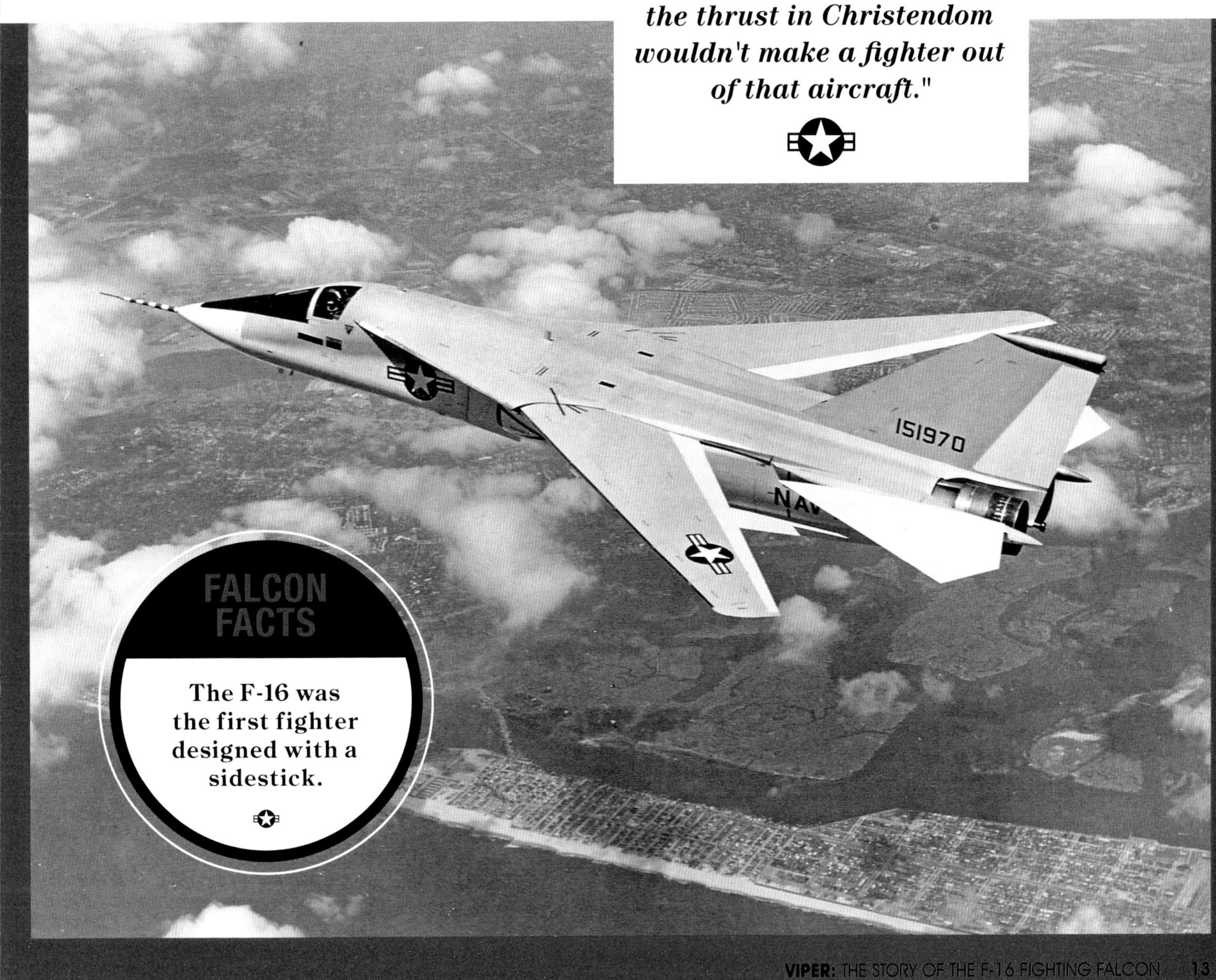

The end result was that the US Government had spent almost $400 million on the F-111B. History shows that the engines and weapons systems involved would be used again on the lighter (but still heavy) F-14 Tomcat and despite the cancellation of both the B-model and a buy for the UK, the General Dynamics F-111 would eventually mature as a fine low-level, high-speed tactical fighter. By the time the project was killed, McNamara had departed the Department of Defence and was head of the World Bank. In an ultimate irony, the US Navy's search for a light-attack aircraft to replace the A-4 Skyhawk led to the adoption of the Vought A-7 Corsair II.

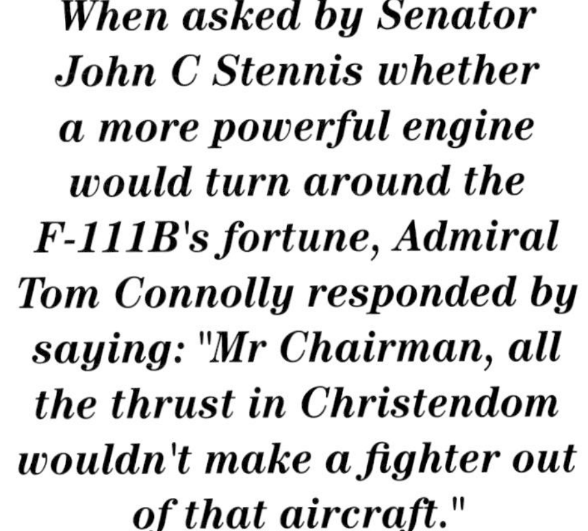

During the request for proposals, it was stated that the aircraft had to be based on an existing model to save money and ensure that it was a proven design. In reality the A-7 only shared the basic shape of the F-8 Crusader and very few common parts, but following the Navy's successful debut of the A-7A into combat over Vietnam in 1967, the USAF quickly adopted its own version – the A-7D – for its own tactical role over South East Asia. So commonality of a sort did come to the Air Force and Navy during the 1970s and 1980s.

With the USAF having both the F-X (F-15 Eagle) and TFX (F-111) on course for service entry in the early 1970s and the US Navy looking to the F-14, many in Washington and beyond were wondering why you had to buy an expensive aircraft, when

> ***When asked by Senator John C Stennis whether a more powerful engine would turn around the F-111B's fortune, Admiral Tom Connolly responded by saying: "Mr Chairman, all the thrust in Christendom wouldn't make a fighter out of that aircraft."***

FALCON FACTS

The F-16 was the first fighter designed with a sidestick.

it makes sense to have more examples of a cheaper machine. Conversely, many in the armed forces were also happy with the way things were.

With the size of the air-arm already set by congress, many in the USAF and US Navy weren't interested in a cheaper, less capable fighter – that would mean a smaller share of the defence budget. Ironically it would be a group of analysts from the same crop of Washington whizz-kids that doomed the F-111B to failure with the idea of reduced costs in commonality that would show what could be done with just a little.

ENTER THE MAFIA

In the late 1960s and early 1970s the F-15 Eagle programme was sacrosanct in the USAF and the Pentagon. Despite the lessons of Vietnam, many within the USAF and the United States Government at the time truly believed that they needed to give the best equipment to their fighting men – and by best they meant biggest, most technologically advanced and most expensive. Ironic, considering that in many cases high-tech F-4s were being beaten by lowly bargain basement MiG-17s. Cost-cutting and cost-sharing clearly had its own problems (as seen with the F-111B) but for some the clear lesson of combat was a need for simpler, cheaper airplanes and more of them. As Lenin once said and as was proved (after a fashion) in the Great Patriotic War: quantity has a quality all of its own.

As Lenin once said and as was proved (after a fashion) in the Great Patriotic War: quantity has a quality all of its own

It was this dictum by which the 'hi-lo' mix of USAF procurement of the 1970s aimed to hedge its bets. Time shows that perhaps the boundaries between 'hi-lo' became blurred, but it's shaped the USAF and air forces around the world ever since. But who were the Lightweight Fighter Mafia and how did such cost-effective lightweight heresy become the equivalent of a Papal Bull?

The core of the Lightweight Fighter Mafia were: Colonel Everest Riccioni, Colonel John Boyd and civilian analyst Pierre Sprey. Others are mentioned as also being 'in the family', including Deputy Defence Secretary David Pickard and General Dynamics' Harry Hillaker, but mainly as a result of history. As the name of the group suggests, perhaps it was from Colonel Everest Riccioni's Italian background that the name first came and it was one that really showed what was thought of the heresy of accepted Pentagon wisdom of the time.

We've seen that the first F-X programme that led to the F-15 Eagle saw the original specifications increase in weight and sophistication, but many inside the Pentagon were vehemently against weight and sophistication. Sprey – a weapons systems analyst – argued for a simple machine in the 25,000lb (11,340kg) class, armed with a simple radar system, a gun and a pair of lightweight missiles. Clearly this would be a simpler, smaller machine which would help bolster the numbers of aircraft in the USAF in comparison to the 'silver bullet' F-15. The US already had such an aircraft in the F-5 family of machines. The Northrop F-5A Freedom Fighter first flew in 1959 and a modernised version of this was offered in the 1970 IFA or 'International Fighter Aircraft' programme. The F-5C Tiger had served in Vietnam, showing itself to be a useful tactical jet, but it was never used in South East Asia in any numbers. Instead many air forces across the world bought the first incarnation of the F-5 in large numbers for their own air forces.

The F-5E Tiger II first flew in 1972 for the IFA programme. It was designed to beat the MiG-21 and offered many of the same advantages as any future lightweight fighter programme for the USAF would. Again, the Air Force did procure them, but didn't field them as a pure fighter, instead later using them for dissimilar air combat training. Outside of the USA they were popular exports and still serve in many air-arms to this day. It's no surprise that Sprey was a big fan, declaring that the F-5 was the most effective US fighter when taking

ABOVE: ***Grumman's F-14 Tomcat was big – but still a dogfighter and had a gun.***

LEFT: ***From the F-X programme came the F-15 Eagle – air-to-air par excellence.***

ABOVE RIGHT: ***The USAF went back to developing prototypes for their programmes: the Northrop A-9 was a contender in the A-X attack plane contest.***

BELOW RIGHT: ***The A-9 lost out in the A-X fight to the Fairchild Republic A-10 Thunderbolt II.***

into consideration cost and performance.

However, as mentioned, the appearance of the MiG-25 Foxbat in 1967 made many think that bigger, faster and more sophisticated was the way forward, so it was that any discussions about lightweight fighters had to be just that. All that could be done was put forward their own F-XX lightweight proposal as a mere back-up to the F-X and F-15 Eagle should anything go wrong.

By 1969 a Pentagon paper on tactical air power – taking into consideration many of the issues that had come to light over South East Asia – suggested that the Navy and Air Force should adopt a machine in the F-XX class as a replacement for the-then current F-15 and F-14 programmes, therefore increasing the numbers of aircraft in both services as they would be considerably cheaper.

With the shadow of the MiG-25 still looming large, this wasn't what the top brass of either service wanted to hear, so they stuck to their guns and waved the flag for the larger, more complex and more costly machines. Colonel Riccioni was among those who believed in a lightweight machine. He was a pilot who was assigned to a staff position in research and development. He had been sent to investigate suggestions of how capable a lightweight fighter (LWF) could be and he liked what he heard.

Riccioni, or 'Rich' as he was known was assigned to the F-15 Office in Tactical Fighter Requirements on the Air Staff, in the Pentagon during 1969. As powerful a fighter as the F-15 Eagle was becoming, Rich himself became deeply uneasy as it grew more and more expensive. In 2014, he recalled: "I achieved little to improve the F-15, but I saw it as a threat to our airpower as its cost would shrink Tactical Air Command and never allow the USAF sufficient numbers for future wars."

With this in mind, Rich decided to see what he could do about it, and that's how he came into contact with Colonel John Boyd and Pierre Sprey. Together they came up with specifications for a small, light fighter; its performance, range, top speed and agility requirements.

"My efforts would have been fruitless but for these two geniuses," Riccioni would later recall. "They believed in me and my programme and joined me to form a triumvirate still renowned as The Fighter Mafia. Boyd and I briefed the USAF and the aircraft contractors on the concept. For some reason the generals only wanted the F-15 for the foreseeable future, but amazingly I was allowed to work on this assignment."

The Fighter Mafia had powerful friends outside of the USAF – most notably in 1969 Deputy Secretary of Defence David Packard (co-founder of the Hewlett-Packard) and 1973-75's Secretary of Defence James Schlesinger, who batted for their ideas. More luck came as there was a move in the Nixon administration to get away from the recent method of procuring aircraft. The policy of Total Package Procurement had resulted in the F-111 debacle, where ➤

THE LIGHTWEIGHT FIGHTER MAFIA

*LEFT: **John Boyd's theories revolutionised combat aircraft thinking.***

*RIGHT: **One of the fathers of the F-16 and A-10, Sprey's thinking dominated combat aircraft design for a generation.***

COLONEL JOHN RICHARD BOYD 1927-1997

Boyd was a former North American F-86 Sabre pilot who ended up having an effect on future fighter development and procurement that went far beyond his combat career.

Boyd joined the USAAF in 1944, missing combat as he was too young although he was stationed in Japan after the end of the Second World War. Arriving in Korea in March 1953 he took part in 22 missions during the conflict, but again he was perhaps a little too late to score any kills. However, his performance as a pilot saw him attend the Fighter Weapons School where he graduated with top honours and where he eventually stayed on as an instructor.

With a long, colourful and distinguished career, Boyd picked up a number of nicknames. These included, 'Forty Second Boyd' to illustrate who quickly he could go from a position of disadvantage to advantage in an F-86 during air-combat manoeuvres, to 'Genghis John' for his spikey personality during a heated debate, to 'The Mad Major' perhaps a negative appellation from those opposed to his heartfelt beliefs. Then he was also known as the 'Ghetto Colonel' as he was believed to lead a 'no frills' lifestyle.

However, there is no mistaking his impact on modern military thinking. During the 1960s, Boyd and a civilian called Thomas Christie developed the Energy-Manoeuvrability or E-M theory of aerial combat. This theory would be used in the development of the F-15 Eagle, but they weren't always met with approval. Using 'E-M', Boyd reportedly told TOPGUN instructors that it was not possible for the F-4 Phantom to win a dogfight with a MiG-17. With two of the Navy instructors having battled and beaten the MiG, they had to disagree, with legendary Navy jock Ron 'Mugs' McKeown later saying: "Never trust anyone who would rather kick your ass with a slide rule than with a jet."

Boyd retired from the Air Force in 1975, but is credited with being one of the architects of modern military thinking. Not only was he the author of many research documents into air warfare, including the Aerial Attack Study which broke down air-to-air combat into what was effectively a manual for the fighter pilot, but he also came up with the OODA Loop, which stands for Observation, Orientation, Decision, Action. In the OODA Loop, victory is assured if one combatant can make the appropriate decisions more quickly than one's opponent. Defense Secretary Dick Cheney had read Boyd's military briefing called Patterns of Conflict in 1981, so by 1990, the retired colonel was called back to work on Operation Desert Storm. For a fighter pilot with no kills, his influence on modern fighter combat, aircraft design and military tactics has been huge.

John Boyd died on March 9, 1997.

PIERRE SPREY BORN 1937

Born in Nice, in the South of France, Pierre Sprey was raised in New York and educated at Yale University.

After studying a diverse range of subjects including mathematical statistics, French literature and aeronautical engineering he worked at naval aircraft manufacturer Grumman before moving to the Office of the Secretary of Defense. As an analyst and

LEFT:* *Northrop's F-5 family had sold in their thousands across the globe as cheap, lightweight fighters.

aircraft were chosen from paper designs.

Many felt it was time to get back to an era where paper designs were whittled down before competing prototypes were built. Packard insisted that the 'old' system was used in the A-X programme, where the Northrop A-9 was built to compete with the Fairchild Republic A-10 prototype. Sprey actually wrote the requirements for the A-X competition, which in September 1970 selected the two companies to build prototypes that would be involved in a fly-off in 1972.

With the success of that programme, a Request for Proposals (RFP) was issued in January 1972 which was similar to the F-XX proposal of a few years before. The F-XX outlined a need for high thrust-to-weight ratio, a maximum 6.5g load, high agility and a weight of 20,000lb (9072kg) or half the weight of the F-X/F-15 proposal. After years of heavyweights, it seemed the Lightweight Fighter really was finally going to be built.

For Riccioni it was to be a bittersweet victory. Back in the 1970s and 1980s the story went that Second World War P-51 Mustang ace General John C Meyer, USAF Vice-Chief of Staff, chatted to Rich about the F-XX proposals over drinks at a party late in 1970 and on hearing the colonel's feelings about the LWF project immediately shipped Riccioni off to Korea.

Speaking in 2014, Rich explained: "Looking back now the F-16 won the competitive fly-off and went into production with the F-15 in 1974. Those two geniuses Sprey and Boyd made my dream of doubling the size of the USAF fighter fleet a reality. Through no effort from The Fighter Mafia, two aircraft contractors convinced the US Navy that a navalised version of either of the two LWF contenders would be a good fighter for them.

"Today the F-15 has essentially disappeared and the F-14 Tomcat is long gone. Meanwhile advanced versions of the F-16 and F-18 are still in production after more than 40 years. Many of the world's countries bought them, bringing much gold to the US. The Fighter Mafia determined the nature of the fighter forces and the order of battle for the USAF, Navy, Marines and much of the free world. As a reward for this achievement I was banished (punished) by the Air Staff to a year in South Korea, as Director of Operations and Training of the 314th Division at Osan airbase in 1973."

History would be kinder to these visionaries and their legacy would be not just the General Dynamics F-16 Fighting Falcon, but also the Northrop/McDonnell-Douglas F-17/18.

Today the F-15 has essentially disappeared and the F-14 Tomcat is long gone. Meanwhile advanced versions of the F-16 and F-18 are still in production after more than 40 years. Many of the world's countries bought them, bringing much gold to the US

consulting statistician many of the figures coming back to Sprey and others in the Pentagon in the late 1960s about the air war over South East Asia didn't add up.

Kill ratios from multi-million dollar aircraft up against low-tech, cheap machines didn't look good. Statistics showed that the impressive weapons and systems carried by US aircraft weren't being used in Vietnam.

With these things in mind he constructed the initial proposals for the A-X programme which eventually matured into the Fairchild A-10 Thunderbolt II close-support aircraft. It's a machine he still has affection for today, saying: "It does the most important job which is to support troops on the ground. To do that it needs to be down low, it needs to turn well and find hard-to-spot targets on the ground. You have to have a big gun and stay near the troops and loiter for hours."

Sprey also spent time on the F-X/F-15 Eagle saying: "Boyd, Riccioni and I had gotten disgusted with the F-15's growing size and complexity and as bureaucratic guerrillas started what became the F-16. This was something half the size and cost and would wax the F-15 in a fight as it's not going to be carrying a bunch of junk."

Despite aircraft such as the F-16 and F-18 coming from his thinking, Sprey often bemoans what happened to these aircraft by the time they became operational, saying that by the time they were in squadron service the lightweight F-16 weighed so much that a great fighter became 'almost' great.

As the last surviving member of the main triumvirate of The Fighter Mafia, Sprey is an outspoken critic of the current Lockheed-Martin F-35 Lightning II and has often poured scorn on its capabilities – much to the annoyance of the aircraft's many supporters. Recently while discussing the project he said: "This plane is a terrible airplane. It's cost us $200 million each, $400 billion so far and with life cycle costs of $200 billion. The problem is that we have three services pulling things different ways and the aircraft has three conflicting jobs to do. It's the worst aircraft we've ever built. They want to make 2500 of them: my prediction is they will stop after 500 – the failings of the plane means it will kill itself."

A music aficionado, Sprey is a lover of jazz and has made a number of albums on his own Mapleshade recording label. Some of his work has even appeared as a sample on a Kanye West song entitled Jesus Walks.

COLONEL EVEREST RICCIONI 1927-2015

Colonel Everest Riccioni joined the US Army Air Force in 1943 and enjoyed a long and distinguished career.

His flying resume during the Second World War includes flying Curtiss C-46 transport aircraft in the Burma theatre and acting as a test pilot on many in-service types of the time, including Consolidated B-24 Liberators, Lockheed P-38 Lightnings and North American P-51 Mustangs. After securing degrees in applied mathematics and aeronautical engineering, he returned to the air force in the early 1950s, with his background leading him to become a test pilot at Edwards Air Force Base. It is thought 'Rich' flew more than 50 aircraft types during his career.

Despite being selected for astronaut training in the late 1950s, Rich refused and instead spent his time instructing and flying many varied jet fighters, including the F-100 Super Sabre and F-104 Starfighter and the F-4 Phantom. By the time he was assigned to the Pentagon in 1969, the F-4's successor – the F-X which became the F-15 was already in an advanced stage on the drawing board.

Riccioni was infamously posted to Korea following his work at the head of The Fighter Mafia. Speaking in 2014 he recalled: "Despite differing with two major generals, I was finally deemed 'rehabilitated' within two years and assigned to command the Flight Mechanics Division at Wright Patterson AFB in 1974. There I managed the research on supersonic cruise fighter design, convened the first nationwide Secret Supersonic-Fighter Design Conference and inspired the second. I retired from the USAF in September of 1976."

That wasn't the end of Rich's story. He began his civilian career with Northrop, looking at advanced projects, including the use of super-cruise – where aircraft can travel at supersonic speeds for long periods of time without the use of afterburner. He also worked on mounting an anti-tank cannon on a small Northrop fighter and worked on the B-2 Spirit programme. He left Northrop in 1981 and in the late 1990s worked on ways to streamline and simplify the F-22 Raptor design. Riccioni saw excessive price as the biggest threat to a sizeable USAF fighter force and sadly the F-22 was to prove him right with its $400 million per plane price tag which led to cuts in the number of airframes purchased.

Riccioni died in 2015 aged 91.

Genesis of a dogfighter

The nascent lightweight fighter concept went from being unloved and unwanted to being a cash-cow for the United States, but how did it all start?

Futuristic and elegant, the YF-16 shows why it was christened 'The Viper'.

FALCON FACTS

'Semper Viper' is an award given for remarkable airmanship by F-16 pilots.

In today's skies across the world its not uncommon to see an F-16 in flight, thanks to more than 4000 being built for air-arms across the globe, but this wasn't always the case.

The Lightweight Fighter concept was almost forced on the US military, but little did they know that the LWF (later the Air Combat Fighter) project would eventually lead to two families of agile machines battling it out across the world for the lucrative export market.

After many deliberations the five competing designs for the Lightweight Fighter (LWF) programme were whittled down to just two – the General Dynamics Model 401 and the Northrop Model P600. At one stage Boeing's design was considered a lead contender, while McDonnell-Douglas and Grumman already had their hands full developing the F-15 Eagle and F-14 Tomcat respectively – even though MDD actually had a LWF design.

With the two front-runners picked, the USAF awarded contracts to both G-D and Northrop for around $38 million each to build two prototypes which would engage in a fierce competition to see which machine was best. Both offered a futuristic look at the shape of fighter aircraft to come and yet both had already been in development since the 1960s.

The General Dynamics machine had been in gestation since around 1965, under the keen eye of Harry Hillaker. Hillaker and his team started out back in the mid-60s with the Model 785 and FX-404 and went through 78 different variations of wing design, tail configuration, strake/canard inclusion, and intake set-up. Exhaustive hours in the wind tunnel – 1272 hours to be exact – let to variations and changes to the design which even went as far as to move the wing forward just 14 inches.

In 1965 General Dynamics' ADF was a 25,000lb (11,364kg) aircraft with a high thrust-to-weight ratio, but when the MiG-25 Foxbat was seen, the design changed from one of simplicity to an all-weather, high-speed machine. By the time 1970 had come around, the design had come full circle. With Pierre Sprey and The Fighter Mafia crunching the numbers which showed that high speed was rarely used in combat and that rules of engagement often negated the advantage of a large radar, GD's design had once more become smaller (around 18,000-20,000lb or 8200-9000kg) and with the bare minimum of avionics and a weapons fit of two, small infra-red heat-seeking missiles and a gun.

LWF Force Models Tested — 78 Significant Variations

	Configurations Tested	WINGS Λ_{LE}	WINGS Fixed Camber	WINGS Variable Camber	WINGS Airfoil(s)	INLETS Side	INLETS Bottom	VERTICAL TAILS Twin	VERTICAL TAILS Single	VORTEX LIFT (Forebody Strakes)	WIND TUNNEL TEST HOURS
Coventional Forebody	785	40°	✓		64A205 & 64A403.5		✓		✓	✓	48
		35°	✓		64004.9 & 64043.5		✓		✓		20
	786 (Twin tail 785)	40°		✓	64A205 & 64A403.5		✓	✓		✓	48
Wing/Forebody Shaping	401F-0	35°		✓	4% BICONVEX		✓	✓		✓ (2) Strakes	187
		40°	✓		64A204		✓	✓			
	401F-2	40°		✓	64A204		✓ ✓	✓	✓	✓	91
		35°		✓	64004.9 & 64043.5			✓			
	401F-3 (Ferri inlet)	40°		✓	64A204		✓	✓			20
	401F-4 (High wing)	40°		✓	64A204		✓	✓	✓	✓ (3) Strakes	39
	401FS	40°		✓	64A204	✓		✓			29
	401F-5	40°		✓	64A204		✓	(3) Horiz tail positions	✓	✓	130
	401F-5A	40°		✓	64A204		✓		✓	✓	30
	401F-10	40°		✓	64A204		✓		✓	✓	30
	401F-10A	40°		✓	64A204		✓		✓	✓	32
	401F-16	40°		✓	64A204		✓		(1) ✓	✓	442
		45°	✓	✓	CONICAL CAMBER 64A(X)5.9/64A203						
	401F-16E	40°		✓	64A204 — Wing Moved Forward 14 inches		✓		(2) ✓	✓	126

TOTAL WIND TUNNEL HOURS 1272

TOP: Unpainted and in natural metal, alongside a dummy F-100 engine, the YF-16 is unmistakably a Viper.

MIDDLE: As a lightweight fighter demonstrator, the YF-16 was 'no frills'.

LEFT: Almost 1300 wind-tunnel hours led General Dynamics to the YF-16 design.

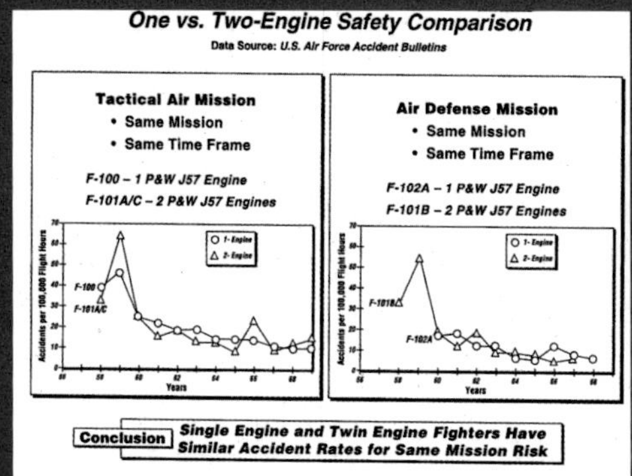

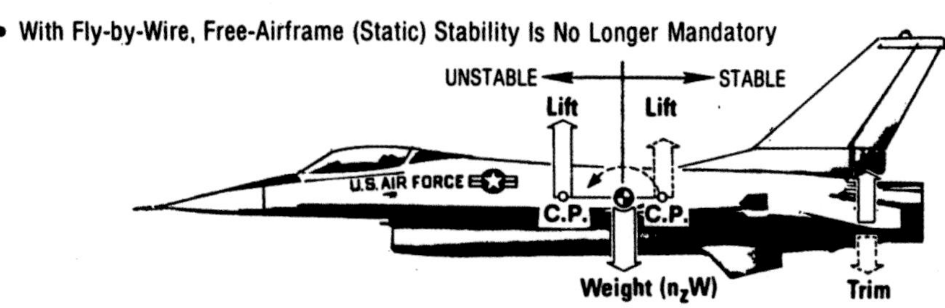

***ABOVE:* Research into single and twin engine configurations found no statistical disadvantage for a single engine design.**

***RIGHT:* The key to the YF-16's agility would be 'relaxed static stability' and its fly-by-wire control system.**

***BELOW:* Hillaker did a number of presentations on how he and the team arrived at the final design.**

***BELOW RIGHT:* General Dynamics tested single and twin inlet designs for the F-100 engine and settled on the single inlet, mounted down low.**

As well as overall design, the choice of one or two engines was also made. Should General Dynamics go with a single or twin-engine layout? Eventually it was felt that a single, Pratt & Whitney F-100 turbofan was the best compromise based on range, weight and fuel efficiency. Two General Electric YJ-101s, as fitted to the Northrop contender, were considered, but the single F-100 offered higher thrust, better thrust-to-weight as well as using 25% less fuel in the cruise and 14% less fuel in combat situations. The other big advantage was that of commonality – the F-15 Eagle utilised two F-100 turbofans so choosing the Pratt & Whitney would lead to attractive potential cost reductions for the USAF when it came to make a decision on the aircraft.

Looking at the various designs today, it is evident that many of the bold aeronautical engineering design cues used by Hillaker and his team at General Dynamics are still valid – in fact one model of the design – the twin-tailed 401-F4 looks very much like today's F-35. The final 'mature' design choice was the Model 401-F10A, with single tail, a low-sweep, straight wing which conferred greater agility at combat speeds especially when coupled with the automatic variable camber flaps and slats and a beautiful blended wing/fuselage body that gave the 401 the ability to carry a large amount of fuel.

Atop the fuselage was a large, blown single-piece canopy, which – thanks to the lack of a bow-pillar for opening (this was moved to the rear) gave the aircraft the best view from the cockpit since the bubble-canopied P-51 and P-47 of the Second World War. The low sill line also meant the pilot had unrivalled side-vision – vital in a turning dogfight. To the left of the pilot on the blended wing/body sat the gun – a 'traditional' GE M61-A1 20mm Vulcan 'Gatling' style cannon, under which sat the engine inlet. Today we take the wide-mouthed look of the F-16 for granted, but the simple, fixed inlet was an elegant solution following many hours in the wind tunnel.

Various configurations were tested, from side-mounted oval, fixed intakes, to rectangular, ramp-style intakes (similar in many ways to today's Eurofighter Typhoon) and a ventral scoop, with centre-mounted shock cone, similar to those found on the side-mounted Lockheed F-104 and General Dynamics' own F-111. The final version was cleverly made as a sub-assembly, so that any design changes

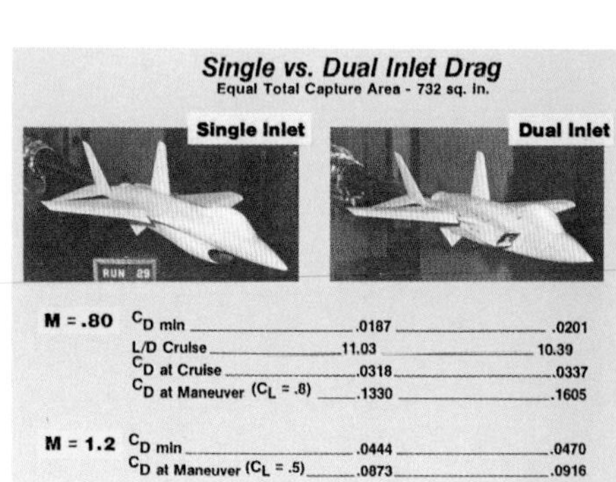
Single vs. Dual Inlet Drag
Equal Total Capture Area - 732 sq. in.

		Single Inlet	Dual Inlet
M = .80	C_D min	.0187	.0201
	L/D Cruise	11.03	10.39
	C_D at Cruise	.0318	.0337
	C_D at Maneuver (C_L = .8)	.1330	.1605
M = 1.2	C_D min	.0444	.0470
	C_D at Maneuver (C_L = .5)	.0873	.0916

RIGHT: **The YF-16 looked good in the General Dynamics house colours.**

BELOW: **The flight programme progressed swiftly and GD knew they had a winner on their hands.**

could be implemented easily. This would later pay dividends when alternative powerplants were being considered.

Having such a low-slung intake had previously led to problems with machines such as the Vought F-8 Crusader and the A-7 Corsair, but the benefits outweighed the problems. Firstly, with a rear-set nose-wheel some 26in behind the inlet, it was found that the wheel was far enough behind the intake so no FOD or 'Foreign Object Damage' material was thrown up by the wheel itself. Secondly as the intake was 39in off the ground (compared to the lower-slung intake of the F-8, which was nicknamed The Gator by deck crews for its voracious FOD-eating habit) the issue wasn't as pronounced. Also, the positioning meant no chance of any ingestion of gas from the 20mm Gatling gun.

If the external shape of the Model 401 looked futuristic, then under the skin it was even more so, as a host of new ideas and technologies were used to help ensure that this small aircraft packed a big punch.

Today many thousands of military pilots would find the F-16 cockpit comfortable and familiar, as many have flown the type, but back in the 1970s it was a brave new world for cockpit design. Today's F-22 Raptor uses a sidestick controller and it was debuted in the F-16. This is where the traditional centre-placed joystick is instead replaced by a smaller stick on the right-hand console. The stick itself has only a small amount of movement and originally didn't have any, instead being pressure sensitive, but production machines had a controller that moved only about half a centimetre back, 2.5mm left and right and hardly moved at all when pushed up – this coming from the natural instinct of pilots to push more negative G than they normally want.

> **Today many thousands of military pilots would find the F-16 cockpit comfortable and familiar, but back in the 1970s it was a brave new world for cockpit design**

The use of a side-stick controller was a curious one. Many felt left-handed pilots would have problems with it – even though in a fighter their left hand would traditionally be on the throttles at least during hectic engagements. The general reception was that pilots – whether left or right-handed – soon got to grips with it, if you pardon the pun. Serious issues were raised by combat-proven pilots who got to fly the plane. The Israelis were worried that any damage to the pilot's right arm from cannon fire, flak or explosions might

BELOW: **The F-16's ejection seat was reclined by 30 degrees: by design or default is a moot point. Some say it was the only way to get the seat to fit.**

BOTTOM: **The YF-16 was every inch the pure dogfighter.**

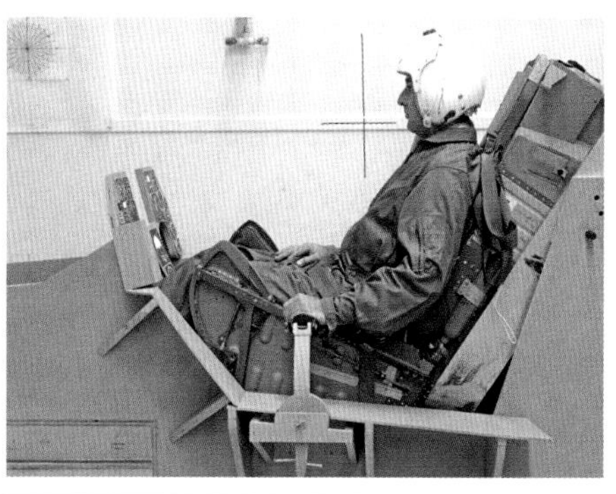

ABOVE: ***The overall shape of the F-16 has changed little in 40 years.***

RIGHT: ***The fly-off against the YF-17 was a busy time for the design and development team.***

BELOW: ***Old and new: YF-16 in comparison with the McDonnell Douglas RF-4C Phantom.***

mean the plane could not be flown back to base. During the Vietnam War at least one A-4 Skyhawk pilot managed to fly back to the carrier with only their left hand on the centre-stick and make it down in one piece, so the argument was valid.

The lack of movement of the stick itself meant that – under high G-load – the pilot wasn't wasting energy trying to move a traditional stick set-up. Another feature of the cockpit that helped during high-G situations was the pilot's seat. The seat (a McDonnell-Douglas ACES II ejection seat) is reclined back 30-degrees, lifting the pilot's heel-line and making him more G-tolerant. Again, some pilots who had seen combat by the early 1970s weren't so impressed by this feature, as they argued it meant it was harder for them to swivel their head around during a high-G aerial engagement. At the time most fighters' seats were tilted between 10-15 degrees, with modern fighters since being around 20-degrees.

Both stick and throttle used the

An early nickname of the F-16 during service was 'Electric Jet' and this came from a number of advances under the skin of the aircraft

then-new ergonomic acronym HOTAS, where the main and important weapons triggers, radio/communication buttons, radar-ranging, missile mode, speed-brakes and other vital functions were clustered on the two controllers, hence 'Hands On Throttle And Stick'. When in the cockpit the pilot would be given all the vital information he or she needed via a HUD, or 'Head Up Display' where speed, altitude, angle of attack, artificial horizon, weapons, targeting and G-rating would be displayed. In heads-down mode, the early models of F-16 featured traditional dials and gauges as well as a multi-function display, threat locator and a number of other panels that would be familiar to any fast-jet pilot of the day.

What wasn't then 'normal' was the sheer amount of visibility through the blown, polycarbonate canopy. Another nod towards dogfighting was the fact that the view ahead and to the sides was completely unobstructed and featured a 40-degree look-down angle over either side of the blended fuselage leading-edge roots and 15-degrees over the nose.

An early nickname of the F-16 during service was 'Electric Jet' and this came from a number of advances under the skin of the aircraft.

With agility high on the list of attributes for a Lightweight Fighter, new ways to make this happen were sought in the late 1960s when the F-16 was on the

THE ACCIDENTAL AIRCRAFT

As first flights go, it wasn't an auspicious start, or maybe it was?

On January 20, 1974, at Edwards AFB, Phil Oestricher was planned to run the YF-16 on a high-speed taxi test.

Oestricher was an ex-Marine pilot, who had flown the Douglas F4-D Skyray and later the Vought Crusader but nothing could prepare him for this accidental 'first flight' that should not have been. The form book said that Oestricher was to split flights in the initial test programme with fellow General Dynamics pilot Neil Anderson. That day he was to taxi the aircraft up to 135 knots and then bring it safely to a halt after checking out the pre-takeoff handling characteristics.

However, that high-speed taxi run turned into a wild series of roll oscillations that caused the right horizontal stabilizer to strike the runway, at which point Oestricher had to fly the YF-16 out of the problem: it was that close to disaster.

Talking to Lockheed Martin's Code One website, 18 years later, Oestricher said he had heard all the various stories, ranging from 'over sensitive flight controls' to a race between himself and Anderson to be the first to fly the YF-16 (in fact Oestricher was always slated to be the first to fly it). He explained: "We'd progressively taxied the airplane faster and faster and wanted to get a better idea of how it handled on the ground. Few people know this, but we actually intended to lift the airplane off the ground that day. Our intention was to move the throttle to military power for a few seconds and let the main gear come up a couple of feet while we went down the runway.

"It was then that we encountered two problems," Oestricher said. "First, the roll control was too sensitive, too much roll rate as a function of stick force. Second, the exhaust nozzle control for the prototype was wired incorrectly. You had to be on the ground for the nozzle to be wide open, so as soon as you took the weight off the wheels, the nozzle closed and essentially doubled the thrust at idle!"

Oestricher rotated the aircraft to about ten degrees when he reached a taxi speed of 130 knots, with the aircraft still accelerating slightly. He made small lateral stick inputs to get a feel for the roll response but got nothing, presumably because the main gear were on the ground, which stopped the airplane from rolling. At this point, he slightly increased the angle of attack.

Immediately upon rotating the second time, the aircraft lifted off with the left wing dropping rapidly. After a right roll command was applied, the aircraft immediately went into a fairly high-frequency, pilot-induced oscillation.

The wingtip Sidewinder rolleron was damaged.

The first F-16 gets airborne – accidentally!

Oestricher said: "Every time I tried to correct the oscillation, I got a full-rate roll. And the airplane was continuing to accelerate all the while because the nozzle had closed, even though I had the throttle at idle power. We had way too much idle thrust to have a practical airplane."

Before the oscillation could be stopped, a rolleron wheel of the dummy AIM-9 missile on the left wingtip lightly touched the runway, the right horizontal tail struck the ground, and the aircraft bounced off its main gear several times. This bouncing pointed the aircraft off the runway. Oestricher now decided to fly the YF-16 out of the situation, as he felt that it would be impossible to keep it on the runway, even if the nose wheel could be quickly brought down.

He applied power and allowed the aircraft to climb slowly in a shallow left turn, flying in a wide pattern to a long flat final approach to touch down six minutes after the 'accidental' take-off. Engineers from General Dynamics solved the problem of control sensitivity that evening. Oestricher said: "We just put in logic where you selected half-gain for taxiing, for take-off, and for landing. You want the controls to be sensitive up-and-away, but you don't want that level of sensitivity down in the pattern."

The knock on the runway badly damaged the right stabiliser. It required repair before the aircraft could fly again. With the control change and a replacement stabiliser in place, Oestricher made the first planned flight on February 2, 1974. That hour and a half sortie was uneventful. Oestricher's report after that first flight included the following: "The airplane was comfortable and enjoyable to fly immediately. No difficulty was experienced in adapting to the sidestick or to the thirty-degree inclined seat... The visibility is so great that it requires some time to adapt... The airplane is highly responsive about all three axes but can be flown smoothly with little effort."

Oestricher always maintained that the first flight of the YF-16 was no big deal, even though it occurred the way it did. In fact, he said: "The F-4 Phantom was flown for the first time in similar circumstances after pitch oscillations occurred during a high-speed taxi so I'm inclined to believe that events like this can be good omens."

- Phil Oestricher was 84 when he died in Fort Worth, Texas, in December 2015. He was a major character in developing the F-16 as well as testing all models of the F-111 swing-wing attack aircraft. Before his career in the US Marine Corps he worked at Consolidated Vultee as an aerodynamics engineer on the huge B-36 intercontinental bomber. After retiring, Oestricher was active in the Lockheed Martin-Fort Worth retirees association and was an avid builder and flyer of radio-controlled model aircraft.

Phil Oestricher in the cockpit of an F-16.

drawing board. The General Dynamics F-16 was the first fighter aircraft to go into production which was designed to be aerodynamically unstable. This is called Relaxed Static Stability, or RSS and it helps to improve an aircraft's agility. An inherently stable aircraft, one with Positive Static Stability, will try to return to level flight if the controls are released, but an unstable one with RSS will not. In effect to keep an RSS aircraft flying, many control inputs or trim changes are needed. With the F-16 a computer makes those instantaneous changes or inputs, thus keeping the aircraft flying.

Another innovation was how those control inputs went from the pilot to the control surfaces. On a conventional aircraft (and even on the YF-17 which was in the fly-off with the YF-16) boosted hydraulic controls from the pilot to the surfaces did the job, but the constant control inputs needed to keep the unstable F-16 flying meant that a computer had to be in between the pilot and the control surface, so with the pilot just needed to send electrical commands to the computer. A 'fly-by-wire' system was built, where the control inputs went electronically from the side-stick, throttle or rudder pedals through the computer and to the actuators on the control surfaces themselves. For many pilots – including the very first – this system would take some getting used to but it was the future.

Finally, the first prototype General Dynamics YF-16 was rolled out at Fort Worth on December 13, 1973, and then delivered to Edwards Air Force Base on January 8, 1974. A very 'unofficial' flight (see panel) took place on January 20 with the official flight taking place on February 2, 1974.

Bugs had to be ironed out, as with every new aircraft, but it was a swift programme with the YF-16. That first machine (code 72-1567) went supersonic on February 5, 1974, and Mach 2 on March 11. The second prototype flew in May 1974 and this machine was fitted with the internal gun and external fuel tanks along with the ability to transfer fuel.

This second prototype was due to attend the Paris Air Show at Le Bourget in 1975 but suffered a wheels-up landing at Fort Worth when pilot Neil Anderson found that the landing gear wouldn't extend following a flight demonstration. This meant that the original prototype would make the first transatlantic crossing for the Paris show. That first prototype would have a long and fruitful life. The aircraft had a busy trip to Europe, showcasing the abilities of the YF-16. It flew 52 times in 50 days at almost 40 air shows and (while by that time the machine was already selected by a number of European air-arms) probably did more to push

The Viper meets the Cobra in the skies over Edwards.

FALCON FACTS

The Fighting Falcon was the first fighter with a completely frameless 'blown' cockpit canopy.

the F-16's case in Europe and further afield than any other single aircraft.

The machine was later refitted as a CCV (Control Configured Vehicle) with canards mounted below the air intake trunking on the forward fuselage. Work commenced at the end of 1975 and 72-1567 first flew in this configuration in spring 1976. CCV aircraft have independently moving or 'decoupled' control surfaces so they can manoeuvre in one plane without movement in another.

Following two hard landings, the CCV tests were brought to an end in the summer of 1977 but still that wasn't the end for 72-1567. It was then involved in studies in the use of an escape module for the F-16. Despite looking a little worse for wear after such a long and varied life – and having been struck off charge from the USAF inventory in 1981 – 72-1567 was (in the early 1990s) fittingly brought back to her best in the corporate General Dynamics colours she wore at the start of her life and displayed at the Hampton Roads History Center in Virginia.

SNAKES AND A PLANE: VIPER VERSUS COBRA

The much-debated LWF/ACF concept was almost a side-line in US military procurement in the late 1960s and early 1970s.

However, by 1974 it had grown into a must-win, all-or-nothing fly-off between two competing designs and companies, with two machines which took very different routes to accomplish the same goal.

By late 1974 the signs were good for any potential winner of the LWF fly-off. The name changed to the 'Air Combat Fighter' and the winner could expect the 650 unit run required by the USAF as well as a chance of becoming a US Navy light fighter and having a crack at the lucrative European market. At the time many air forces across the continent of Europe were flying the Lockheed F-104 Starfighter: a 'hot-ship' in its day, but really a generation or so behind even the likes of the McDonnell Douglas F-4 Phantom.

Against the General Dynamics YF-16 was pitched the Northrop YF-17. This machine looked very different from the

ABOVE: ***The YF-17, seen here in use by NASA, was a logical development of previous Northrop lightweight designs.***

MAIN: ***The designs were different but both would mature as superb fourth generation fighters.***

> ***Instead of a single engine inlet, the YF-17 was a twin engine design, featuring low, cheek-mounted air-inlets and twin, out-canted tails***

WHEN HILLAKER MET BOYD...

Harry Hillaker – the father of the F-16.

During an interview in 1997 Harry Hillaker – the man who would lead the design team for what became the F-16 – described his first meeting with John Boyd. It would prove to be a pivotal encounter.

"As I sat sipping an after-dinner drink in the Officer's Club at Eglin Air Force Base in the Florida panhandle, I was distracted by the antics of three pilots, still in their flight suits, standing at the bar. One of them, tall with dark curly hair and a cigar in his mouth, talked in a loud animated manner. He used his hands to emphasise his words as fighter pilots are prone to do. I commented to my host, a colonel and chief of development planning: 'There's a guy who obviously thinks he's the world's hottest fighter pilot.' 'That's John Boyd, who may well be one of the hottest fighter pilots,' my host responded. 'You should meet him.'

"I wasn't too interested because I don't go for loud, showy people. My host, however, insisted. It turned out that Boyd didn't cotton to me either. Upon learning that I was from industry and working on the F-111, he really blistered me. *'You call the F-111 a fighter?'* he asked. 'It's designated a fighter-bomber,' I countered, which didn't placate him. *'You guys in industry this, and you contractors that,'* he ranted. He thought I didn't know *'beans'* (not the exact word he used) about fighters. The atmosphere, to say the least, was icy. Our lively discussion continued. As we bantered, we slowly began to understand each other. We parted on somewhat more amiable terms."

Hillaker didn't realise how profound and important that meeting would be. A few days later back in the office one of Boyd's associates called Harry, asking if he wanted to meet up with Boyd again, to transfer Boyd's energy-manoeuvrability theory into relevant and meaningful aircraft parameters. He agreed.

Hillaker recalled: "Over the next six years, I participated in many all-night sessions in Washington DC with Boyd and his small elite group. The group came to be known as The Fighter Mafia because of its close-knit underground operation. The mafia dissected and analysed every facet of air combat and its relevance to aircraft parameters. In the process, we defined a concept for what became known as the Lightweight Fighter, progenitor to the F-16.

"Boyd had a passion for insight and an unbending commitment for truth and understanding. He sought to understand the intricacies of manoeuvring flight – what was it about an airplane that would limit or prevent him from making it do what he wanted it to do? To gain a finer understanding, he probed the principles of thermodynamics. He wanted to understand the states of energy; their conversion and their equilibrium.

"He knew that, when turning from a steady-state flight condition, the airplane under a given power setting would either slow down or lose altitude or both. The result meant he was losing energy (the drag exceeded the thrust available from the engine). From these observations, he concluded that manoeuvring for position was basically an energy problem. Winning required the proper management of energy available at the conditions existing at any point during a combat engagement."

From these thoughts Boyd would develop his various ideas and theories and together with Hillaker, Sprey and the other members of The Fighter Mafia, a new way of designing fighter aircraft was born.

Hillaker added: "Boyd's theories didn't make him too popular within the Air Force – many couldn't accept his premise that speed was not as important as agility – nor did his criticisms of how the Air Force conducted itself on certain matters. His direct, forthright manner, often very blunt on controversial issues, didn't help his popularity much either. Many people saw Boyd as either a madman or a genius.

"Boyd savoured that image as a tactical advantage. He was always seeking ways to seize the advantage and keep a firm grip on it. For Boyd, conversation was often a contact sport. With a booming voice, he would engage others nose-to-nose, thrusting his forefinger into a chest to emphasize a point and punctuating his conversation with, *"Do you hear what I'm saying?"* or *"Do you get my meaning?"*

> ***I wasn't too interested in meeting Boyd as I don't like loud, showy people, but we got to like each other. No F-16 would be flying today if it were not for his efforts.***

Boyd's theories did get to have some impact on the F-X/F-15 programme and helped lead to the Lightweight Fighter (LWF) concept. At the end of the contract study that led to the YF-16 and YF-17 each contractor was required to give a briefing on the results of its efforts to USAF officials at Wright-Patterson Air Force Base in Dayton, Ohio. "Being project leader of the study," says Hillaker, "I gave the briefing. Afterwards, I was complimented on the results and particularly on how I handled *'that major,'* with his continuously probing and challenging questions. What they didn't know was that this was John Boyd. We had spent the previous evening orchestrating the presentation, devising the questions and answers to emphasise the important and meaningful points. Boyd was willing to be used to make a point for the cause."

Hillaker adds: "Boyd planted the seeds for the Lightweight Fighter, cultivated those seeds, and helped harvest them in 1972 while playing a major role in defining the requirements that were put into the request for proposal for the Lightweight Fighter. The proposal led directly to the YF-16 and YF-17 technology demonstration prototypes. His influences can be seen in world-class fighters such as the F-15, F-16, and F/A-18. After his retirement from the Air Force, Boyd elevated his theories to a higher plane to encompass the total battle – not just the air battle. He refined and expanded his combat theories of fast reaction and mobility and incorporated them into a four-hour Patterns of Conflict briefing that he presented to the Army and Marines to illustrate how his concepts could be adapted to the land battle. Many of the tactics used in Desert Storm were patterned after Boyd's theories.

"Many years after that chance meeting in Florida, the F-16 has done John Boyd proud. It will continue to honour his memory. John left his mark, wanting only to do what he thought was best for the Air Force, his Air Force. He changed the complexion of air combat and fighter design. No F-16 would be flying today were it not for his tenacious efforts. His legacy lives on in the hundreds of F-16s that grace the skies worldwide."

- **Harry Hillaker – the chief designer of the General Dynamics F-16 died on February 8, 2009, aged 89.**

Excerpts from Lockheed Martin's July 1997 issue of Code One.

MAIN: *Even more striking in warpaint, the F-16 could easily run an F-4 out of fuel during test sessions.*

BELOW: *The very basic, simple cockpit would change dramatically over the years with the introduction of multi-function displays.*

F-16 itself. Instead of a single engine and single tail machine with a single engine inlet, the YF-17 was a twin engine design, featuring low, cheek-mounted air-inlets and twin, out-canted tails. The design had – like that of the F-16 – been long in the making, having its roots in the 1960s.

Northrop had considerable success with small, lightweight fighters. Their F-5 Freedom Fighter/T-38 family of fighters and fighter trainers were in service with a number of air-arms around the world by the early 1970s, coming as they did from earlier designs such as the N-102 Fang. From Canada, to South America, across Europe and even in the US, this family of twin-engined light fighters and supersonic trainers would eventually sell almost 4000 units worldwide to more than 30 air forces around the globe. Little wonder it was such a success, as – at the head of the design team – was Edgar Schmued, who had been part of the North American team responsible for the legendary P-51 Mustang.

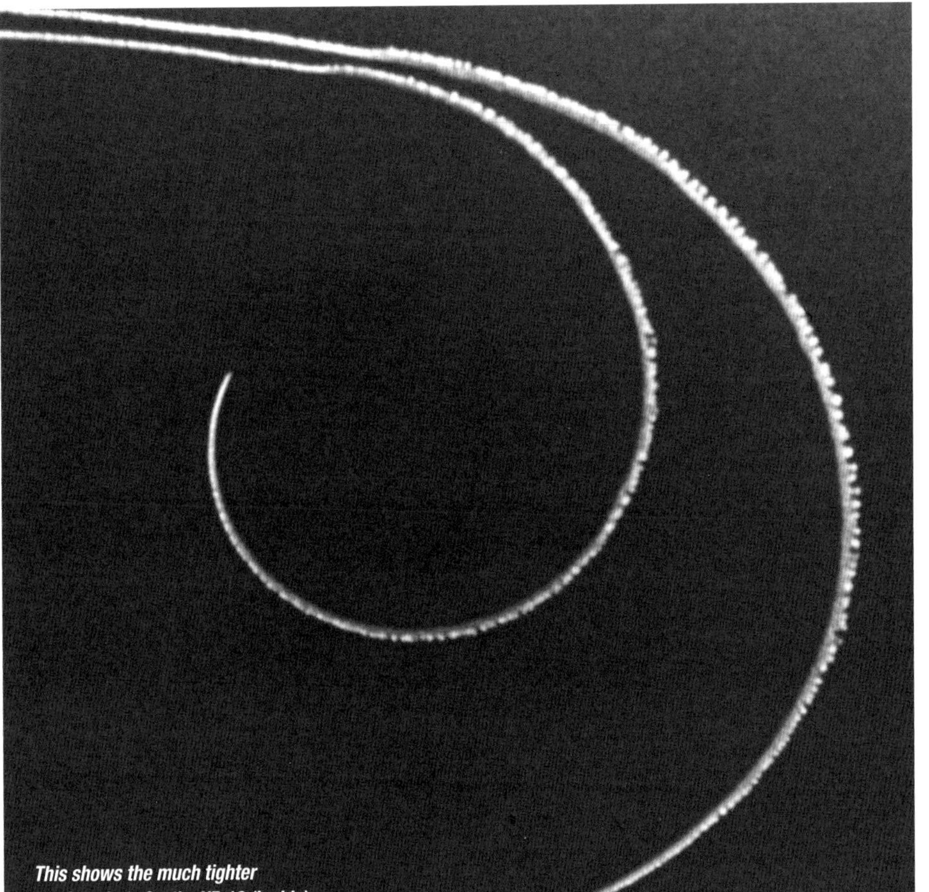

This shows the much tighter turning circle for the YF-16 (inside) compared to the Phantom II.

In 1970, the developed Northrop F-5 had won the International Fighter Aircraft competition, which saw the US try and sell low-cost, high-performance aircraft to its close allies around the world. By 1972 the F-5E and F (two-seat) Tiger II aircraft was introduced with more powerful General Electric J-85 engines and it became a popular multi-role aircraft, no doubt helped by the USAF's use of F-5C machines in Vietnam as part of its Skoshi Tiger project. With the F-5E, many air forces had a high-performance, cost-effective machine which was a notable dogfighter. Little wonder the aircraft was later bought and used by both the USAF and US Navy as a dissimilar/aggressor aircraft against the main fighter/attack aircraft in their inventory.

The F-5E was the inspiration for the next Northrop light fighter design, 1965's N-300, which had become the P.530 Cobra by 1971. So why 'Cobra'? The design by this stage had matured into a twin-engined, twin-tailed machine ➤

with what was called 'Leading Edge Root Extensions' or 'LERX'. These came from the high/mid-set wing, forward past the cockpit canopy. So, when seen in plan-view, it almost looked like the flared defensive hood of a striking Cobra snake. The LERX themselves had come about thanks to research into a fighter that could stay in controlled flight in regimes of high angle of attack or AOA.

Most fighters would stall or depart at anything past 16 degrees AOA, but any aircraft that could go beyond 25, 30 or approach 40 degrees of AOA and still be in controlled flight had a 'pointability' that would make it an impressive, almost unbeatable performer during close-in dogfighting.

Other advances – not just aerodynamic – had to come. General Electric had worked closely with Northrop for many years. Their ubiquitous J-79 engine was supposed to power the N-102 Fang, J-85s had powered the T38 Talons and F-5s and now they were designing a new engine for the fighter of the future. Originally a version of the GE J-97 turbojet was proposed for the P.530, but as the world moved towards the start of the 1970s, it was clear that a clean-sheet design could offer bigger advantages.

Eventually the GE-15 engine design was selected for the Cobra. This based on core parts used in the F-101 turbofan planned for use in the Rockwell B-1 swing-wing bomber. The GE15 would be a twin-spool engine and this basically reduced the number of compressor stages and cut down dimensions and weight. Eventually the YJ-101-GE-100 'turbojets' used in the YF-17 prototype would be rated at 14,400lb of thrust (64.08kN) each.

Like the YF-16, the Cobra (by 1971-72 the P.600) came at the wrong time, a time when congress and the military were looking at larger, higher-performance fighters. Despite this, Northrop knew that there was money to be made; even in the time of the high-end F-104 and F-4 they had sold more than 3000 lightweight fighters. By using simple, existing equipment such as the M-61

RIGHT: ***In clean fit, bereft of pylons the F-16 looked purposeful.***

The YF-17 became the F-18 and the Hornet family of multi-role fighter aircraft for the fleet - another great aircraft for the US and another export success around world

Fitting the second prototype with pylons and AIM-7 Sparrow medium-range air-to-air missiles was a nod to the future.

FALCON FACTS

The Viper was the first fighter designed to be able to pull 9Gs.

Vulcan Gatling gun and existing avionics, the flyaway cost per aircraft was looked to be between $2m and $3.5m.

By the time the YF-17 entered the fray with the YF-16 in the LWF/ACF competition it had gone from being envisaged as a true multi-role machine like the F-4 and having a maximum take-off weight of around 40,000lb (18,144kg) to being the LWF that the YF-16 was always envisaged as. The YF-17 was simplified and lightened (thanks to use of some composite materials) so that when the two aircraft lined up the take-off weight was in the 23,000lb (10,433 kilo) class.

The biggest problem the YF-17 faced was in the use of the GE engine. With the P&W F-100 being used in the already-flown F-15, the General Dynamics YF-16 was running ahead of schedule and the YF-17 finally flew for the first time on June 9, 1974, some six months after the YF-16. By now the programme was gathering pace and interest both in the US and abroad.

It's beyond the scope of this book to go into detail of the fly-off between the two aircraft, but one of the biggest factors had to be the relative immaturity of the GE engine compared to the Pratt & Whitney F-100 (and this despite future issues with that engine). With the Northrop Cobra being later to fly, this put enormous pressure on the team to play catch-up with the General Dynamics team. Broadly speaking, the YF-16 had some advantages in the rolling plane, the YF-17 in the high-AOA slow-speed dogfight arena. Many Navy pilots expressed a preference for the twin-engine YF-17, while others preferred the YF-16.

With hindsight we can now see that both the YF-16 and the YF-17 gave great value to the US military. The F-16 has sold more than 4300 units and a mooted F-16 for the US Navy was also considered in 1974/75. Not to be confused with the later, Navy Fighter Weapons School 'TOPGUN' models, this was going to be in conjunction with Vought, after they teamed up with GD to 'navalise' the F-16 in a deal brokered in September 1974. Despite much work by Vought 'beefing up' the standard F-16 structure to withstand brutal landings aboard a carrier and looking at adapting the AIM-7 Sparrow for fitment onto the slender F-16 body, on May 2, 1975, the US Navy decided it wanted a twin-engined machine for its own LWF.

ABOVE: One of the schemes suggested for the F-16 was this one. Note drop tanks are fitted.

BELOW: The evolution from demonstrator (the YF-16 is now the CCV test ship) through to one of the FSD aircraft.

And so the YF-17 became the F-18 and the Hornet family of multi-role fighter aircraft for the fleet – another great aircraft for the US and another export success around the world. Meanwhile the Pratt & Whitney F-100 developed into a fine engine as did the YJ-101 when it became the GE F-110 series of engines that – ironically – would power later versions of the F-16 family. The greater irony was that both the F-16 and F-18 would pile on the weight and become more than just simple, lightweight fighters, much to the annoyance of the original 'Lightweight Fighter Mafia'. Indeed the Super Hornet in F-18E and F guises would be in the 47,000lb class in fighter guise (21,320kg) compared to the 44,500lb F-15C!

Perhaps the only loser in all this was Northrop. This forward-thinking firm ended up pushing land-based versions of the Cobra – as the F-18L – but instead the winners were McDonnell Douglas (later Boeing) who got the lion's share of the work when the F/A-18 Hornet, which first flew in 1978, was eventually selected for the USN and Marines and entered service in 1983-1984.

SALE OF THE CENTURY!

FALCON FACTS

The F-16 was the first combat aircraft with a fly-by-wire system.

Winning the ACF fly-off was just the beginning. Now the F-16 had to develop and mature into a fighting machine ready for combat – and future military sales.

When the General Dynamics F-16 won the Air Combat Fighter competition, it could be argued that this was when the hard work was really about to start for those involved in the project.

Because from here it was time to turn the YF-16 Lightweight Fighter concept into the F-16 Air Combat fighter. The differences between 'LWF' and 'ACF' were not just two letters. Back in April 1974, Defense Secretary James Schlesinger wrote to the chairman of the Senate Armed Services Committee that he wanted to move the programme from a lightweight, simple day fighter to an 'Air Combat Fighter' with a true multi-role or 'swing' capability. This phrase 'swing force fighter' meant that the winner of the ACF competition would be more capable than the original machine and carry a much more sophisticated fire control radar and avionics suite to enable it to get to targets with accuracy, find them on the ground and bomb them then navigate home.

It would also be expected to haul bombs and use external fuel tanks to get to and return from a target. In terms of range/fuel efficiency the YF-16 had already shown itself to be excellent as during the 90 minute first flight, Phil Oestricher claimed to have been able to run two T-38 Talons and almost run an F-4 out of fuel while still having around 40 minutes' worth of flying time left.

Originally the main mission envisaged for both the YF-16 and YF-17 had been an air-combat mission with a radius of 500 miles with the aircraft carrying two lightweight air-to-air missiles (Sidewinders) and around 400 rounds of ammunition for the 20mm ➤

Three Block 1 F-16s (black radomes) in flight. The middle aircraft has an early single-colour camouflage scheme

RIGHT: To evaluate the ASPJ and ALR-69 antenna systems the second YF-16 was mounted atop a 30ft pedestal. Saves flight time and money...

BELOW: A 'clean' early production F-16 at altitude.

Gatling gun and an ECM pod. However, both aircraft had also shown their ability to use air-to-ground ordnance during the ACF trials (the rumour was the YF-17 showed a greater ability for growth in this area) but now these capabilities would be expanded. Even with the YF-16, General Dynamics had made provision of four hard-points under the wings and one under the fuselage.

To develop the YF-16 into a multi-role combat machine, firstly, the simple General Electric ranging gun radar would be swapped for a full-on multi-mode mission radar. From initially contacting 19 companies for radar proposals, it was in October 1974 that the Aeronautical Systems Division announced that the winner would provide a full radar and avionics package. By early November, two firms – Westinghouse and Hughes – were given around $4m each to develop a radar package and their associated systems. Westinghouse would eventually win the contract with the APG-66 radar.

The APG-66 was a small, well-packaged pulse-doppler radar considered to be one of the most capable designed in the mid-1970s. The original radar system weighed just 296lb (134kg) and benefited from being modular, with units that could be replaced in the field, for ease of maintenance. In use, the APG-66 would be able to detect fighter-sized targets at well over 30 miles and had a number of air-to-air, navigation and air-to-ground modes. Usefully – and with a nod to the future – while the employment of continuous-wave illumination for the likes of radar-guided AIM-7 Sparrow missiles was not part of the original ACF design brief, General Dynamics did make provision for such a unit.

As the capabilities of the F-16 grew so did the airframe itself. With both the LWF aircraft effectively being aerodynamic demonstrators, the external load capacity of the machines was in the order of 8000lb for the YF-16 (around 3268kg) and 10,000lb for the YF-17 (around 4535kg). For these mere demonstrators to become deadly destroyers, they needed to grow.

> ***To develop the YF-16 into a multi-role combat machine, firstly, the simple General Electric ranging gun radar would be swapped for a full-on multi-mode mission radar***

For the FSD (or Full Scale Development) planning the dialled-in capability that was latent in the F-16 design began to be taken up. The number of hard-points rose from five to nine and by mid-1975 the loadout with full internal fuel had risen to 11,000lb (4989kg) and by the time the aircraft got into production the load had gone to almost 12,000lb (5442kg) with the ability for 9g sustained agility, or up to 20,500lb (9297kg)

with reduced agility: interesting when you consider that the clean all-up weight of the first YF-16 was just in the order of 16,500lb (7483kg). To haul this warload and to detect the enemy, the actual size of the F-16 had to change – it had to beef up.

With the radar fit, the nose profile of the aircraft had to broaden and lengthen to fit the planned 24in (61cm) antenna. With the proposed growth of the ability of the F-16, came physical growth too. The original shaped tailplanes would not deal with the increased loads, so a new design was made which was 15% bigger in area. The airbrakes situated either side of the jet nozzle grew larger, the strakes under the rear of the engine grew by 15.8% and the wing area by 7.1%, going from 280 to 300 square feet (26sqm to 28sqm). The fuselage was also lengthened by 13in (33cm). Along with the changes in dimension, the F-16 was also strengthened in key areas.

The ultimate irony to the original members of 'The Lightweight Fighter Mafia' was that the F-16 was getting bigger and going beyond the concept that they originally put forward, but there were many positives, including with the rate of roll. With the production F-16 needing more roll-power with the prospect of heavier external loads for the strike mission, the dimension changes, larger tail-planes and larger flaperons meant that roll-rate was improved significantly, from anything between 30-80% and at 10,000ft at maximum airspeed the time for a 360-degree roll was cut almost by half and improvements were also seen at low speeds.

Other advantages with the changes made included the muzzle of the Vulcan gun shifting 2ft (61cm) rearward. This was important for a pilot to avoid the dazzle of a night-time mission, just as early BAC Lightning pilots who used the nose-mounted Aden cannon had found in the 1960s. The wheelbase from nose-wheel to main-gear was also lengthened, which made the F-16 more stable in the taxi and on touch-down.

Changes from YF to Full Scale Development 'F-16A' airframes would see both the USAF and General Dynamics go through the YF-16's specifications in detail to see where improvements and/or savings could be made. In some instances partners who supplied parts and expertise

***ABOVE:* Hill Air Force Base in Utah was to be the first 'home' of the Fighting Falcon.**

***RIGHT:* Inert 500lb dumb bombs are under the wings of this F-16A from Hill.**

***BELOW:* Even in this configuration the F-16A had put on the pounds to become a viable combat aircraft.**

The F-16B lost just 17% internal fuel over the F-16A. This aircraft flew with the 61st Tactical Fighter Training Squadron from the 56th TTW in 1983.

for the demonstrator programme would not necessarily make it through onto the production airframe. Thankfully General Dynamics' ethos of keeping the production machine as close to the prototypes as possible helped, as did a forward-thinking decision to make the F-16A as 'user-friendly' for the USAF as possible and this went beyond simply using the same engines as the-then 'new-into-service' F-15 Eagle.

The end result – almost two years after winning the ACF competition – was that the first production General Dynamics F-16A flew on December 8, 1976, with the F-16B flying the following August. The twin-seater would (unlike many foreign fighters, especially Soviet machines) be fully combat capable with the Westinghouse APG-66 radar fitted in the nose. Both the F-16A and B models would also share identical dimensions with the only reduction being around 17% of internal fuel capacity.

Overall the F-16A was slightly larger, considerably more capable, much stronger and even had a bigger internal fuel capacity than the demonstrator YF-16s. It could also carry twice the load of the McDonnell Douglas F-4E over the same distance and handily turn inside and outfight any opposition.

With the USAF slated to receive 650 F-16s in the late 1970s, the appeal of this futuristic new fighter was not lost on the world's 'free' air forces.

'THE SALE OF THE CENTURY'

Legend has it that the name for this lucrative sale of aircraft across the European

ABOVE: *The Norwegian F-16As had a single colour scheme and extended tail-base housing a braking parachute for operations on icy runways.*
RIGHT: *An early Danish Block 1 F-16B.*
BELOW: *F-16s were soon coming off a number of production lines across the world.*

continent either came from the American TV programme of the same name, or the fact that the French national newspaper Le Monde called the battle between the F-16 and its European rivals 'La Marche du Siècle', (Sale of the Century) after their own version of the licensed TV show.

Either way, the title was apt, for the winner of the European competition for (effectively) a Lockheed F-104 replacement was really going to be a winner-take-all event. The stakes were very high and the resultant political ebb and flow could almost make for a good spy novel.

Belgium, the Netherlands, Norway and Denmark all needed replacement multi-role fighter aircraft to replace the aging machines currently in their inventories. In late 1973, the four nations had discussed the potential bargaining power they would have, should they go shopping together. As is always the case politics played a big part: the Dutch had been part of the original European MRCA (Multi-Role Combat Aircraft) programme, that would lead to the Panavia Tornado, meanwhile Belgium – thanks to their operation of Dassault Mirage 5 aircraft and the French firm owning shares in that country's aircraft manufacturer SABCA – was strongly linked with any future or existing French fighter.

In the summer of 1974 the four NATO nations (having formed the Multinational Fighter Programme Group or MFPG) had arrived in the capital city of the US to discuss their options. The US already knew that the much vaunted McDonnell Douglas Eagle would not be on the shopping list – it was too expensive for the kind of numbers the Europeans wanted to buy. The Northrop F-5E could possibly fit the bill (Norway had operated the earlier F-5A from 1966 and Switzerland would buy F-5Es later) but a more modern option was needed. The numbers required between the four nations stood at around 350 aircraft, a lucrative deal for any military aircraft manufacturer.

Soon the combatants for the competition became clear. In the American corner were the F-17 and F-16, then Northrop's own P.530 Cobra – the original 'multi-role' version of the later P.600 that became the YF-17 demonstrator. For the Europeans it was the Dassault Mirage F1, the SAAB Eurofighter – a version of the Swedish firm's JA37 Viggen – and the SEPECAT Jaguar. The Anglo-French Jaguar was dismissed early on, being more of a dedicated strike aircraft and soon the options were the Mirage F1E, or a more powerful version the F1/M53 (which wasn't in service with the French Air Force) the Viggen and any winner of the US's Air Combat Fighter fly-off. With this in mind, the pressure was on the Americans not only to get to Europe and showcase the aircraft, but also to make a decision as to which machine the US military would buy.

Over the months to come, teams from

"

Belgium, the Netherlands, Norway and Denmark all needed replacement multi-role fighter aircraft to replace the aging machines currently in their inventories

ABOVE: ***The classic 'Sale of the Century' shot of the first four European nations who bought the F-16.***
BELOW: ***When the F-16 came to display – most air show visitors had never seen anything like it before.***

the NATO countries in the form of the MFPG would visit the likes of Dassault, SNECMA (manufacturer of the Mirage's powerplant) SAAB, Volvo Flygmotor (which powered the Viggen) and then criss-cross the Atlantic to spend three weeks evaluating both of the ACF aircraft. With the potential market being billions of dollars and offset manufacturing agreements with the home nations at stake – lavish entertaining and some dirty tricks would be the order of the day.

It can be assumed that, as Belgium had already signed a non-binding letter of intent to buy the F1, Dassault felt they only had the other three nations to convince. The result was some 'creative' evidence from some companies as to the performance of their aircraft and the issues with the opposition. The French, it seems, were particularly good at boosting the performance of their F1/M3 on paper, while rubbishing the opposition.

The YF-16 and YF-17 embodied technology that was at least five or more years younger than the opposition; in fact both the Viggen and the Mirage were really products more of the 1960s, than the 1970s like the ACF contenders. Northrop with its knowledge of the European market already had 'agents on the ground' on the continent and General Dynamics had to catch up, opening an office in Brussels in 1974 staffed with some key players in the F-16's development.

The financial implications of purchasing 'foreign' aircraft and the off-set manufacture agreements would also rumble on in the USA: after all, if any agreement saw European companies build parts of aircraft destined for the USAF, what if any industrial action halted production progress? Politicians also got more involved with French Prime Minister Jacques Chirac effectively telling the four NATO members that a choice for the Dassault product would show some form of European unity.

More intrigue was to follow. General Paul Stehlin – the then most senior retired French Air Force officer – sent a document in September 1974 detailing why the American aircraft were superior to the French/Dassault proposals to the French President, Valery ➤

*BELOW: **Pushing the product carried on and still does today. This is Farnborough 1980.***

FAILING FALCON

Every new aircraft designed has teething troubles and even the General Dynamics F-16A and B had its fair share.

Despite the advantages of sharing a 'common' powerplant – the Pratt & Whitney F-100 – there were still some issues with the engine itself during its early days of development for both the F-15 and the F-16. The engines suffered from stalls, afterburner flameouts and high wear levels. The modern modular approach to engine design exhibited in the F-100 meant that the motor itself was easily upgradeable. Since service entry the F-100 has – according to USAF statistics – become the safest single-engine fighter engine ever: that's some achievement.

Other issues would also come to light with the aircraft, but again all the bugs would be ironed out – in time. In this telling account, Sergeant William M Eckberg recalls what it was like switching from his beloved McDonnell Douglas F-4D Phantom to the new 'Electric Jet' in the late 1970s. We stress that the words and feelings are Bill's own!

"Way back in 1974, I joined the USAF and my chosen career field was 'aircraft maintenance 43131C jet engines 1&2.' After tech school at Sheppard AFB, Texas, my set of orders would send me to Hill AFB, Utah and to the 388th TFW. I got to Hill in March of 1975 but there were no jets yet and we waited for two weeks for the first F-4Ds to show up from Udorn, in Thailand. These jets were beat up from the Vietnam War and it was a true testament to how tough they were as many went through our heavy depot to be fully repaired, at Ogden Air Logistics Centre, Utah, which was the F-4 depot repair facility.

"My first jet was an F-4D, tail number 650712, and it was my pride in joy: I got so many 'attaboys' for how clean and operational my jet was. I took as many courses as I could, so I could learn the jet inside and out. I moved up in rank to E-3 and became a full crew chief with my own jet. The jet flew more missions than most jets in the 4th TFS. Then the secret got out on how much I knew about the F-4, so that was when I became (volunteered) as one of the 388th wing trainers, teaching newbies how to work on the F-4 jets. I spent time in the 34th and 421st squadrons as we got more jets into the 388th wing.

"I had a great time working on that old hunk of junk: the F-4. You know, 'The Love Sick Ground Brick', 'Hog', 'Pig', proof that; 'with enough power bricks can fly' and 'Lead Sled': these were all crew chief nicknames for the Phantom II but we said this with love and affection. The F-4 was a tough jet to work on and if it flew for an hour and half it took eight hours to fix. Most of the old jets where labour-intensive but very reliable in the air: it could fly with several systems inoperative. The fun I had on the F-4 was figuring out what was broken and how to fix it. Many jets came back from flight broken with something new that few in maintenance had seen.

"Then there were what we called 'the ultimate problems'. These were 'pilot-induced aviation screw-ups' where the pilot would not admit it, to save face. The very best thing was when the pilots forgot something in the cockpit. Depending if the crew chief found the item or the pilot came back before we found it determined the fine they were subjected to. It usually was a six-pack of beer for a minor incident or a case of beer for a major FOD (Foreign Object Debris) incident. The worst problem was if a pilot lost something in the cockpit that would ground the jet until it was found.

"Many nights were spent looking for something 'lost'. This often meant pulling out ejection seats and black boxes and stripping the cockpit to find an object and this was not cheap. Then there was that time when the lost item was not lost, the back-seater found the item in his helmet bag just after we had pulled the cockpit apart. The culprit would then get a chance to help put things back together and pay a couple cases of beer! Crew chiefs are still brutal about FOD in cockpit – and rightly so. I am glad to have been a part of the USAF and being a crew chief in my time of service on the F-4D it was tough and fun.

"Then I remember the day in November 1978 when they asked for volunteers to switch over to the new F-16: that's right I did it. The USAF picked the 388th to become the first operational wing and they would form the 16th Training Squadron for the fleet. Oh boy! Something new and we were all excited. The first jet came in around February of 1979 from Edwards AFB and it put on a show for us: it zipped around and performed some fabulous stunts and then landed. There it was: 78001 and from a distance it was a great looking jet.

"Now let's investigate the reason why you never volunteer for anything in the service because it usually proves to be a bad choice! The F-16s that we got were far from being the operational jet it was supposed to be. In the beginning the jet had so many problems I can't even go into every detail and item. It took many months to work the bugs out of the jets to even get full flights out them. I thought about going back to the old F-4 and was told that I couldn't: "Remember you volunteered, Bill!" I learned more about aircraft maintenance and repairs then I ever wanted to know and I got to learn many of the systems: damn I got to be a trainer on these jets too, go figure.

"So what went wrong? Well, we had various gearbox failures, engine shut downs and electrical wiring nightmares which were the main troubles. Then there was that pesky little problem of the In Flight Refuelling (IFR) door system. General Dynamics the manufacturer at the time forgot to place an indicator light to show if the IFR door was open or closed. We lost a jet because of that simple little thing. One fine day a Belgian pilot in training with an A-model jet,

took fuel from a tanker so the pilot could qualify and after full tanks he flew off to complete the mission.

"Twenty maybe 30 minutes later the pilot radios that he was bingo internal fuel but he had full wing tanks: turns out that when the IFR door is open the fuel will not transfer from the wing tanks. Even the check list forgot to add this to the possibility of problems and so he never verified the door was closed. That's right he flamed out on finals into Hill and he lost control. So, he punched out and the jet gently ploughed into the marsh area on the north-end of the field, breaking a few parts off the jet. We cleaned it out and fixed the jet and it flew for a few months more before being retired. To solve the issue, we added the new wiring kit to the fleet that added a door switch, master caution and IFR door open warning lights: another problem solved, but I still wanted to go back to the old F-4, my first love!

"Many of us felt that the F-16 was rushed through production and put it into service where General Dynamics would fix the problems while in service. Many of the first jets from GD were real piles of junk! Then I was privy to work on the first two training jets from overseas: one Belgian FA-01 and one Dutch J-212, F-16A model jets. It was a case of the same problems, but with different builders. Now, don't get me wrong: when the jets flew they were (and still are) one the best jets ever, but they came out before they were ready and a little ahead of their time. The fly-by-wire controls, a laid-back seat and a side control stick made the jet alien to most conventional jet pilots and it did take many hours for pilots to get used to the controls: even we crew chiefs had trouble getting used to all the issues with the cockpit, such as the all-new glass displays and various integrated controls.

> *Many nights were spent looking for something'lost'. This often meant pulling out ejection seats and black boxes and stripping the cockpit to find an object and this was not cheap*

"Three things that made our job really miserable: the first was the JFS (Jet Fuel Starter) this was a secondary jet engine used to start the main engine. If it was not metered correctly, then usually it would not start because the charge cylinder would dump all the pressure at once and the engine would not light up and it took 200 strokes of the pump handle to recharge it. At Hill, we would actually keep the hydraulic mule hooked-up to the jet until the JFS was successfully started.

"It took time to isolate the problem and install a flow limiter for the fix. Then there were the wire-routing issues because many wires would get stretched and then fail because of improper routing. The main gearbox was also just a cheap design that later was fixed, but when the gearbox failed it would shut-off the generators, fuel pump and hydraulic pumps. This would cause the EPU (Emergency Power Unit) to fire off. This unit was a serious thing, it was powered by rocket fuel called hydrazine a very dangerous fuel. We were constantly reminded to safe the system when we could, so it would not accidentally fire off. When in the hanger we placed chemical sniffers around the EPU to detect possible fuel leaks, as one whiff of hydrazine could kill you!

"So, no: I cannot say the F-16 was a stellar jet when it first came out but it finally turned out to be a great fighter. It just took a long time to mature, maybe too long, because some of the stories I heard about the jet after I left the service in 1980 were truly scary. The problem with the F-16 is that General Dynamics never asked anyone what they wanted or needed in the multi role, multi-national fighter jet. I learned later with a 30 year career at Boeing that great aircraft designs happen when pilots, air-crew, maintenance, engineers and planners get together and help design and build a jet. The testament to this concept is the Boeing 777 aircraft: the best commercial jet ever built because of the 'working together' design concept."

- Sergeant William M Eckberg, USAF 1975-1980

ABOVE: **The General Electric M61 A1 'Vulcan' cannon had been in use since the F-104 Starfighter.**

LEFT: **The standard F-16B on the right, next to the version which was going to be the export model of choice for the early 1980s, the F-16/79, powered by the older GE J-79 turbojet.**

Giscard d'Estaing. The result was that Stehlin was ostracised and forced to resign from the French Assemblée Nationale.

The USAF finally announced their winner for the ACF fly-off on January 13, 1975, and behind the scenes in Europe the details had to be thrashed out as to how to make it all work. By March a document was produced showing why the F-16 had won. The report said that it was a cut above the other candidates in outright performance and was cheaper, even if some of the offsets for production and technology transfer were not quite as lucrative as the opposition's offers.

In a dramatic turn, on June 6, 1975 a report on Northrop's activities was made public showing that the Frenchman Paul Stehlin had been – effectively – on the company's payroll since 1964. That night in Paris, Stehlin was knocked down by a bus as he was crossing the Avenue de l'Opéra. He suffered a number of injuries including a fractured skull and died on June 22.

The next day, June 7, the NATO nations had selected the F-16 following an impressive display by General Dynamics test pilot Neil Anderson in the YF-16 demonstrator, after which the legendary Marcel Dassault himself told Anderson: "You have a fine aeroplane." This was the ultimate accolade considering that –following the news of the sale – the atmosphere in the Dassault sales chalet was distinctly icy. Worse was to follow. On July 21, 1980, the USAF announced the name for that the General Dynamics F-16 would adopt. Folklore suggests the name was the result of a 'name the plane' competition, won by a TSgt. Joseph A. Kurdell from MacDill AFB in Florida. He came up with 'Fighting Falcon'. Falcon as it's the emblem and mascot of the Air Force Academy, but – rumour has it – the prefix 'Fighting' was foisted upon the F-16 to avoid any legal issues confusing it with the Falcon family of business jets manufactured by... Dassault.

WORLDWIDE PRODUCTION

With the F-16 winning the 'Sale of the Century' it was now time to put the aircraft into production across the world.

Even 40 years later the sheer scale of the task seems humbling. Buying a total of 348 airframes cost the four European nations $2.168 billion and now work on actually building them had to begin. The manufacturers involved in the production of the F-16 in the USA (around 50 of them) now had to find other companies in Europe who could help them co-produce parts. In three of the countries it would lead to conferences and bids to get a slice of the pie – all except for Norway, whose government chose the companies that would get involved.

Politics – more local this time – still got in the way. For example in Belgium work had to be shared (or seen to be shared) equally between the French-speaking south and the Flemish north. In the Netherlands, Fokker had to move manufacturing to a number of different sites, whereas in other countries laws against the manufacture or shipment of 'war material' or anything considered to be such had to be dealt with or circumvented.

By 1977 things were beginning to come together across Europe so that the various parts were being produced and also going to General Dynamics' own production line in Fort Worth, Texas. The Europeans were to eventually look at manufacturing six aircraft a month from two assembly lines (Societé Anonyme Belge de Constructions Aéronautiques or SABCA at Gosselies, Belgium and Fokker, Schipol in The Netherlands).

The fact that this undertaking happened was thanks in no small part to GD's F-16 programme director for Europe, Jerry Jones. Despite thinking everything possible through before cranking up production it was understandable that lessons were going to be learnt on the hoof. It was found that tooling costs were higher than anticipated, the merging of US and European contractual laws and quality control was sometimes not smooth and – at one point – a holiday shutdown in Europe almost left a number of USAF-bound aircraft without their wings!

The 'told you so' contingent, were quick to jump on the fact that the F-16 was more expensive when made this way and may not have produced the promised jobs in the region. In 1977 the French newspapers carried headlines not of 'La Marche du Siècle' but instead 'La Marche des Dupes' and in March of that year Le Figaro even carried headlines suggesting deception, following the loss of a radar/avionics contract to a Belgian firm.

With hindsight – and while looking at similar programmes such as the Pan-European MRCA – which became the Tornado, and today's F-35 programme, the F-16 programme could be seen as relatively smooth in comparison. Also, it was thought that by 1981 around 30 sub-contractors in Europe and many hundreds of associated suppliers had received contracts totalling more than $1.5 billion dollars.

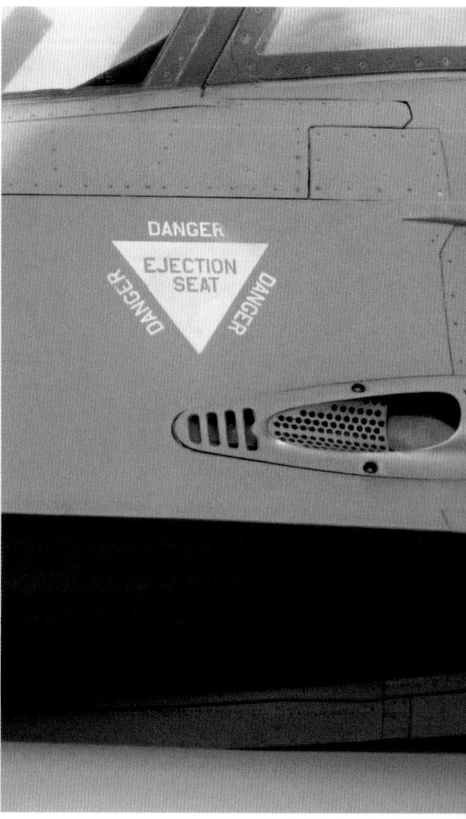

With the F-16 winning the 'Sale of the Century' it was now time to put the aircraft into production across the world

Belgium, Denmark, The Netherlands and Norway had operated around 300 Starfighters and they needed replacement by the early 1970s. The overall need was greater still as older types in the inventory of the four nations also required replacement. Types flown by various European air forces that could be a target for replacement by any victor of the ACF fly-off included North American F-100 Super Sabres, Northop (and Canadair licence-built) F-5As and Bs, Dassault Mirage Vs as well as other models, including the Fiat G.91.

INTO SERVICE

The F-16 era was ushered in almost simultaneously in the USA and Europe. On January 6, 1979, the first operational F-16A arrived at Hill Air Force Base, Utah and was seen arriving by more than 50,000 people and the Governor of Utah himself. It was that big of a deal.

Brigadier General Davis Rohr commanded the 388th Tactical Fighter Wing which was taking the new and futuristic fighter and by the end of the following year the Wing would have more than 100 F-16s with which to train pilots for Tactical Air Command and the European nations. By October of 1979 the first deliveries had also begun to the 56th Tactical Fighter Wing at MacDill AFB in Florida.

In a lightning series of events, the F-16 came on-stream for the four European nations, also. On January 26, 1979, the first European-built machine – an F-16B – was accepted by the Belgian air force. By early May of that year the first Fokker-built F-16 (J-259) first flew and by June 6 the Dutch air force had accepted their first F-16A. Close ties were forged between the operating nations of this new fighter.

On July 20, 1979, Majors Steve Heyboer and Jeff DeHeyn of the Dutch

ABOVE: An F-16B test fires an AIM-9N/P version of the ubiquitous Sidewinder family.

LEFT: The siting of the Vulcan cannon and the design of the muzzle cover changed over the years.

Inert Mk84, 2000lb bombs tumble from an F-16 from Hill on a training mission.

FALCON FACTS

For ease-of-service 80% of the F-16's access panels can be opened without needing a ladder!

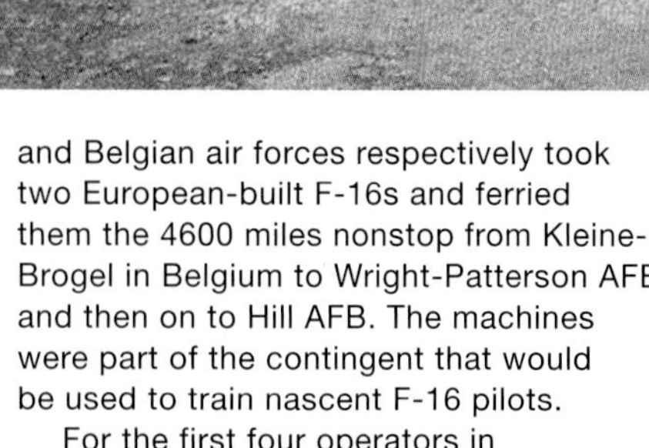

and Belgian air forces respectively took two European-built F-16s and ferried them the 4600 miles nonstop from Kleine-Brogel in Belgium to Wright-Patterson AFB and then on to Hill AFB. The machines were part of the contingent that would be used to train nascent F-16 pilots.

For the first four operators in Europe, the F-16 was a massive leap in capability in many areas, even with the first model's simplicity. All the machines were virtually identical to production F-16As being made for the USAF, with some small detail differences.

For operation in the cold extremes of Scandinavia, all 72 Norwegian F-16s were to be delivered with an extended fairing at the base of the aircraft's tail which would house a braking parachute for increased safety on icy runways. This also allowed the aircraft to use shorter, civilian runways dotted around the country. The Dutch also later adopted the parachute tail. Any aircraft received after 1987 had the extended tail fitted and the fleet was retrofitted with the parachute tail in 1992 under the 'Pacer Tail' programme.

The Norwegian machines would also carry the indigenous Penguin anti-ship missile and a searchlight was also fitted to the forward fuselage to aid with night-time interceptions, a modification the Dutch also adopted. From 1982-on, Belgian F-16s also had an extended tail fairing but this was occupied by Loral

***ABOVE:** The AGM-65 Maverick series of air-to-ground missiles was soon used by the F-16 force.*

***RIGHT:** These Hill F-16s feature the then-new AIM-9L Sidewinder with an 'all-aspect' seeker in the nose.*

***BELOW LEFT:** Crew chiefs take the potential for foreign object damage very seriously!*

RAPPORT III (Rapid Alert Programmed Power Management and Radar) Electronic Counter-Measures equipment, a suite of ECM equipment originally given the go ahead in 1979 and intended for the Belgian Air Force's own Mirage 5 aircraft.

On delivery, each F-16 was painted an attractive – if muted – series of greys. During original flight-testing before and during the ACF fly-off, a number of schemes were tested including a single-colour grey and a very attractive sky-blue/powder-blue 'wraparound' scheme. Eventually a compromise was reached and the USAF adopted a three-tone blue/grey scheme with the darker of the trio ghosted over the main wing and tailplanes.

Initial aircraft from Block 1 had black nosecones but this later changed to grey on the further production aircraft from Block 5 onwards with the Block 1 machines being retro-fitted with grey radomes at a later date. The main reason was that the colour of the nose showed up strongly during against the camouflage used on the aircraft and at altitude and during mock air engagements. European aircraft colour schemes were almost identical to the one used by the USAF, except for the Danes – who used semi-gloss finish – and the Norwegians who used a single shade of semi-gloss grey.

As the world went into the 1980s, it was clear that this was going to be the start of the F-16's decade of dominance. As more aircraft trundled off the production lines in Fort Worth and Europe, a number of firsts took place. On March 25, 1980, the 34th Tactical Fighter Squadron from ➤

the 388th TFW took their 12 aircraft on a simulated deployment called Red Max Alpha which was similar to what they would be expected to endure in time of war.

The exercise included two days of intensive combat flying, many simulated missions and a nonstop 4300 mile plus flight, utilising a number of in-flight refuelling slots with KC-135 tanker aircraft. By this time more than 100 production F-16s were flying and more than 14,500 flight hours had been logged, almost two-thirds of that total on production aircraft. By June, Yellow Max Alpha – another intensive test – this time over five days, proved the operational effectiveness of the F-16 as it topped previous bests set with other aircraft for the number of operational sorties flown and other criteria.

A name for the futuristic new fighter still hadn't been officially bestowed by the end of the 1970s, although one popular appellation was 'Viper'. Some say it was due to the serpent-eque lines of the wingroot/fuselage blend, while some say that the name came from the space-fighter aircraft seen in the film and television series Battlestar Galactica.

The General Dynamics F-16 was finally christened 'Fighting Falcon' on July 20, 1980, and by October of that year Tactical Air Command declared that the 4th Tactical Fighter Squadron had achieved 'Initial Operational Capability' or IOC. By November 18, 1980, all three combat squadrons at Hill AFB – the 4th, 34th and 421st TFS were fully equipped with F-16A aircraft and the first aircraft were on their way to the 474th Tactical Fighter Wing at Nellis, in Nevada.

By the time the F-16 had been declared combat-ready and received its operational name other nations had declared an interest in this new and promising fighter.

Way back in October 1976 Iran had signed a letter of intent to order 160 F-16s from a total of 300. It was said that the technology and aviation-obsessed Shah of Iran wanted the best for his air-force and the F-16s were to join the F-4s, the recently-acquired F-14 fleet and the rumoured F-17/F-18L fighters. The Shah was deposed before the order started and this meant that early deliveries could be made to the Israeli Air Force, who tested the F-16A with the 388th TFW soon after aircraft delivery. They accepted their first aircraft at the end of January 1980. Also in the Middle East, Egypt was offered 40 F-16s by the US in June 1980.

ABOVE: ***King of the castle in one of the finest fighter aircraft ever built.***

LEFT: ***Take-off for an F-16A of the 50th TFW.***

> ***A name for the futuristic new fighter still hadn't been officially bestowed by the end of the 1970s, although one popular appellation was 'Viper'***

By this time a number of other prospective versions of the F-16 had flown, including the F-16/79 on October 29, 1980, and the F-16/101 the following December. The F-16/79 was basically an F-16B, fitted with the earlier J-79 engine as used in the F-104 and F-4. Seen as a simplified machine for export, it won little favour with the export market but was evaluated as a potential adversary aircraft for the United States Navy. The F-16/101 would lead on to bigger things. This machine ironically used a General Electric engine derived from the YJ-101 used in the YF-17 LWF. The GE F-101 engine was called the Derivative Fighter Engine and the aircraft – which first flew on December 19, 1980 – made a total of 58 test flights before the programme ended in July 1981. Although the F-101 was not adopted for early F-16s, we shall see later that the engine developed into the F-110 which would power later variants of the Viper.

One of the existing European operators steadily began to increase their purchase in 1980 as the Dutch increased their initial order of 102 airframes to 213 in yearly increments of 22 aircraft. Meanwhile the aircraft itself was proving to be a potent multi-role fighter. The Belgian Air Force took their new fighter to their Corsican training ranges and found that their new mounts could record the highest scores ever attained in both air-to-air and air-to-ground training missions. The following year would see not just more foreign interest in the Fighting Falcon, but also further vindication of the platform and package itself.

In January 1981, the Belgian Air Force's 349th Squadron was the first F-16 unit assigned to NATO while in March, 12 aircraft from the USAF's 4th TFS took part in a month-long deployment to Norway where they experienced first-hand the tough conditions experienced by their F-16-flying brethren in the Norwegian Air Force. And all without a landing drag chute. During the sorties they would also take part in combat with various dissimilar aircraft including Northrop F-5s and SAAB Drakens.

Spring and summer 1981 would see yet more firsts. Two more European squadrons were declared operational for NATO (for the Dutch and the Belgians) and the 400th aircraft would leave the General Dynamics assembly line at Fort Worth. The month of June would ram home the capabilities of the F-16. Firstly on June 7 when a stunned world heard that the Israeli Air Force had attacked and destroyed the Osirak nuclear power station in Iraq and then on June 24 seven aircraft from the 388th TFW won a tactical bombing competition at RAF Lossiemouth. Not bad for a new aircraft.

With a look to the future, 1981 also saw the successful guided firing of a Hughes Advanced Medium Range Air-to-Air Missile (AMRAAM) in August which destroyed the drone target successfully. It was another nod to the future, with General Dynamics shrewdly leaving a capability for future radar-guided missiles latent in the design.

***ABOVE:* The AIM-9L was the wingtip weapon of choice for the F-16A and B.**

***BELOW:* F-16As over Hawaii.**

Various configurations and artists' impressions of the development aircraft had been seen or flown with dummy AIM-7 Sparrows – most notably during development for the proposed US Navy LWF/F-16 which was in conjunction with Vought, but which lost out to the McDonnell Douglas/Northrop proposed F-18. In fact the AIM-7 Sparrow had already been fired from an F-16 back in November 1977 over China Lake – the missile test facility in California – as had the UK's advanced Sparrow derivative the SkyFlash back in November 1978, at Point Mugu.

At the close of 1981, more than 500 General Dynamics F-16s had been built. One pilot had already logged a 1000 hours in the type and aircraft had been delivered to six air forces around the world. It had also been selected by both Egypt and Pakistan for delivery the following year. The aircraft had shown itself not just adept in competition with other aircraft both in the USAF and other air forces but had been fully bloodied in combat with the Israeli Air Force. The F-16 Fighting Falcon had truly arrived and by December of 1981 the 50th TFW at Hahn AFB in West Germany began to convert to the new fighter. The Viper was about to get involved in the cold war.

VIPER ENTERS THE COLD WAR

As soon as the F-16 won the LWF competition it was a given that it would go to war: a cold war...

Looking back now to the beginning of the 1980s, it's hard to believe that the USAF had been enjoying a few years of peace – albeit under the dark cloud of the Cold War.

Following on from the end of the Vietnam War, USAF squadrons would enjoy a long period of relative calm, before the start of Operation Desert Shield and later Desert Storm in 1990/91. It was left to other air forces to show the Viper's bite, but for a young USAF pilot, the tip of the spear for deployment had to be USAFE – the United States Air Force in Europe.

The F-16 – despite being conceived as a lightweight, clear-weather dogfighter – was going to its own phoney war in Europe, loaded with bombs, where the rain, clouds and clag were about as far from the gin-clear skies of the USA as you could get.

At the end of 1978 it was announced that the 50th Tactical Fighter Wing would adopt the new F-16A fighter but first would come a series of tests to evaluate the new aircraft on the continent. A number of F-16s from the full-scale development batch were flown to Hahn Air Force Base during 1979 to embark ➤

The sharp end of the USAF during The Cold War included the F-15A, F-16A, A-10A and the long-in-the-tooth F-4E Phantom II.

on what was to become known as the European Test and Evaluation programme.

The first four European nations to buy the F-16 were already learning hands-on how the aircraft performed in the demanding conditions of Northern Europe. It made sense then that the ET&E aircraft used the existing expertise, travelling from Hahn to Norway (for cold weather trials), to Denmark, and even to RAF Lakenheath as well as other USAFE bases. More than four months of testing, as well as some dissimilar air combat training with RAF Alconbury's 'Aggressor' F-5E Tiger IIs.

Although not from the USAFE, a detachment of seven aircraft from the 388th TFW deployed to RAF Lossiemouth, Scotland, to take part in a tactical bombing competition on June 24, 1981. The results were staggering. The 388th TFW team scored a record 7831 from a possible 8000 points. In second was an RAF Jaguar team that scored 6401. It was reported that all ordnance hit the correct ground targets, while the

***ABOVE:* Exercises like Operation Bright Star in Egypt in 1982 often threw up interesting formations. Here an F-16 and A-10A fly over the Pyramids alongside a MiG-21 and MiG-15 trainer.**

***RIGHT:* Returning to its shelter after a 'Certain Sentinel' mission in 1986 is this F-16A from the 10th Tactical Fighter Squadron.**

F-16s soon made their mark. In 1981 an F-16 team wiped the floor with the opposition at a bombing competition at RAF Lossiemouth, also scoring an 86-0 kill ratio against Lightnings and Phantoms.

team scored an 86-0 kill ratio against the defending BAC Lightnings and McDonnell Douglas F-4 Phantoms.

Unsurprisingly 388th pilots took first and second places overall in the Sir John Mogg Bombing Trophy (Captain Roger Riggs and Captain Wayne C Edwards respectively) which was awarded during the deployment. Edwards was particularly excited by the potential of the F-16. He said at the time: "The machine, now wearing its operational colours of mottled grey, looked devastatingly effective. I found myself thinking that if the

LAWN DART: NOT THIS TIME

It's fair to say that – like most modern military jets – the General Dynamics F-16 wasn't a happy ship to fly with an engine out. Okay, with its only engine out.

Numerous crew chiefs christened the F-16 'the lawn dart' during an engine failure, stating that the only thing the inherently unstable F-16 would do without power was plough into the ground. However, pilots could – and sometimes did – make engine-out landings in the F-16.

Captain James Trinka was an instructor with the 311th Tactical Fighter Training Squadron at Luke Air Force Base. And one day in 1986 he performed an emergency dead-stick, downwind landing following a bird-strike in his F-16A.

There is no real 'good time' to suffer a bird-strike but accelerating to climb speed just after take-off while leading a flight of three F-16s is perhaps one of the worst. Glancing over his shoulder, Trinka saw his wingman moving gradually back into echelon position off his wing. Then, as he moved his head forward he saw a shape coming towards him. It was a large bird, maybe 200-300ft directly in front of his F-16 and on a collision course with his aircraft.

There's never any 'good place' for a large bird to hit, but taking a heavy object at speed on the canopy doesn't bear thinking about. For Trinka his training immediately kicked in as the incident unfolded before him. Recounting his experience to the US Navy's flight safety magazine Approach he recalls: "We were always told that a bird when it sees an airplane will immediately fold back its wings and try to dive and that's just what this bird did. There was no time for any manoeuvres to miss the thing and it went right down my jet intake."

It was a worst-case scenario for Trinka. As soon as the bird was ingested into the engine, the engine unsurprisingly failed. Trinka needed to get as much height as he could, so he went into a climb to get a better altitude for ejection and moved the throttles back from full military power to idle. As the rpm of the engine declined the motor's generator dropped offline, which signalled the EPU or Emergency Power Unit to kick in as the engine's revs went below 35%.

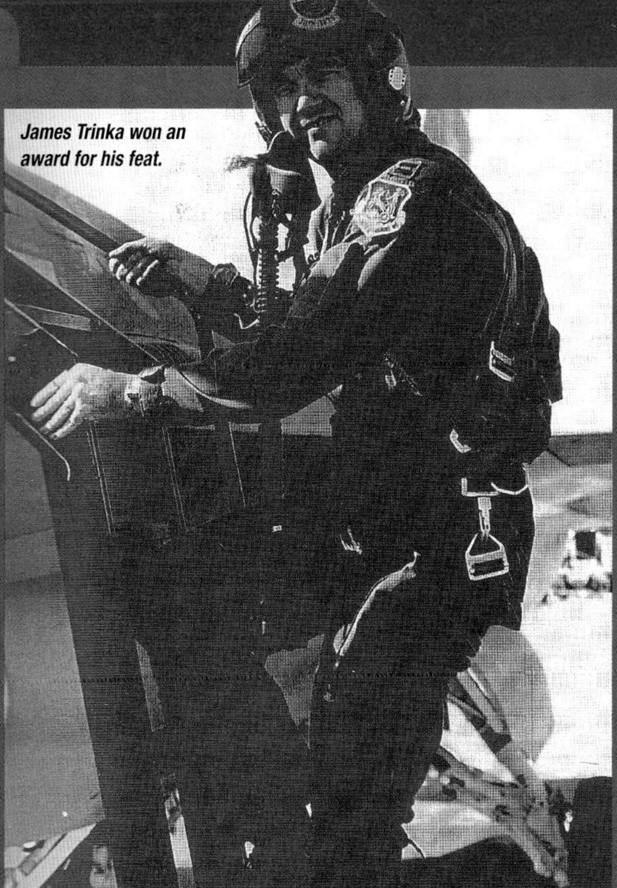
James Trinka won an award for his feat.

With the vital EPU working, Trinka then turned on the Jet Fuel Starter (JFS), which is basically a small jet engine which can keep even an F-110 at minimum rpm. The bird had struck the engine, smashing its way through a 6in section of the first stage of fan blades. The fan section was seized as a result, but the core section of the motor was kept spinning by the JFS, which ran the hydraulics. With these systems functioning and with the reassuring whine coming from the JFS, Trinka decided to try and save the aircraft by making a dead-stick, downwind landing.

Trinka was at 750ft altitude and he turned the F-16 270-degrees then made a 90-degree turn back in the direction he had been coming from, so as to head back to the end of the same runway he had just left. The recommended procedure was to eject from the aircraft, but with altitude in hand and airspeed of 210 knots, he called the tower, lowered his emergency arrestor hook and then his landing gear. Again the gear was lowered thanks to hydraulic pressure from the JFS.

Trinka said: "My heart was beating so fast during the event and I didn't have much time to think. My reactions were a result of the training programme. It was interesting also to find that the aircraft behaved just as it had during 'routine' flameout approaches that I had flown previously."

With his F-16 aiming halfway up the runway, Trinka told the tower to raise the arresting cable at the end of it. He made the touchdown half way down the runway and thankfully caught the arresting cable and came to a stop.

The whole incident showed the benefits of exhaustive training. USAF instructors are some of the best pilots in the world and Captain James Trinka had just saved US taxpayers a $25 million F-16. As a result, Trinka was awarded the Air Force's 1986 Aviator's Valour Award for a "conspicuous act of valour or courage performed during aerial flight, in or out of combat".

And what of the aircraft? Well, it was a Block 10 F-16A delivered on July 31, 1980, and it had a long and impressive career in the USAF. Joining the 311th in 1984 after its early years at the 421st Tactical Fighter Squadron at Hill Air Force Base, the aircraft became the squadron flagship, adopting the '311' as part of its tail code.

Following the incident and a full repair the aircraft was used as a demo flight aircraft at Edwards AFB, adopting the striking white/red colour scheme of EAFB from 1991 before being retired to the AMARC Boneyard in 1995, where it still sits to this day. S.Sgt. Joni Kelsey (retired), a recipient of the 2015 Katherine and Marjorie Stinson Trophy no less used to work on 311 and she recalls: "I always remember 311. After that incident there we were cleaning out a dead bird and engine debris in Arizona in 100 degree heat plus, but I wouldn't have given the job up on the Viper for the world."

Currently, 311 is in storage at the Davis Monthan 'boneyard'.

CURIOUS CONFIGURATIONS

ABOVE & LEFT: ***Old-school aviator 'Gums' McAdoo.***

TOP LEFT: ***Gums says goodbye to the F-16.***

BOTTOM LEFT: ***Poor quality shot shows the angle of the leading-edge flaperon.***

With so many F-16s in service with air forces around the world, many hair-raising failures would occur and strange landing configurations would be encountered. One during 1982 was when the starboard leading edge flap failed, while being flown by Lieutenant Colonel Pat 'Gums' McAdoo.

Gums was old-school and a Vietnam veteran. He'd flown the F-102 Delta Dagger, the F-101 Voodoo, old T-33 trainers as well as combat in South East Asia with the likes of the A-37 Tweet and A-7D Corsair. McAdoo was on hand when the F-16s first came to Hill AFB in 1979. McAdoo would retire with 600 hours on the F-16 and recalls it was an eye-opener when the first 'Electric Jets' arrived.

He recalls: "The really neatest thing about flying a new jet, a really new jet, was we didn't have official USAF tech orders. No kidding. First few months I was there we used a Xerox copy of the Edwards' flight test Dash One. We also had no 'rules'. So all of our emergency procedures were word-of-mouth until the official technical orders and flight manuals came out. Man, those were the days."

I flew so many great aircraft and the Viper turned like an F-102, climbed like the Voodoo, dropped bombs as good as (or better than) the A-7D and had the best visibility of anything out there

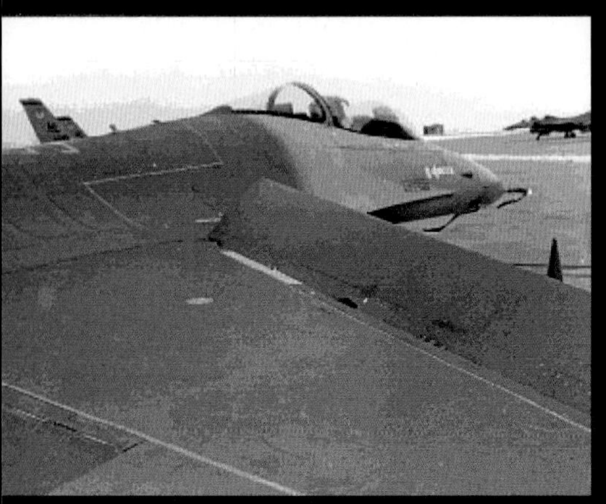

And some days were better than others. In 1982 Gums was able (just) to land F-16A, tail number 044, which had a starboard leading edge flap failure. He recalls: "It was maybe March 1982. Maintenance had failed to insert a 'keeper' bolt that is supposed to keep the flap drive tubes from slipping apart. It's like a cotter key on a bolt. The flap drive motor has a spline gear on it and the drive tube has gear teeth that match up. So the drive tube gradually slipped out from the motor spline gear.

"When I rotated on take-off the drive tube slid all the way out and the leading edge flap went up until the wing upper surface stopped it. It was maybe at 50-60 degrees. Another troop had his fail a few months later and the flap went to 90 degrees because he was going a lot faster when the drive tube failed. So I was at 160 knots and holding full left stick. Post-flight data revealed that I had about one pound of control authority for banking left. So I was holding 15-16 pounds of left stick the whole time.

"I stayed at 170-180 knots as I could still maintain control and wasn't gonna play Chuck Yeager any more than I had to. Nevertheless, I was the first guy to fly the thing in that configuration, so everything was new territory. I was bunted over to get the opposite leading edge flap two degrees up (LEFs go up when bunting over, or when weight is on the wheels). I now had both LEFs up and it seemed to help with the roll authority.

"Additionally, that other flap wasn't gonna be moving all over the place, and this kept things a little more predictable for me on the approach. I came round and landed in one helluva crab. The drag was so great that I almost landed short when I pulled off the power. As I was coming in a lot hotter than normal, I thought I would land long but that sucker dropped like a rock and I was able to make a mid-field turn off!

"I flew so many great aircraft and the Viper turned like an F-102, climbed like the Voodoo, dropped bombs as good as (or better than) the A-7D and had the best visibility of anything out there."

FALCON FACTS

F-16s have been embroiled in coup attempts in Venezuela and Turkey.

TOP: The 1980s saw the General Dynamic F-16 mature as a combat aircraft.

ABOVE: The successful USAF team were a resounding success at the RAF Lossiemouth bombing competition in 1981.

RIGHT: The USAF crews took the overall award and proved that the F-16 could bomb and fight its way to and from the target.

airplane could do half of what it looked to be capable of, it would be unreal." Riggs and Edwards and the 388th had given the F-16 a stunning start in Europe and one which paved the way for the arrival of the first Block 15 F-16A at Hahn on December 29, 1981. The Viper was finally in Europe.

The 50th TFW had been based at Hahn Air Force Base since 1959 and before the F-16 arrived, it was equipped with the battle-proven McDonnell F-4E Phantom II which it had been using for the previous 12 years. The switch from a two-seat aircraft to a single-seat would take some adaptation. The main roles for the new General Dynamics aircraft would be conventional attack, nuclear strike and air-to-air, so it was understandable that many pilots would come to the 50th TFW with a strike background, such as from the General Dynamics F-111 – another two-seater.

Training was intense and deployments were made away from the overcast of central Europe to the likes of Zaragoza, Spain. Problems with their new mounts were also found, as they were in the fledgling F-16 units during the early 1980s. These issues included difficulties with the Westinghouse APG-66 with clutter against air-to-air targets (especially in mountainous terrain) problems with the afterburner suffering a 'blow out' thanks to fuel flow issues, landing issues with such a relatively 'lightweight' aircraft and some problems with the flight control system.

A 'Wolfpack' F-16 with centreline tank and Mk84s.

Under-fuselage ECM pod and training rocket pods are toted by these F-16s.

Eventually all three squadrons: the 10th, 313th and 496th Tactical Fighter Squadrons were operationally ready in April 1983. Retired Lieutenant Colonel Dana Purifoy had come from the F-111E community and he recalls the challenges flying the – still relatively simple – F-16A in Europe. He says: "Initially I was surprised we were doing more air-to-ground work than air-to-air in the F-16. For F-111 pilots flying air-to-ground missions in Europe, the F-16 seemed like a step backward: I thought I'd traded one bad deal with an airplane I thought had at least some possibility of survival in for an airplane I thought had zero possibility of survival."

In the F-111E, Purifoy had the benefit of an all-weather radar and an automated terrain-following system that enabled him to fly at 200ft above the ground: at night or in bad weather (or at night and in bad weather) and still hit a target. Meanwhile the ex-F-4E drivers were having to juggle using the new radar themselves (having lost their Weapon Systems Officers or WSOs) and were bemoaning the lack of a radar-guided missile for longer-ranged intercepts. And the aircraft's much-vaunted agility was not much of a bonus when weighed down with an air-to-ground

ADVANCED AGGRESSOR, ADVERSARY

The USAF's aggressor squadrons came about as a result of some poor performance in the early part of the conflict in South East Asia.

Experienced hands like Robin Olds knew the score. A Second World War ace on P-38 Lightnings and P-51 Mustangs, he'd led Uborn's 8th TFW to success from September 1966 to the following September. He knew that to fight air-to-air you had to practice it – and against aircraft other than your own.

"The air force just wanted guys who could take off, do the job and not crash," he once said. This was again the case when the offensive operations started again up north in early 1972, but not so the US Navy. On the quiet after taking up his post at the Air Force Academy, Olds would get some unofficial training with the US Navy.

In his autobiography he wrote: "To get in some real flying I'd head down to San Diego and fly with the Navy at Miramar. Damn, those guys were for real! It was dog-eat-dog – no pussyfooting around! Their air-to-air programme was realistic and aggressive. They had their act together on training."

This was of course as a result of the US Navy's own issues over Vietnam – they weren't going to suffer that way again. Meanwhile, Olds was sent back to Vietnam to check on the readiness of the USAF in both air-to-air and air-to-ground missions and what he saw shocked him so much that he reputedly told his superior General John D Ryan that the USAF forces in theatre in Vietnam "couldn't fight their way out of a wet paper bag". Olds offered to be reduced in rank if he could be sent back to South East Asia and rectify the situation but was not taken up on his offer. He retired in 1973.

History would prove Olds right. While the Navy had learned the earlier lessons from Vietnam the USAF had to learn the hard way – again. As a result 18 months of study on combat in South East Asia led to The Red Baron I and II reports. They explained what much of what the 'old hands' already knew. When it came to air combat the pilots would only dogfight each other – in the same aircraft. And even then sometimes this was frowned upon and could end up with the pilot losing his wings.

Over in Europe this was not so much the case. The dissimilar aircraft used by the various NATO forces in the 1960s and 1970s meant that aircraft were often 'bounced' by RAF Hunters, Lightnings, West German F-104s and USAFE types.

The Red Baron reports effectively said that air combat training needed to be realistic and

ABOVE: *Aggressor pilots are trained to fly and fight like Russian-trained pilots.*

preferably against aircraft of dissimilar type. It also said that intelligence needed to trickle down to operations level in the squadron, keeping them abreast of all the latest tactics and capabilities of any potential enemy and also that training needed to help front-line pilots get the best out of the equipment they were trying to employ.

> *To get in some real flying I'd head down to San Diego and fly with the Navy at Miramar. Damn, those guys were for real! It was dog-eat-dog - no pussyfooting around! Their air-to-air programme was realistic and aggressive. They had their act together on training*

Out of this came the Dissimilar Air Combat Training programme or DACT. Simply setting up various DACT arrangements between squadrons, commands, service branches or even with friendly countries wouldn't do the job. Sure, it would be interesting to take on RAF BAC Lightnings, or French Mirages – but the level of the threat and the tactics employed had to be the same (or near as dammit) to that used by and exported from the Soviet bloc.

This meant pilots had to fly the same way – even if it meant getting beaten by the opposition. The 'threat manual' had to be kept bang up to date (which meant regular liaising with the intelligence community) and the strict use of GCI or 'Ground Control Intercept' so favoured by the Soviets (and customers such as Vietnam) had to be slavishly adhered to and replicated.

From this came the formation of 'Aggressor' squadrons, the first of which was formed at Nellis Air Force Base, Nevada in 1972. The choice of aircraft was what was on hand at the time – the Northrop T-38 Talon. This was the standard, supersonic advanced trainer in use with the USAF. Twenty T-38s were borrowed from Air Training Command and – eventually – painted up to look suitably 'warlike', normally in colours seen on Soviet bloc tactical fighters.

As good as the Talon was, what was

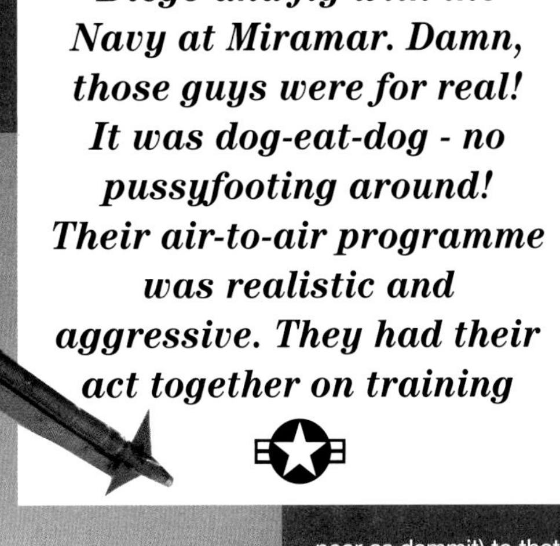

As well as in Europe, the F-16 was at the tip of the spear during The Cold War in the Korean peninsula.

ABOVE: The US Navy moved to the F-16C following the phase-out of the F-16N.

BELOW: Wheels up on another ACM sortie for the Aggressors.

needed was a proper fighter aircraft, preferably with a simple radar and with the end of the war in Vietnam in 1975, came the windfall of around 100 Northrop F-5E Tiger II, single-seat fighters that were going to be used in the conflict in South East Asia. As the news of the good work done by the first unit – the 64th Aggressor Squadron – filtered down others were formed, most notably the 65th (also at Nellis) followed by the 527th Tactical Fighter Training Aggressor Squadron, formed in 1976 at RAF Alconbury and the 26th Aggressor Squadron formed at Clark Air Force Base in the Philippines.

The activation of the aggressors also saw a marked increase in the 'train as you fight, fight as you train' dictum. From this came the various flag exercises held even to this day. Red Flag began in 1975, following The Red Baron III report, where it showed that – in Vietnam – pilot survivability soared when 10 successful missions had been accomplished. Red Flag (and the subsequent other 'Flag' exercises) aims to give pilots those 10 realistic missions in a variety of environments – albeit in peacetime. The popularity has led over the years to invites from the US to many other nationalities to take part, including the RAF, the Indian Air Force, the Israeli Air Force, the Greek Air Force and many more.

For a decade until the mid-1980s the F-5E was the workhorse of the Aggressor squadrons, replicating – with some degree of accuracy – the main threat faced at the time – the MiG-21 – but as the 'threat manual' got updated so the weapons employed by the Aggressors had to too. And besides, a decade of use in the high-G environment aged airframes quicker than those out on the front-line.

The USAF and the US Navy looked at procuring the same 'new' equipment, but while the Navy went for a stripped-down specific model (the F-16N, see below) the USAF took an off-the-shelf option with the F-16C. The adoption of the F-16C wasn't the perfect scenario for a number of reasons. Firstly, the whole point is 'dissimilar', which the F-16 is not, if you're flying an F-16 in the USAF.

Thankfully, the addition of some Soviet warpaint and the later adoption of F-15 airframes helped. Other issues included the worry that the F-16C couldn't replicate the high-alpha dogfight attributes of the MIG-29 Fulcrum, or the off-boresight capability of some of its missiles and its passive infrared tracking system. The big problem was numbers. With insufficient F-16 airframes available the 65th Aggressor Squadron was deactivated in 1988.

In Europe the 527th moved from Alconbury to RAF Bentwaters and kept their F-16Cs in standard F-16 camouflage, but the large, red Soviet-style 'bort' numbers often painted on the intake trunking remained.

Back in the mid-1990s, Colonel Doug Melson, a 4000-hour fighter pilot with 1000 instructor hours under his belt heaped praise on the F-16C. He said: "If we fought as ourselves using the F-16 to its best advantage we would win 90% of the time and you would see the disparaging effect that would have on the young fighter pilots we were teaching.

"Even when we stay within the Soviet aircraft's limitations there will be many times when we can win the engagement easily, but we don't press home the attack. It's about teaching. Sometimes giving the young pilot the chance to 'live' means we can talk about it back on the ground: although if he's really cocky, shooting him down might just be the best thing!"

The constant demands on the USAF over many conflicts has shown that the best training gives the best results out on the cutting edge – even if today's 'modern wars' aren't given to dogfighting – but Desert Storm showed that it worked.

With the deactivation of the 65th Aggressor squadron late in 2014 came a shift from using both the F-15C and the F-16 to – now – just the F-16. Meanwhile, the US Navy still uses versions of the F-5 Tiger II as well as the Boeing F/A-18 Hornet and the F-16C as adversary aircraft.

Time will tell if this is the right tactic for the USAF, especially against the new breed of 'Blue Air' with the likes of the F-22 Raptor and the F-35 Lightning II joining the latest Red Flag exercises, not to mention the more-modern 'foreign' fighters like the Rafale and Typhoon taking part. And with the USAF's current crop of F-16Cs being the oldest Block 25s and 32s, perhaps a limited-run upgrade to a 'modest F-16V' level be the future answer?

MAIN: ***F-16s utilising a KC-135 air-to-air tanker.***

BELOW LEFT: ***Bitburg's F-15 Eagles often worked with Hahn's F-16s.***

BELOW RIGHT: ***While dumb iron bombs were the normal load for F-16s in USAFE…***

BOTTOM: ***This F-16 is carrying a BDU-38 practice B61 Tactical Nuclear bomb.***

load either – pilots reckoned that with tactical ordnance hanging of the plane, the F-16 was no more agile than an F-4.

Other air forces in Europe were finding the same issues with the basic F-16A and Bs. One Belgian pilot confessed that – in reality – things hadn't changed much and that a lack of radar-guided missile actually meant that the new F-16s were less capable than the French Air Force's Mirage F1-C that they were 'playing' with in exercises. "The early F-16As were just day fighters, in the same mould as the Mirage V and F-104 and in bad weather we were grounded…"

Hard work with the 50th TFW saw rapid improvements in weapon delivery. Purifoy ➤

In 1985 this F-16A flew with the 401st Tactical Fighter Wing out of Torrejón in Spain.

A 10th TFS F-16C in 1987 with practice Mk84s.

***ABOVE:** The F-16 and F-4G would form a 'hunter-killer' anti-SAM team following the F-4E's retirement in Europe.*

***ABOVE:** Airman Sylvia Wagner inserts a HUD video tape into the F-16 before the pilot climbs aboard.*

The AN/ALQ-131 ECM pod was a common fit for F-16s.

recalls: "When I got to the 10th TFS, we just completed our NATO TACEVAL (Tactical Evaluation) qualifications. We put about 30 airplanes across the target over a period of a week. The average error for the whole squadron was under a metre and bomb time on target was less than two seconds off desired TOT. And this is from toss manoeuvres from up to four nautical miles distant."

Ramming the Hahn Wing's results home was the fact that in October 1983 six pilots from the 50th TFW took their mounts to the Gunsmoke air-to-ground gunnery and bombing contest. They were overall winners, as well as taking the honours in the 200ft level bombing competition and the 30-degree dive-bombing competition.

The 50th TFW would carve their own glorious history in USAFE and further afield over the years following the introduction of the F-16A and B. In 1986 the Wing converted over to the new F-16C/D model, with APG-68 radar and (finally) a medium-range missile capability. They also participated in Desert Shield and then Desert Storm in 1990/91, before being deactivated on September 30, 1991.

It could have all been so different.

Instead of the F-16Ns that the US Navy eventually used for adversary training they could have had Vipers flying off the decks of carriers by the early 1980s.

Following on from the F-16's win over the YF-17, the US Navy was being pushed to accept its own Light Weight Fighter, ostensibly to replace the aging A-4 Skyhawk, F-4 Phantom II and (younger) A-7 Corsair II. With the thought of another lucrative contract in mind, General Dynamics teamed up with Ling-Temco Vought (LTV) – creator of the F-8 Crusader and A-7 Corsair – while Northrop teamed up with McDonnell Douglas of A-4 and F-4 fame.

Vought and GD came up with three proposals for a shipboard F-16: the V-1600, V-1601 and V-1602. Each would have a different engine, a Pratt & Whitney F-401, Pratt & Whitney F-100 and General Electric F-101 respectively.

Much was changed to get the F-16 close to carrier-capable. The F-401-powered V-1600 was longer than an F-16A, with a stretched fuselage, bigger wingspan, flaps and horizontal tail. The landing gear was strengthened, twin-nosewheels added at the front, along with catapult bar. The radar was to be a pulse-doppler set married to the medium-range AIM-7 Sparrow missiles carried on wing pylons. The V-1600 was going to be around 10,000lb heavier than the standard F-16A.

The V-1601 was more like the standard F-16A, sharing the same F-100 powerplant. This too had a fuselage stretch, a larger (but not as large as V-1600) wing and reduced fuel capacity, while the V-1602 was to use the heavier GE engine, a further reconfigured wing and widened fuselage. The capacity to use the Sparrow family of missiles was vital to the US Navy's requirement, hence mock-ups and artists' impressions showed them being carried under the wings or conformally on the fuselage.

History shows that the McDonnell/Northrop development of the YF-17 seemed more suited to the US Navy's needs, with its twin-engined safety, but you can't help wonder 'what if' one of

THE NAVY'S F-16s

these three versions had made it onto the carriers of the early 1980s. Maybe Tom Cruise wouldn't have been flying a Tomcat in TOPGUN…

The Navy, like the Aggressors, like to go for colourful paint schemes.

ENTER THE F-16N

The US Navy finally did get to fly the F-16 and it was one hot ship, but first a brief history lesson.

The US Navy – like the USAF – was shocked by its relative poor performance air-to-air in Vietnam. So, during a pause in the air battles during 1968 the Ault Report into the performance of the air-to-air missiles in the first three years of the conflict was set up and the findings were sobering. The most striking were the fact that many missiles fired by crews in Vietnam weren't made inside of launch or kill parameters and that proper employment of the aircraft they were flying often wasn't made.

To this end the creation of the Navy Fighter Weapons School or 'TOPGUN' was made and the US Navy made their own adversary squadrons, using the Northrop F-5E Tiger II and the ubiquitous A-4 Skyhawk. The NFWS was then to hold a number of 'power projection' courses during the year for a number of crews from various squadrons who would then go back to the fleet and pass on their knowledge and experiences. It worked, as the US Navy would record an F-4J crew as their first aces of the campaign.

> *It could have all been so different. Instead of the F-16Ns that the US Navy eventually used, they could have had Vipers flying off the decks*

The US Navy made a decision in 1985 to adopt its own version of the then-current F-16 in service with the USAF. The US Navy urgently needed something to bridge the gap between the Northrop F-5s and up-engined Skyhawks they were using in the adversary role. With the mid-1980s threats changing from the MiG-21 and MiG-23 to the latest MiG-29 Fulcrum and Sukhoi Su-27, like the USAF's Aggressor squadrons, the US Navy needed an agile, more capable threat replicator.

This was to come in the shape of the F-16N. Based on the F-16C/D Block 30, it was powered by the General Electric F-110-GE-100 turbofan fed by the small-inlet intake, with the APG-66 radar. The N had the 20mm Vulcan cannon removed along with a number of avionics, but they did have radar warning receivers and chaff/flare dispensers.

A brace of F-16s from the 50th TFW at Hahn.

Free from the shackles of weight for the carrier role and without much land-based F-16 gear, the emergent F-16N was a prize fighter stripped for purpose. A total of 26 aircraft were made, 22 single-seat F-16Ns and four two-seat TF-16Ns.

Of course the F-16 wasn't originally the first choice, but it had to be a dissimilar one. With such a long connection with Northrop's F-5E and F-5F family, initially it was the F-20 Tigershark that was in the running for the Navy's fourth-generation adversary, but with no bulk buyer on the horizon, it would have been expensive to fire up the production line for just 20-30 aircraft.

Of course the F-16 was in production and in the very early 1980s there already was a downgraded F-16 available: the F-16/79, powered by the venerable J-79 turbojet. Rumours have it that TOPGUN instructors did get to fly the F-16/79 and found it good enough for the job. As time marched on, Northrop could only let Navy instructors fly the F-20 simulator and then the F-16/79 was dismissed as no orders would be likely with 'full fat' F-16As now being allowed for foreign sale by the Reagan administration. Sadly, by October 1984 the F-20 programme had suffered a loss of one of the prototypes and despite Northrop touting the machine across the globe, no production-start orders were forthcoming. As the US Navy didn't need a large amount of dissimilar adversary aircraft, the announcement was made in 1985 and the F-16N was born and produced in very modest numbers.

The F-16N and TF-16N had a tough, 11-year career with the US Navy, with the first being delivered in 1987 and the last being retired in 1998. With them often being flown in 'clean' configuration, with weight down (250lb was lost by deleting the gun) and with a hi-G nature of their jobs, it wasn't surprising that fatigue led them to be retired early.

So, it was a 'hot-ship' but how hot? Paul Nickell was a former F-14 Tomcat pilot and became an instructor at TOPGUN and flew the F-16N. He says: "The jet would do supersonic cruise (super-cruise) in the configuration that we flew it. Generally slick, at altitude (no pylons or missiles – just an ACMI pod on the right wing tip) it could go supersonic with no afterburner with the help of its powerful General Electric engine.

ABOVE: A 13th Tactical Fighter Squadron F-16A is seen on a snowy flightline in 1985.

"This was something we had to keep in mind transiting around the country. Unlike the F-14, there was not a noticeable reduction in acceleration as you approached Mach 1. Bottom line, it was sleek and it was fast. I've personally seen it achieving Mach 2 and a burner take-off in the stripped-down N was the next best thing to a cat-shot off the deck."

For some the N model was perhaps still a little too basic considering the rumours coming out of Eastern Europe over the beyond visual range (BVR) capability of the Fulcrum and Flanker. The F-16N had the Westinghouse APG-66 from the standard F-16A/B, but the leap in capability meant that – if well flown (and they were) the F-16N could replicate any real threat from MiG-17-up. Nickell adds: "The F-5 could simulate the MiG-23 if it stayed fast and made large arcing turns. However, neither the A-4 nor F-5 could properly simulate the fourth generation threats.

"The beauty of the F-16N was that it could simulate all of these threats well if flown properly by the adversary pilot. To simulate the MiG-17, we simply flew the F-16 full-up, except we never used the afterburner. To simulate the MiG-21 we flew it full-up, except we would select no more than zone two in afterburner. To simulate the MiG-23 we flew the F-16N at the speed of heat and made no turns greater than about 4g. On top of that, we could simulate the fourth generation Soviet fighters, the Su-27 and MiG-29, if we flew it full up, full burner and at any speed."

The IAF has had much use from its Netz fleet since delivery.

FALCON FACTS

The F-16 is the second most common military aircraft in the world.

The General Dynamics F-16A Netz or 'Hawk' gave a boost in capability to the IAF. This is one of the Block 10 aircraft delivered.

Legendary airframe 107 with its kill tally, after retirement. It also took part in Operation Opera. Of the 67 F-16 kills to date, 47 have been made by Israeli F-16s.

The Netz was chosen to supplement and eventually replace the mighty F-4E Phantom II in IAF service.

VIPER'S BITE

Israel needed a modern, multi-role combat aircraft with which to fight the many enemies clustered around her borders. She needed something deadly and cost effective. She needed the General Dynamics F-16.

Less than a year after its introduction into the Israel Defence Force/Air Force and General Dynamic F-16 Fighting Falcon had scored its first kill and dropped its first bomb in anger.

With multi-role a priority for the IAF – especially as the F-16 was initially envisaged as a replacement for its ageing McDonnell-Douglas A-4 and F-4 fighter-bombers – it's not surprising that the first blooding of the F-16 was in the air-to-ground role. The first operational General Dynamics F-16 Fighting Falcon squadron was No.117 – The First Jet Squadron – under the command of Lieutenant Colonel Ze'ev Raz. On November 21, 1980, it was declared fully operational with 18 aircraft on charge and yet reportedly the aircraft flew its first combat mission prior to that, during August of 1980, striking Palestinian targets in Southern Lebanon – such was the pace of life on the front-line for the IAF. On April 22, 1981, the Northern Knights Squadron put up a four aircraft formation led by Squadron Commander Amir Nachumi which bombed suspected Palestinian Liberation Organisation targets in The Lebanon.

Both of the first two squadrons of F-16s – No.110 (The Knights of the North) and No.117 – held typical Quick Reaction Alert or QRA flights, but it wasn't until April 28 that the first air-to-air victory came.

Syrian Mil Mi-8 helicopters armed with rockets and guns and airlifting PLO troops had been supporting the Syrian offensive against Lebanese Christian Militia at El Matan as well as ranging in and out of Israeli-held territory. So, at 12.14pm on the 28th Lieutenant Rafl of No.117 Squadron – widely claimed to be the youngest pilot in the IAF at the time – engaged the Mi-8 Hips in F-16 code-numbered 78-0314 (local nose-code 112) with heat-seeking missiles and cannon fire. It is reported that a missile was fired first, but missed, so that the young pilot had to switch to the 20mm cannon to bring the helicopter down.

> ***Colonel Dov 'Doobie' Yoffe was the second F-16 pilot to destroy an enemy when he too shot down a Mi-8 with an AIM-9L Sidewinder***

Later that day squadron-mate Colonel Dov 'Doobie' Yoffe was the second F-16 pilot to destroy an enemy when he too shot down a Mi-8 with an AIM-9L Sidewinder. These actions, while not quite showing the F-16's prowess as a dogfighter, showed that the IAF was prepared to hit Syria hard, a taste of things to come for 1982 when the F-16 would finally meet a more worthy opponent – the Mikoyan-Gurevich MiG-21.

Why was the F-16 even in the Middle East? With Israel's then-recent dependence on US arms and weapons, it was little wonder that the IAF kept close tabs on the Lightweight Fighter fly-off. Indeed, even during initial design and development stages both Israel and Iran were interested in what small, simple lightweight aircraft could do – Israel especially, as she was surrounded by hostile neighbours with larger quantities of aircraft. If Israel could get larger numbers of more modern warplanes, the balance could swing the other way.

In September 1975, the Israeli government began talking to the US about the F-16, but the US President, Jimmy Carter, was very reluctant to alter the delicate balance of power in the Middle East with the introduction of advanced warplanes. Despite this, an order was placed for 68 F-16As and eight F-16Bs in August 1978 in a deal worth a reported $1.2 billion. In the typically ironic shorthand of the time, this deal was prefixed with 'Peace' and was entitled 'Peace Marble.' The Peace Marble order was finally agreed in 1979, following the

ABOVE: ***This is one of the F-16A Block 5s delivered during 'Peace Marble IV' in 1994.***

RIGHT: ***The Israelis had already enjoyed great service from a small fighter-bomber in the form of the A-4 Skyhawk family.***

BELOW: ***One of the original two-seater F-16B Netz aircraft delivered in the early 1980s.***

signing of the Camp David Accords of a year before, by Israel's Menachem Begin and Egyptian President Anwar Sadat.

Everything in the Middle East was linked, however. At the time Saudi Arabia was also negotiating for new, modern fighters (the Saudis would buy McDonnell Douglas F-15 Eagles and later Panavia Tornado F.3s to replace BAC Lightnings) and Egypt too would turn to the US for its military aviation needs, buying McDonnell Douglas F-4 Phantoms and later F-16s. For Israel 70+ F-16s was a big statement on what they thought of the little fighter in terms of both combat capability and value for money – with their own F-15 order they had initially purchased just 25 of the big McDonnell fighter.

Israel felt it had a need for anything from 150-400 F-16 type aircraft and was also interested in building them under licence – Israeli Aircraft Industries more than had the capability to do so. However, as seen to this day with the F-35 Lightning II, the Americans were a little shy about technology transfer of this new fighter – not surprising considering Israel's use of subterfuge when it came to reworking

the Mirage for its own needs. In the end there was plenty of kick-back for Israel with the F-16 purchase with local firms being chosen subcontractors, as well as building spares for the F-100 engine (used on both F-15 and F-16 in IAF service) as well as main structural parts such as tail fins and drop tanks and pylons.

The Peace Marble order was made up of Block 5 and Block 10 aircraft. A number of modifications were made to the basic F-16 to make them inter-operable with IDF/AF systems, these included software updates and changes and different radio equipment. It's said that the IAF aircraft were the first to get chaff/flare launchers fitted too. Doubtless this was a lesson learned from the 1973 Yom Kippur war, where many IAF fighter aircraft were lost to surface-to-air missiles.

Rumoured changes to the F-16's Westinghouse APG-66 radar with an-indigenous pulse-doppler radar didn't happen as the IAF wanted the aircraft as soon as it could get them. This is where other incidents in the Middle East had an influence on early delivery for the IAF. The Iranian Revolution of 1979 and the ousting of the pro-western Shah in favour of a hard-line Islamic Republic meant that the US equipment that was slated for delivery would now not arrive.

The Shah had already purchased

Grumman F-14 Tomcats, had ordered F-16s and was looking at Northrop F-18Ls. For Northrop this meant the end of another chance to market the F-18L but for the Israelis it meant they could get their F-16s a whole year earlier by using machines originally earmarked for Iran. While welcome, the knock-on effect added greater cost to the aircraft for the Israelis.

The IAF took delivery of the first F-16 on January 31 at Fort Worth, Texas, in a formal handover ceremony. This machine – with IAF local designation 003 – presumably followed two aircraft that were sent to Hill Air Force Base in Utah, where the initial training of IAF air and ground crews took place. From late 1979 Israeli crews were receiving training with the first pilots graduating in spring 1980. Following on from tradition, the F-16 was not to get its 'Fighting Falcon' name in IAF service, but was instead called the Netz – which in Hebrew means 'Hawk'. It was to be an entirely fitting sobriquet.

As deliveries began apace, a third squadron – 253, The Negev Squadron – was formed and began training with the first two squadrons at Ramat David, just south east of Haifa. By October of 1981 they would move to Ramon, not far from the Egyptian border and become the training unit for the fledgling Netz community.

Following Operation Babylon/Opera in June 1981 (see panel) shipments of the new Netz multi-role fighter were halted off and on until around May 1982, leading to only sporadic deliveries. What the arrival of the F-16 Netz and F-15 Eagle meant in real terms in the area could not be ignored – the Israeli Air Defence/Air Force had the edge in quality over all their enemies in the area and it would soon tell in 1982.

In Israeli tradition, the F-16 wasn't called 'Fighting Falcon' in IAF service, but instead was called 'Netz' which in Hebrew means 'Hawk.' A fitting name indeed.

By June 1982 and the eve of the Bekaa Valley air battles, four F-16s had been lost in accidents so around 70 were ready for action. It's reported that they had been extensively modified to use some sort of joint information sharing with Grumman E-2C Hawkeyes and other aircraft, so they could have target data shared as a back-up to their own installed APG-66 radars. This along with rumoured chaff/flare countermeasure capability probably made these aircraft the most capable combat aircraft in the world at the time.

***ABOVE:* Day-Glo orange centreline tank and wingtip Sidewinders add a dash of colour to this Netz. The final Netz was retired by the IAF at the end of 2016.**

Up to this point, Israeli forces had already been battling Palestinian Liberation Organisation troops in Lebanon in 1978, but withdrew when United Nations forces took over policing checkpoints. Slowly but surely the PLO returned to the borders to begin shelling Israeli positions.

The F-16 engagements in 1981 were as a result of the issues and losses the IAF had suffered in the Yom Kippur war of 1973 – the placement or rumoured placement of Syrian or enemy surface-to-air missiles and anti-aircraft defences

Many Israeli-developed equipment would find its way into not only the Netz, but later versions of the IAF's F-16 fleet.

It's cosy, it's built like a glove, it's built for the pilot, by pilots, it's easier to fly than an F-15 it's built so you can do a lot of things at the same time. You can operate the radar systems and weapons systems while maneuvering around the skies: it's a fighter pilot's plane.

were to be met with force. In Yom Kippur, 37 F-4 Phantoms were lost to enemy fire and six were so badly damaged they never flew again. The A-4 Skyhawk suffered even heavier losses. Never again would Israel allow surface-to-air missiles to take such a toll of its forces, therefore they were proactive in a bid to ensure their borders were clear.

SAM supression, or SEAD (Suppression of Enemy Air Defences) was of vital importance if the IAF was to retain air superiority over the battlefield so it could support ground troops. During 1981 the Syrians had placed several SAM batteries in East Lebanon, just across the border from Israel. In any other theatre of operations this would be considered normal, but to the Israelis it was deemed a threat that would have to be dealt with.

Operations against any SAM sites were called off in the run-up to Operation Babylon/Opera, and for most of 1981 and early 1982 the US tried to negotiate between the two sides. In the meantime the IAF flew many sorties over the sensitive border areas, including reconnaissance and strikes such as – including the July 17, 1981, attack on the PLO headquarters. The IAF was often probing the border area with Remote Pilotless Vehicles (RPVs) and RF-4E Phantoms to gather intelligence. On July 29, 1981, a Syrian MiG-25 Foxbat was shot down by F-15 Eagles as it tried to close on a recon RF-4E.

Adding fuel to the fire on June 3, 1982, was the shooting and wounding of Shlomo Argov, the Israeli ambassador in London by Arab terrorists from a PLO splinter group – it was an attack that would lead to his death in hospital in 2003 after more than 21 years of permanent hospital care. More airstrikes from the IAF followed the day after as retaliation and – in turn – the PLO hit Israeli settlements with artillery fire. By June 6 Israeli forces, including armoured divisions, crossed into Southern Lebanon. Operation 'Peace for Galilee' was aimed at wiping out the PLO threat that could make any attacks on Israeli border towns and settlements. What followed were ground clashes between the mismatched sides: the PLO and associated groups couldn't match the Israeli Defence Force on the ground.

The air war over the Bekaa Valley began the day after the attempted assassination. During the mid-afternoon of June 4, seven waves of IAF aircraft, including F-4 Phantoms, A-4 Skyhawks, IAI Kfirs and F-16s hit a number of known PLO targets in southern Lebanon. For their part, the PLO retaliated with artillery fire on Israeli border settlements and during the air attacks managed to shoot-down a Skyhawk with an SA-7 SAM. On June 6 a large armoured force, supported by combat helicopters including Bell AH-1S Cobras and Hughes 500 Defenders, moved north into southern Lebanon. The assault was intended to destroy known refuges for the PLO, push back any Syrian units in the area and eventually form a buffer zone so that Israel's border towns would be free from the threat of rocket or artillery fire.

***ABOVE LEFT:** Although often used for training, the IAF's two-seaters remain combat capable.*

***ABOVE:** Great use was made by the IAF of its qualitative edge in the 1980s/1990s – including the use of Grumman Hawkeye E-2 AWACs aircraft.*

***BELOW:** An early air-to-air shot of an F-16B freshly delivered from Fort Worth.*

AIRCRAFT AND PILOTS OF OPERATION OPERA

USAF	ISRAELI	SQUADRON	PILOTS
#78-0315	#113	117 Squadron	Commander Ze'ev Raz
#78-0311	#107	117 Squadron	Commander Amos Yadlin
#78-0318	#118	117 Squadron	Colonel Doobi Yoffe
#78-0322	#129	117 Squadron	Colonel Relik Shafir
#78-0332	#228	110 Squadron	Squadron Commander Amir Nachumi
#78-0329	#223	110 Squadron	Commander Yiftach Spector (Base Commander of Ramat)
#78-0339	#239	110 Squadron	Deputy Squadron Commander Hagi Katz
#78-0342	#243	110 Squadron	Captain Ilan Ramon *(later died in the Columbia Space Shuttle disaster of 2003 and is the only foreign recipient of the US Congressional Medal of Honour. In 2009, shortly after graduating top of his class, Ilan Ramon's son crashed his own F-16 jet and perished.)*

TOP: **Brimming the F-16's tanks before take-off.**
MIDDLE: **The crews for the successful mission.**
BOTTOM: **Captain Ilan Ramon used this Netz during the attack on the Osirak nuclear reactor, hence the triangle on the nose. He died in the Space Shuttle Columbia disaster of 2003.**

The attack pushed back the PLO and Arab terrorist units meaning that by June 7 their allies – Syria – had to intervene. Israel announced that it would only attack Syrian units if they were first fired upon, and in the air reports were that the Syrian Air Force suffered losses over the next two days – six MiGs were claimed by the IAF for no losses with the SAF claiming three IAF aircraft and a drone. Other sources put the IAF claims at a more modest three.

On June 9 the IAF orchestrated a stunning victory over Soviet-built surface-to-air missile sites with Operation Artzav or 'Mole Cricket' – the Mole Cricket being an insect that largely stays on the ground and burrows into the earth. The Israelis had used remote pilotless vehicles since the early 1970s and it was in the Bekaa Valley war that these came into their own.

In the Bekaa, such drones would be used both for decoy work – where Ryan Firebees were used to provoke the Syrians into targeting the drones themselves – and in reconnaissance work, where the lower-level, propeller-driven Scout and Mastiff RPV's wide-angle and real-time TV cameras would give controllers on the ground immediate intelligence on what was happening.

So, not only were RPVs probing the SAM umbrella, getting the Syrians to switch on their systems so the IAF could pinpoint their locations, RPVs also flew near to Syrian air force bases to report on any activity. Intelligence showed that Syria had 19 SAM sites in the Bekaa: 15 SA-6 units, two SA-3 units and a pair of SA-2 batteries, making a total of around 200 missiles which posed a serious threat to the IAF's domination of the area.

On the afternoon of the 9th, Operation Mole Cricket 19 was launched, when around 90 aircraft from the IAF took part in a closely-orchestrated demonstration of tactical airpower and one which the Israelis and their closest allies had been working on since the dreadful losses in Yom Kippur a decade before.

With Scout and Mastiff RPVs watching the SAM sites and the three main Syrian airfields, the attacking forces had an overwhelming advantage. With two of the IAF's four Grumman E-2C Hawkeyes AEW (Airborne Early Warning) machines on-station off the coast, providing consistent command and control, the Syrian radars which targeted the SAM systems were confused with a range of techniques – including with the use of modified Boeing 707s with side-looking radar and a stand-off jamming ability.

While the radars were being jammed and Syrian communications disrupted, Israeli long-range surface-to-surface missiles, rockets and artillery also pounded the positions. Then in came the IAF, with A-4, F-4 and Kfirs popping up and rolling in on the SAM sites. First the radars were taken out of action with a mix of AGM-45 Shrike and AGM-78 Standard Anti-Radiation Missiles and AGM-65 Maverick air-to-surface missiles, then aircraft armed with iron bombs, GBU-15 guided bombs and more Maverick missiles would deal with the missile launchers themselves. ➤

For many years the Netz was the backbone of the IAF and at one point had a 44-0 kill ration against its Arab neighbours.

***ABOVE:* The IAF, its pilots and maintenance personnel are highly professional.**

Reports said that 10 out of the 19 sites were offline within the first 10 minutes and that by the end of the attack 17 of the sites were destroyed. The attacks came in three waves and reports were that the Israelis didn't lose a single aircraft.

The Syrian Air Force had to react when the first attacks came, but the IAF were waiting. The backbone of the SAF during the Bekaa Valley strikes were the Mikoyan-Gurevich MiG-21 and MiG-23 'swing-wing' interceptors. With E-2C Hawkeye AEWs watching from above and RPVs operating near the Syrian air-bases, it is thought that the IAF knew exactly when the SAF had launched a fighter – and reports indicated that around 100 were in the air following the attacks on their SAM sites.

The result was one-sided. The IAF claimed 29 SAF aircraft that day without a single loss, while on their side, the Syrians claimed to have shot-down 26 Israelis. The SAF later admitted to losing 16 aircraft. After the decisive victory on June 9, Syria tried to rush reinforcements to the area, including new SAM missiles and targeting radars to try and halt the Israeli armoured thrust. Once more Israeli ground and air units hampered the Syrians, with further IAF claims for 26 MiGs and three attack helicopters. On June 11, a further 18 SAF aircraft were claimed before a ceasefire between Syria (not the PLO) and Israel came into effect.

The battle itself would rumble on for a further month, as Israel moved towards Beirut, pushing back PLO units and re-engaging with Syrian forces in the air and on the ground. Eventually, late in 1982 an international peace-keeping force had to be placed between the warring factions to maintain order. They left in 1984 following a series of terrorist attacks.

The air-to-ground war of 1982 was an impressive co-ordination of forces, tactics and superior equipment that showed SAMs could be beaten. Meanwhile, the air war over the Bekaa Valley forever became known as the 'turkey shoot'. The Israeli claim of 85-92 Syrian aircraft (depending on sources) for no losses ➤

PAKISTAN VIPER KILLS

It wasn't just the Israelis that counted on the killing power of the F-16. The Pakistan Air Force also was an early user of the Viper in anger.

The USSR's involvement in Afghanistan lasted almost a decade from December 1979 to February 1989 and it had far-reaching consequences for Pakistan – which ultimately led to the country being the second General Dynamics F-16 customer to blood the aircraft in combat.

From today's viewpoint we can see the ugly irony of the same war being fought twice: back in the 1980s it was the USA/CIA and the West backing the guerrillas against the invader with Pakistan as the haven from which the US operated. Then in the 2000s the US and her allies were the invaders, chasing the Taliban guerrillas who often had a safe haven in Pakistan…

During the Soviet invasion, Pakistan took in millions of Afghan refugees who were fleeing the fighting and Soviet occupation – some of whom were guerrilla fighters looking for a safe place from which to prosecute continued action against the Soviets. At one point Pakistan was believed to have absorbed the largest refugee population in the world. This was made more difficult when you realise that the border between the two countries is both geographically large (1510 miles long) and politically sensitive – following the border being determined back in 1893 – with arguments continuing to this day about its legitimacy.

The terrain goes from mountain ranges in the east to deserts in the south. The border is hard to defend thanks to both the sheer size of it and the terrain itself, making border incursions a regular occurrence. During the Soviet-Afghan war it was the job of the Pakistan Air Force to defend this border against any airborne incursions.

The Pakistan Air Force (PAF) was established in 1947, largely along the lines of the Royal Air Force and today is one of the largest Islamic air forces in the world. During the latter part of the 20th Century the PAF has fought a series of wars and skirmishes with India, most notably in 1965-1971 where Pakistan was outnumbered by her much bigger neighbour. During the 1960s India began to accrue knowledge and material to construct her own nuclear weapon.

In May 1974 the ridiculously titled 'Smiling Buddha' nuclear test in India was successful and it was only logical that Pakistan wanted to follow suit. In 1979 Air Chief Marshal Anwar Shamim heard intelligence that India had plans to attack Pakistan's nuclear research facility at Kahuta. The argument was that the PAF didn't have the capability or range to defend the facility

PAF F-16s have been in combat since their first introduction and the service has a number of versions, including this Block 52 F-16D.

before Indian Air Force aircraft were overhead and attacking it – as it was close to the Indian border. Advanced fourth-generation fighters were needed to help defend this important facility.

Historically, the PAF has used equipment from the French, Soviets, Chinese and Americans and so Pakistan soon went to the US with money to purchase new aircraft. The PAF had already decided on the F-16, following dalliances with the French Mirage 2000 and even the Panavia Tornado (presumably the UK's Air Defence Variant), but the US government tried to palm the Pakistanis off with either Fairchild A-10 Thunderbolt II ground-attack machines, Northrop F-5E Tiger fighters or the later F-5G/F-20 Tigershark, which was then an unproven machine. But the PAF won out and the F-16 sale was eventually agreed.

In 1981 the Peace Gate I agreement was sealed, seeing the country order 40 F-16A and B Block 15 aircraft, the first six of which (two single-seaters and four two-seaters) were delivered to the PAF in January 1983. The remaining 34 came between 1983 and 1987. The first PAF F-16 was accepted in a ceremony at General Dynamics' Forth Worth factory in October 1982 and the first PAF F-16 was flown by Squadron Leader Shahid Javed, landing at the Sargodha Air Base on January 15, 1983.

The Pakistan Air Force F-16 Fighting Falcons were given USAF serial numbers but had a small three-digit PAF serial number on their noses, just ahead of the radome. Single-seaters had a number sequence beginning with 701 and the two-seaters began with 601. On the tail the two digits preceding this number indicated the year of delivery. PAF F-16s came in an altered version of the standard USAF two-grey scheme, with the darker grey covering less of the wings and not going so far forward of the blended fuselage. In typical 1980s fashion, PAF fin-flashes and roundels were subdued and very low-vis.

The purchase of F-16s was a wise one – although it wasn't India that would be the aggressor they would be taking on. Following the 1979 invasion of Afghanistan by the Soviets, Pakistan was placed in a difficult and delicate situation. Border violations became frequent and these were both accidental and deliberate. Pakistan could not ignore these incursions, but neither did it want to be drawn into the wider war. The PAF decided to act on border violations with two squadrons at Kamra and Peshawar (just 16 miles from the border) in the front line.

Tough rules of engagement saw that only military aircraft would be intercepted and that any wreckage had to fall on the Pakistan side of the border. Even before the F-16 was introduced into service, border infringements were many – but the PAF's Dassault Mirage IIIEPs and Shenyang F6s (Chinese-built MiG-19s) were unable to make a kill. This was thanks to the Pakistan government's fear of interference in the larger conflict and PAF pilots were instructed to avoid engagements if at all possible.

To show this, No.15 Squadron PAF intercepted a Soviet Il-26 on March 1, 1980, and later in February 1986 two MiG-21s but both times they were told to keep 'weapons tight', much to the consternation of the PAF pilots. In 1986 a wider-range of Soviet-built machines were seen over the border, including Mi-24 Hind helicopters, Sukhoi Su-22 fighter-bombers, MiG-21s and MiG-23s.

PAF F-16 pilots in the early 1980s: the new aircraft soon showed its teeth.

It wasn't until later in 1986, that PAF fighters were actually able to engage, as Afghan and Soviet fighter-bombers began flying missions over Pakistan as they tried to target Mujahideen camps near the border. On May 17, 1986, a pair of Afghan Air Force Sukhoi Su-22 Fitter variable-geometry ground-attack aircraft were intercepted by PAF F-16s and shot down. In the encounter an AIM-9L all-aspect Sidewinder missile fired by Squadron Leader Abdul Hameed Qadri of No.9 Squadron took out an Su-22 while its wingman escaped on fire from 20mm Vulcan gunfire and was claimed as a probable, although other sources say it was a definite kill.

During this engagement his number two was Squadron Leader Mohammed Yousaf. It has been reported that two pairs of aircraft were picked up on radar, but that one pair had exited the region by heading south. The other pair were heading east. Qadri locked onto the nearest target and got Yousaf to lock onto the leader. With both F-16s dropping their fuel tanks the fight was on. After reports of an alleged unsuccessful head-on intercept with an AIM-9L, the pair made a climbing turn to get onto the tails of the aircraft which were now identified as Su-22s.

> ***I watched my wingman cross to my right side and called visual. I called 'engaged' and quickly locked-on to one of the Sukhois***

After a 180-degree turn reports from Qadri said: "I watched my wingman cross to my right side and called visual. I called 'engaged' and quickly locked-on to one of the Sukhois. I got all parameters right on one of them, uncaged the missile seeker head and fired my second AIM-9L missile. With a plume of fire and smoke, the missile from the right rail raced in a wild semi-circle to the right. Taking tremendous lead, it soon reversed towards the target and exploded on impact with the turning Su-22."

Clearing his tail, with a look over his shoulder, Qadri instructed Yousaf to keep his tail clear while he went after the final Su-22. Qadri continued: "The other aircraft was in a left turn. His radius of turn and my energy state gave me confidence that I could get him with either missile or guns. During the turn, I found myself hitting too close for AIM-9P missile parameters. I pulled a high yo-yo as my target was now in a nose-down position and heading towards Afghan territory. I quickly rolled back and fired a three-second cannon burst on the exiting Su-22. I stopped firing when a trail of smoke and flash from his aircraft confirmed a lethal kill."

From this, it's likely that the PAF weapons fit of the time was the common 1980s fit of wingtip mounted AIM-9Ls and underwing AIM-9Ps – with a centreline fuel tank. The AIM-9L was the 'all-aspect' version of the venerable Sidewinder missile, with increased lethality and the ability to engage targets from high angles of deflection and even head-on. Despite the later suffix, the AIM-9P is older than the 9-Lima. This was a version of the AIM-9J/N model of Sidewinder designed mainly for export. Introduced in the mid-1970s, its capabilities were less than that of the 9L, featuring much lower agility and (at least on early 9P versions) a seeker head that was much more suited to the traditional tail-chase intercept. PAF F-16s were also able to carry the French-built Matra Magic 2 air-to-air missiles.

On March 30, 1987, Wing Commander Abdul Razzaq and his number two, Squadron Leader Sikander Hayat were in F-16As – again from No.9 Sqn – when they were vectored towards two bogies. One of these aircraft was an Antonov An-26 machine – an electronics-intelligence (ELINT) gathering machine. Both were on a heading towards a sensitive area of Pakistan where the country had a radar station. Razzaq later said: "The bandits were reported close to Parachinar; another 30-40 miles had to be covered before intercept. Soon the controller reported that now only one bandit was violating the border. The second had turned away.

"When I brought the target into the Target Designator box at three or four nautical miles, I realised that it was a slow moving, larger aircraft. I asked for permission to shoot, which was quickly given. With an overtake rate of well over 200 knots and a low infra-red signature, the minimum range cue was lying close to 4000ft.

Effectively, I had no more than a 1.5 second firing window available. Everything worked as conceived and with the press of the button, the missile was on its way. As I was breaking off, I saw the missile impact the target. My wingman also released his missile, which also impacted the target. The enemy aircraft crashed on the snow-clad mountains below." According to Soviet sources, all 39 on board the An-26 perished. After rising to the rank of Air-Vice Marshall, Razzaq himself would die in a PAF Fokker F-27 crash in February 2003.

Between May 1986 and January 1989 PAF F-16s accounted for anything from 10-15 intruders from Afghanistan, although some put the number lower and some higher – stating that many clashes occurred the wrong side of the border and therefore were not reported. Some unofficial sources also state that PAF F-16 pilots were so confident in their mounts' capabilities that they often had certain kills taken away from them due to the very stringent rules of engagement (ROE.) Victims ranged from the Su-22 to the An-26 and -24 transports, a Sukhoi Su-25 Frogfoot as well as a couple of MiG-23 MLD Floggers. In the Eighties the highest-scoring PAF F-16 pilot was Lieutenant Khalid Mahmood, who was credited with three kills: two MiG-23s and one Su-22. The An-24 kill was apparently a 'manoeuvre' kill at night.

In one incident a PAF F-16A actually shot down a squadron mate. This was during a six-aircraft melee between two PAF F-16s and four Soviet MiG-23s. The victim was rumoured to be Flight Lieutenant Shahid Sikandar Khan whose F-16 was hit by an AIM-9 fired by another F-16 piloted by Squadron Leader Amjad Javed, but Sikandar Khan was able to eject safely.

Following the successful performance of the aircraft and the shoot-downs, a further 11 F-16A/B Block 15 aircraft were ordered under Peace Gate III in December 1988 and a further 60 were requested in December 1989 under Peace Gate IV. Pakistan had already paid $685 million for the Peace Gate III airframes but all 71 machines were embargoed by the USA in October 1990 when it was revealed that Pakistan had a nuclear weapons programme.

Of the 71 ordered 28 were built and these aircraft were sent directly to the huge AMARC storage facility at Davis-Monthan Air Force Base for storage. Pakistan either wanted the planes or their money back, but despite these being offered to a number of different nations they were finally taken out of mothballs and used by the USAF and US Navy as aggressor aircraft.

By 1997 eight of the Peace Gate I and II orders had been lost, leaving 32 still in service. Despite the embargo by the US from 1990, the F-16s were still able to be supported with only a marginal loss in availability, thanks to civilian support contracts that were in place.

A decade or more after the embargo and things were very different. Thanks to the intervening terrorist atrocities and the subsequent 'war on terror' – where the front-line was on Pakistan's doorstep and where the US-led forces had needed Pakistan's help. Suddenly the country was off the naughty list. In March 2005 the US Government agreed to sell new F-16s to Pakistan – these would be comprised of 24 Block 50/52 F-16C and Ds with options for as many as 55 aircraft.

Ironically called 'Peace Drive' (the Pakistanis were reluctant to have another 'Peace Gate' name following the embargo) this new initiative saw a further strengthening and modernisation of the Pakistan Air Force including an updating of the older F-16A and Bs still in service. The US also finally also supplied airframes still covered under the Peace Gate III and IV programmes. Contracts were finally signed at the end of September 2006 for 18 F-16C/D Block 52 aircraft with an option for 18 more. The delivery of 26-28 Peace Gate III and IV aircraft was also part of the deal, as was a mid-life update to these machines and existing PAF F-16A and Bs.

The Pakistan Air Force was strengthened still further by the buy of existing F-16s from Jordan. The deal was struck in late 2013 and covered 13 aircraft – 12 F-16As and one F-16B. These machines were from Jordan's Peace Falcon I programme. These machines were the ADF version of the ubiquitous F-16 (see F-16 variants chapter for a breakdown of this version.) Deliveries began in May 2014 and it is expected that these will all be brought up to a relevant MLU standard.

The skill of the PAF crews and the technological advantage of their mount showed through in the 1980s. While it is said that the PAF suffered one loss in air-to-air combat in that decade (to a MiG-23 MLD in September 1988) the end result is that the F-16 once more showed itself to be an air-combat fighter of some prowess when employed by skilled pilots.

Pakistan's F-16s have even taken part in Red Flag exercises.

To supplement the Netz (F-16A/B) the 'Barak'(F-16C/D) was ordered in the mid-late 1980s and entered combat for the first time in 1988.

between June 8-11 may or may not be entirely accurate depending on whose side you're on. Meanwhile more even-handed observers claim that three IAF aircraft were shot down during the air-to-ground phase, along with up to 10 other IAF aircraft (including an F-16) being badly damaged by enemy fire.

So how did the F-16 Netz do in air-combat? Very favourably, it seems. Depending on sources it's hard to verify exact numbers, but around 40 SAF machines were destroyed by F-15 Eagles, of which the IAF had acquired 37 by that time. One McDonnell-Douglas F-4 Phantom managed to get a kill with an indigenous Python-3 heat-seeking air-to-air missile – the last kill in IAF service for the F-4 – while the rest of the kills (around 43/44) were made by the F-16, of which 72 were then in service with the IAF.

The spread of victims is said to be an almost equal amount of MiG-21s of various versions and MiG-23s. Although it was then lacking a precision guided munitions capability, unlike the F-4s the F-16s joined the A-4s and Kfirs in attacking the missile sites when their associated radars had been put out of action. It is thought that on one of these missions on June 9, two F-16 Netz aircraft switched role from striker, to fighter and each downed a Syrian MiG-21 each.

It's also thought that on that day a pilot from The First Jet Squadron made three kills in 45 seconds and may have shot down four in one mission. The breakdown of figures shows around 17 kills by F-16s on June 9, eight kills on June 10 and 15 on June 11. The split by squadron was 19 each to The First Jet Squadron and The Northern Knights Squadron and five to The Negev Squadron.

Adding to the aircraft shot down before the Bekaa Valley Turkey Shoot, the IAF's F-16 Netz fleet was responsible for the destruction of 50 enemy aircraft by the

Final checks before taxying to the runway.

ABOVE: **While the cockpit of an F-15 is highly prized among IAF pilots, the F-16 has long been a favourite posting since the 1980s.**

end of 1982, including 20 MiG-21s, 19 MiG-23s, seven Su-22s, two Mi-8s and two Aerospatiale Gazelle light attack helicopters, all for one 'probable' loss.

OPERATION BABYLON/OPERA

A year earlier, on June 7, 1981, Israel shocked the world with its daring raid against the Iraqi nuclear reactor at Al Tuwaitha, near Baghdad.

The story began in 1976 when the French government sold an Osiris-class nuclear reactor to Iraq, along with 72kg of 93% enriched uranium for a sum of around $300 million. Dubbed 'Osiraq' or 'Osirak' by the French, it was maintained by both Iraqi and French personnel.

In the intervening years there have been some very persuasive arguments and direct evidence to say that the tightly-controlled reactor could not have had anything to do with any direct nuclear weapons programme, rather it was to produce nuclear-powered electricity.

Despite the overtly peaceful nature of the reactor itself, at the time both the Israelis and Iraq's other neighbours (most notably Iran) were worried about Iraq and its leader Saddam Hussein having such a capability and Hussein had also been boasting around that time that he was going to have a nuclear weapon and that it would be used, but against who?

Israel's secret service – Mossad – was working hard behind the scenes to find out just what the reactor was for. In fact the murder of Egyptian nuclear scientist

This two-seat Netz taxis out with just the pilot for a training mission.

Yahya El Mashad in a Paris hotel room on June 14, 1980, was considered to be the work of Mossad. It is thought that, following unsuccessful attempts to bribe El Mashad – who was known to be working on the Iraqi reactor – he had his throat cut.

The worry as to what the Iraqi nuclear programme was for was shown during the Iran-Iraq war of 1980-1989. On September 30, 1980, Iranian McDonnell-Douglas F-4E fighter-bombers attacked the facility in Operation Scorch Sword, causing some damage but not destroying the Osirak reactor but by February 1980 French technicians had returned to repair the damage.

A later recce mission by Iranian RF-4Es took pictures of the facility – pictures that were rumoured to have been sent to Israel.

In the background during the late 1970s, Israel persisted with diplomatic means to try and halt use and development of the reactor, but without success. The rumours were that other, more clandestine means were used, including using planted bombs in the facility and more threats and attempted assassinations to those connected with the Iraqi project. By late 1979 Israeli President Menachem Begin was apparently in favour of a policy of 'first strike' to neutralise the threat from the Iraq nuclear facility.

The Israel Defence Force/Air Force delayed their own mission long enough to get the machines it needed for the attack – the F-16 Netz. Initially the mission was assigned to the venerable McDonnell Douglas A-4H/N Skyhawk (Hebrew name Ayit) but this soon changed. With Netz deliveries at around four a month, it took time for the IAF to get the aircraft and spares available for the attack. They wanted around eight aircraft with a number of machines ready in case any aircraft went unserviceable.

The F-16 was the weapon of choice due to its considerable range, which meant that the target which was 700 miles away from Israeli territory was within striking distance – just. Also, the Netz could carry the 2000lb Mk.84 free-fall bomb, which was the IAF's weapon of choice for the mission. And finally, the F-16's modern weapons delivery suite and Continuous Computed Impact Point (CCIP) imagery in the head-up display would make delivery from low-level more assured.

Israeli President Begin was a staunch advocate of the planned attack on the Osirak nuclear facility, insisting it was vital to the future safety of the Israeli people – Iraq could not be allowed to get weapons-grade material at any cost. With this highest-level seal of approval, when the

The F-16I Sufa 'Storm' was a Block 52 Plus made just for the Israelis and is more strike-oriented.

The Barak or 'Lightning' is heavier than its USAF counterparts, using changes to the landing gear and wheels. The extended fin-base doesn't house a braking parachute, but more avionics.

PAKISTAN F-16 KILLS

May 17, 1986 Squadron Leader Abdul Hameed Qadri
No.9 Squadron, PAF
F-16A Fighting Falcon
Sukhoi Su-22 destroyed by AIM-9L and second Su-22 probably destroyed by 20mm gunfire.

March 30, 1987 Wing Commader Abdul Razzaq
No.9 Squadron, PAF
F-16A Fighting Falcon
Aircraft destroyed Soviet/Afghan An-26.

April 16, 1987 Squadron Leader Badar Islam
No. 14 Squadron, PAF
F-16A Fighting Falcon
Soviet/Afghan Su-22 Shot down after strafing Pakistani villages near Tull, Pakistan along with another Su-22 and with a pair of MiG-23MLDs flying top cover.

April 8, 1988 Squadron Leader Athar Bokhari
No. 14 Squadron, PAF
F-16A Fighting Falcon
Soviet Su-25: single PAF F-16 versus four Soviet Su-25s in a night interception. AIM-9L Sidewinder Kill. Su-25 pilot, Colonel Ruskoi Alexander Valadimirovich, (later Vice-President of Russia) was taken prisoner by Pakistani authorities.

With the raid planned for as early as November 1980 and later May 1981, eventually the time was set. On Sunday, June 7, 1981, at the Etzion airbase, 12 miles from Eilat, on the Red Sea, the plan was to be put into operation. Eight F-16 Netz aircraft would be supported by six McDonnell Douglas F-15 Eagles. The timing of the attack itself was critical for a number of reasons.

Firstly intelligence told the Israelis that the fuel rods were to be loaded into the reactor and any time after could lead to radiation being spread over a wide area – although reports since claim that there was limited danger of this, other than radiation exposure in the direct area of the reactor. Secondly – and with the international fallout in mind – it was supposed that

***ABOVE:* While the Sufa is powered by the Pratt & Whitney F-100, the F-16D Baraks (known also as IF-16Ds) are powered by the General Electric F-110. The IF-16Ds were the first to use the avionics dorsal spine and are thought to be used in the anti-SAM role.**

F-16 airframes became available, it was game on for Operation Ofra – or Opera.

While the F-16's considerable range and pinpoint weapons delivery made it perfect for the mission, there were doubts raised about its vulnerability with a single engine. Despite this, training began in the Negev desert in the summer of 1980, where a replica of the reactor was built so that the pilots could familiarise themselves with the facility they would be attacking. The first simulated attack took place on August 23, 1980, and cabinet approval for the mission was given in the October. A second simulated attack happened in November.

The timescale for the attack was fluid, thanks to on-going combat in the Iran-Iraq war and intelligence on the number of French workers at the facility. Training was based on precision low-level navigation in the difficult desert/mountain terrain with much use of mutual support and quick reaction to any significant threat. After months of training the IAF pilots were highly proficient in both their mounts and in being able to deliver weapons on the intended target.

Colonel Aviem Sella – who was one of the architects of the raid – later said that the training was like that of an orchestra, where everyone could go straight into a concerto and know exactly what music to play. Eventually, one day before the attack, Colonel Iftach Spector – who was to participate in the raid himself – announced when they would be going.

The Sufa shows the lumps and bumps that the F-16 has inherited over the years in Israeli service.

The conformal fuel tanks add around 40% to the F-16's range.

September 12, 1988 Flight Lieutenant Khalid Mahmood
No. 14 Squadron, PAF
F-16A Fighting Falcon
Two Soviet MiG-23MLDs destroyed. Both Kills in a single sortie with AIM-9L and AIM-9P Sidewinders.

November 3, 1988 Flight Lieutenant Khalid Mahmood
No. 14 Squadron, PAF
F-16A Fighting Falcon
One Afghan Air Force Su-22 destroyed with two AIM-9Ls.

November 20- 21, 1988 Muhammad Abbas Khattak
No. 14 Squadron, PAF
F-16A Fighting Falcon
Soviet An-26 Shot down while on a recce mission inside Pakistan.

January 31, 1989 Flight Lieutenant Khalid Mahmood
No. 14 Squadron, PAF
F-16B Fighting Falcon
One Soviet An-24 crashed while allegedly attempting to surrender: thus credited as a manoeuvre kill.

the French technicians would be on their weekend off as it was a Sunday.

Thirdly, action in the on-going Iran-Iraq war had seen a constant erosion of Iraqi interception capability, which worked well for the IAF. Timing would also see them make their attack with the sun at their tails. Just-delivered Grumman E-2C Hawkeyes and CH-53 Sea Stallions would provide search and rescue should any pilots be shot down – and the IAF was expecting one or two losses. Each Netz carried two Mk.84 2000lb bombs, two external wing tanks, a centreline tank and two AIM-9 Sidewinders.

This was a tricky mission as the tanks would have to be jettisoned alongside the live ordnance. Normally external weapons would be dropped before tanks were dropped – but not this time. Colonel Ze'ev Raz said: "This is something that I don't think is even done today. The problem is that the tanks are near the bombs and when you carry bombs on the wings you're not allowed to jettison them until the bombs are dropped." It's thought that the 16 wing tanks are still out in the desert somewhere.

ABOVE: **The CFTs mar the wing-fuselage blend, but otherwise do not affect performance.**

BELOW: **It's rare to see a Sufa without ordnance or wing tanks.**

Other issues had already been dealt with. With some pilots expressing doubt as to whether the F-16 had the range for the mission, pilots had flown the Netz down to the Red Sea and back in an effort to check the range of the aircraft.

Before take-off, the pilots were told that the very survival of the state of Israel could depend on the success of this mission. Squadron Commander Amir Nachumi said all the pilots felt the gravity of the situation and that in the briefing, IAF General David Ivry told them that: "If you guys succeed, you will save Israel. We know they can't stop you getting there, but we don't know if they can stop you getting back."

Colonel Relik Shafir recalls in a documentary about the strike that he and Ilan Ramon both felt that they would not return from the mission. He says: "I couldn't tell my family or my wife this before we took off but I came to peace with myself about that just before the flight. I'm named after my grandfather who died in a concentration camp and I felt I was flying for him and there was

F-16I Sufa from 107 Squadron in 2008.

RIGHT TOP: ***The Sufa complements the Boeing F-15I Ra'am in IAF service. The P&W F-100-PW-229 powering the Sufa is the most powerful version of the F-100 yet for the F-16.***

RIGHT BELOW: ***The Northrop Grumman APG-68 radar in the Sufa gives a 30% increase of range air-to-air and gives a hi-res ground mapping capability.***

some calm in it that there's a meaning in whatever happens to you. When doing the walk-around the aircraft, I found myself caressing the plane, as you want it to have a personality and you ask it not to go wrong on this flight: any flight but this flight."

At 3pm local time the aircraft took off and history was about to be made. The F-16 Netz machines were made up of aircraft and crews from both 110 and 117 Squadrons, and using extremely experienced personnel – after all, this was to be a low level mission into and through three hostile nations' airspace. Discipline and radio-silence had to be maintained at all times and despite some fears as to whether all of the heavily-laden aircraft could get off the ground, around an hour after the F-16s staggered into the air from Etzion.

General Ivry said in the documentary that: "With extra fuel and no jamming pods or anything, they were like flying ducks with no capability to defend themselves." Alone the F-16s were vulnerable to air-to-air attack, but together with the F-15s, the formation crossed north-east from Saudi Arabia, into Iraq by an indirect route often flying over empty swathes of desert to get to their destination. The route would see them fly at low-level over deserted areas of Jordan and northern Saudi Arabia before they crossed the Iraqi border.

It is thought that while on their way to the target, the Israeli aircraft flew over the yacht of King Hussein of Jordan, who was on holiday at the time. Hussein – himself a pilot – recognised the markings on the aircraft and guessed at their destination. It is said that the King tried to contact his Government and enable them to take a message to the Iraqi regime, but it is thought that this message did not arrive in time. The fight was on.

At around 5.30pm local time, the formation broke – with the F-15 Eagles screaming for height to protect the attacking F-16s. Meanwhile the attack pilots, with fuel burnt off and wing-tanks jettisoned, gained some height to acquire their target. With some extra altitude, the Netz pilots could identify the Osirak Nuclear Reactor itself: it was unmistakable; the dome was 60ft in diameter and around 11ft thick.

If you guys succeed, you will save Israel. We know they can't stop you getting there, but we don't know if they can stop you getting back

The attack went in at around 5.35pm, with first section leader Ze'ev Raz in F-16 Netz, coded 113 with Amos Yadlin in the historic Netz 107 airframe with him and 'Doobi' Yoffe and Colonel Relik Shafir, deputy commander from 117 Squadron in Netz 129 just behind. The other four machines followed their lead. Reports indicate that the weapons were delivered on the target by two waves of two pairs of Netz aircraft. Around 10 miles from the target they popped up from ground level to just under 10,000ft to deliver the ordnance in a 35-degree dive at around 600 knots.

Commander Ze'ev Raz said: "We knew they should have been able to see us 15 minutes before we got there, but their attention was on the east not the west. We dropped our ordnance and saw nothing fired at us. After two minutes at low level we climbed to 40,000ft and still they didn't attack us. We saw no fighters and were surprised and even a little disappointed."

Some reports indicate that all 16 Mk.84 bombs hit the target but one failed to explode. Others claimed that one or two failed to explode and that one went wide of the facility. Either way, considering that it was thought two Mk.84s could destroy the facility, it was an excellent piece of airmanship, with the aircraft being over the target for just around one-and-a-half minutes. Apart from sporadic anti-aircraft fire and some reported surface-to-air missile launches greeting the second element led by Amir Nachumi, the defenders did little to hinder the attackers.

It's thought that chaff and countermeasures were used when the attackers exited the target area and other reports claim that some Iraqi targeting radars were turned off as personnel were away on a break. Either way, the eight F-16 Netz machines linked up with the F-15 Eagles and headed for home with no losses.

It was rumoured that as part of the deal for gaining intel for the attack, Israeli ➤

aircraft were granted a safe haven in Iran should any aircraft be damaged and not be able to make the long flight back to their homeland, but even if it was true, it was not needed. It is believed that Saddam Hussein had a number of his Air Force's top brass executed for their failure to intercept the mission. It was also reported that 10 Iraqis were killed and one French civilian and engineer Damien Chaussepied. Later in 1981 the Israeli Government made a payment of restitution to his family.

After a three hour flight which saw no form of interception, the aircraft landed at Etzion and were quickly re-distributed to their parent units. It was said that on the flight back, the crews recited sections of Joshua 10-12 to each other, a section of The Bible where God grants Joshua victory over his enemies with a rain of hailstones and commands the very sun and moon to stand still so that Israel could have the victory.

Outwardly the attack was criticised around the world – even if secretly a number of Middle East and Western nations were supportive of the attack, one would assume the same from the US, who – while criticising the attack, had supplied intel from various spy satellites. On hearing of the attack President Ronald Reagan was reportedly shocked, asking; "They did what?" before saying: "Well, boys will be boys." The majority of his chiefs of staff were against the action, including the-then Vice-President George Bush Senior, but Alexander Haig, US Secretary of State said: "Mr President, before this is over, we will be on our knees thanking God Israel did what it did."

The Americans went as far as endorsing the UN resolution which condemned the attack and the US Government withheld the last 22 F-16s earmarked for Israel, although this lasted just a month, then it was extended by another month when the IAF attacked the PLO headquarters in Beirut on July 17 where more than 300 people were killed. The US Government would adopt this 'on-off' policy with the IDF/AF and the Israeli Government throughout the 1980s.

Before the attack the Israeli government itself was divided as to how they would be perceived after such an attack. Some felt it would scupper the recent Egyptian-Israeli Camp David Accords, while others felt it would lead to an irrevocable breakdown in relations with France. At the time the UK sided with the UN also, saying that Iraq could not have the

TOP: This IF-16D Barak appears to have a training round for the Delilah precision stand-off missile.

ABOVE: Whether a P&W or GE-powered F-16 (as here with this D Barak) any IAF F-16 take-off is impressive.

THE CURIOUS TALE OF EMBARGOED F-16S

With the embargo on military sales to Pakistan, this left a tricky political situation between the two countries which took many years to sort out – and in the interim the airframes were offered to many other countries.

In March 1996, nine aircraft out of those already manufactured for Pakistan were sold to Indonesia, but this country cancelled the order in June 1997. This gave President Clinton and his administration a headache, as they had already promised recompense to then-Pakistan Prime Minisier Benazir Bhutto that the money her country had already paid for the aircraft would be reimbursed if they were not delivered. Islamabad wanted their money back and so the US tried to sell the aircraft to yet another third party in the hope to pass on the proceeds of the sale to Pakistan.

Despite a sale being mooted to Taiwan, the PAF F-16s that were built were taken straight to the AMARC Boneyard at Davis-Monthan. Yet again they were being touted around the world, with the Philippine Air Force (still flying aged F-8 Crusaders) being likely candidates, but sadly they couldn't close the deal. Another deal put the 28 airframes in the hands of the Air Force of Bosnia and Herzegovina in 1998, as part of the US 'Train and Equip' initiative. Again this fell flat. Later that year with nuclear sabre rattling in the area by both India and Pakistan a proposed redelivery of the aircraft was cancelled when Pakistan detonated nuclear devices in response to India doing so close to her borders.

At the end of 1998 New Zealand was looking to buy the Pakistani F-16s stored at AMARC, which Pakistan had paid $658 million for around a decade earlier. With the US having already paid $157 million to Pakistan and with New Zealand agreeing to pay $105 million to 'lease' the aircraft it looked as if the deal was done; the US would pay $327 million in hard currency (which Pakistan badly needed at the time) and $140 million in other compensation. The remaining $80 million would be down to negotiation. Sadly in 1999 a new government in New Zealand was elected and they cancelled the F-16 contract meaning the aircraft stayed in the Boneyard.

Three years later the US eventually moved the aircraft to the USAF and US Navy aggressor squadrons, filling an important technological gap with the early retirement of the Aggressor-dedicated F-16N for the US Navy in the early 1990s.

material for nuclear weapons. The site was to be rebuilt, but difficulties during the Iran-Iraq war meant that a timescale for such a project could not be pinned down. Eventually in 1984 France pulled out of the project and – in the 1991 Gulf War following Iraq's invasion of Kuwait the previous summer – Coalition forces attacked and destroyed the structure.

Depending on your point of view politically, the attack was either a pointless exercise targeting a civilian facility which had zero military worth or a far-sighted political and military decision that was to be proved correct as the 1990s began. With the hindsight of almost 35 years, the ramifications and echoes through history of this attack still rumble on. While Israel initially said the attack put the Iraqi nuclear programme back a decade, others felt it could do nothing but accelerate it.

Whatever truth you believe, Vice-President Dick Cheney following Desert Storm sent David Ivry, later Israeli Ambassador to the United States, a satellite photo of the destroyed Osirak reactor with the hand-written note on it. It said: "If it weren't for you Desert Storm wouldn't have been a success."

Relik Shafir: "Many of us were sons or grandsons of people who had survived the Holocaust and for us we were on a mission to prevent another Holocaust." Perhaps the last word should be with the man who led the raid – Ze'ev Raz. Cutting through the politics to the very basics, he said in 2010: "There was clearly no doubt in the mind of the decision makers that we couldn't take a chance. We knew that the Iraqis could do exactly what we did with our own nuclear research centre."

An F-16D from The Scorpions Squadron prepares for take-off.

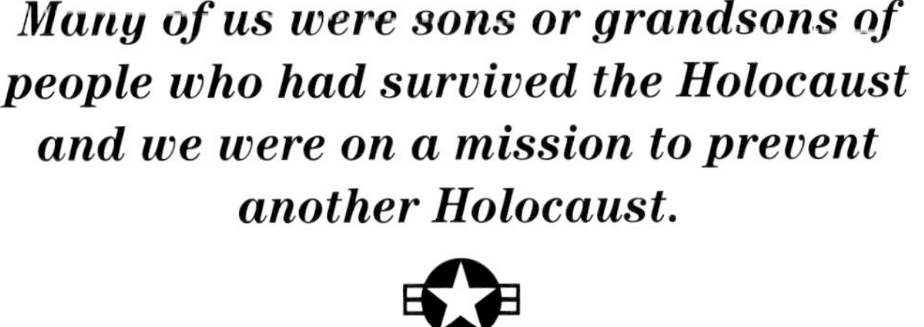

Many of us were sons or grandsons of people who had survived the Holocaust and we were on a mission to prevent another Holocaust.

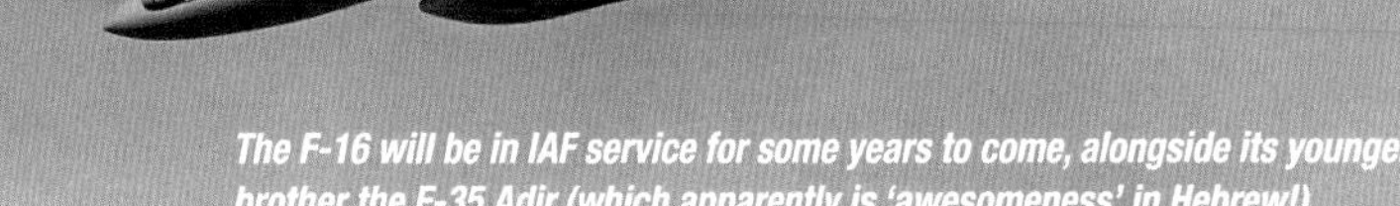

The F-16 will be in IAF service for some years to come, alongside its younger brother the F-35 Adir (which apparently is 'awesomeness' in Hebrew!)

Touchdown for an F-16D Barak.

Viper variants & building

Belgium received some of the first F-16s after the USAF and has upgraded them constantly. This is an F-16AM and BM.

blocks

:PART 1

With around 4500 built over a 40 year period the F-16 has spawned a vast array of variants most of which have seen combat.

Looking at today's F-16 models or the latest upgrades for existing airframes, it is clear how 'right' the original design was.

The latest F-16E/F Block 60 or Block 70 F-16V-configured aircraft still carries that basic shape, penned by General Dynamics more than 40 years previously, but the latest machine has capabilities that far outstrip those of the original F-16A Block 1 of the late 1970s. This has been down to the impressive scope for growth found in the basic airframe, along with its intrinsic strength and the onward march – and miniaturisation – of modern electronics and technology.

The F-16 has seen around 140 different configurations and around nine major models in its lifetime, giving it the modernity and massive capability that sees it currently equip 27 nations across the globe.

The A in F-16A refers to Blocks 1 through 20 single-seat aircraft. The B in F-16B refers to the two-seat version. The letters C and D were substituted for A and B, beginning with the Block 25 airframes. The new series letters emphasise the major differences occurring between Blocks 15 and 25. Block 60 denotes the transition from the F-16C/D to the F-16E/F. But, let's start from the beginning and go through the building blocks and versions of the earliest versions of the F-16 family.

BUILDING BLOCKS

Major changes made to the F-16 airframe during its long life have come in the form of 'blocks'. Logically any new production configuration for the F-16 sees a new block number and this has stayed true throughout the aircraft's long and fruitful life.

Following on from the two YF-16 prototypes came the eight FSD (Full Scale Development) aircraft. These aircraft are often called Block 0 F-16s, while the first production aircraft that followed were Blocks 1 and 5.

F-16A/B BLOCKS 1 AND 5

The first Block 1 F-16 (number 78-0001) first flew in August 1978 and was delivered to the 388th Tactical Fighter Wing at Hill AFB, Utah, and is now on display at Langley AFB, Virginia. The original Block 1 machines featured an all-black radome, but this was later changed on following blocks. A total of 94 Block 1 and 197 Block 5 F-16s were built up until 1981, both for the USAF and the four 'Sale of the Century' European customers. The majority of Block 1 and Block 5 aircraft were upgraded in 1982 to a Block 10 standard through the Pacer Loft I and II initiative, which saw the fitment of grey radomes and other changes. Block 10 machines came through the assembly line in 1980-1981 and numbered 312 machines and were essentially very similar to the preceding machines. The powerplant ➤

LEFT: ***The Block 1-5 aircraft were delivered with a black radome.***

BELOW: ***Norway's F-16s featured a single-grey scheme and extended tail which houses a braking 'chute. Many have been upgraded to AM/BM standard.***

was the Pratt & Whitney F-100-PW-200, producing around 12,240lb of thrust in dry military power and 23,830lb with afterburner.

F-16A/B BLOCK 15

Block 15 F-16s are the most numerous of all the various marks and – in updated form – many are still serving today, following a 14-year production run. The 330th production F-16 was the first Block 15 aircraft manufactured of a total of 983. Block 15 machines were built over three production lines (Fort Worth, Texas and one each in Belgium and The Netherlands.)

Changes made from Block 10 included a 30% larger horizontal stabiliser to help cope with the weight of two further sensor stations mounted on the engine inlet as well as helping with high angle of attack agility. Block 15 machines also enjoyed an Operational Capability Upgrade (OCU) and the first of a number of MSIP (Multi-Stage Improvement Program) upgrades. The Westinghouse AN/APG-66 (V)2 radar now had a 'track-while-scan' mode and could now launch radar-guided AIM-7 Sparrow and AIM-120 AMRAAM missiles. Block 15s were equipped with new Have Quick UHF radios, enjoyed cockpit upgrades/re-wiring and had updated mission/fire control computers as well as a radar altimeter. Provision was made to fire the AGM-65 Maverick air to ground missile and the Norwegian Kongsberg AGM-119 Penguin anti-shipping missile. Dominating the cockpit was also a wider HUD or 'Head Up Display'.

One of the biggest improvements was that the Pratt & Whitney F-100-PW-220 was introduced. This engine upgrade produced a little more power and also more reliability. The final Block 15 OCU aircraft was delivered to Thailand in 1996. Around 15 air forces worldwide still fly the Block 15 F-16A, including the US Navy.

> ***By 1992 the USAF had left the programme, but for the Europeans, around 360 MLU packages were ordered in early 1993***

F-16A BLOCK 15 AIR DEFENCE FIGHTER (ADF)

The F-16 ADF came about due to the need for a new fighter to protect the continental United States, replacing F-4 Phantom II and Convair F-106 Delta Darts in the role.

The model fought against the Northrop F-5G/F-20 Tigershark for the contract and once again the General Dynamics aircraft won. In the late 1980s and early 1990s 271 Block 15 F-16s were modified into ADF configuration. This included systems more suited to the pure air-to-air role.

Changes included an improved Westinghouse APG-66A radar to provide continuous-wave illumination for Sparrow and later AMRAAM medium range missiles, a 'look-down, shoot-down' capability, and better detection ranges for smaller, fast-moving targets such as cruise missiles. A 150,000 candle power searchlight was also installed in the port side of the nose of the ADFs.

The easiest way to recognise an ADF F-16 was by the four blade antennas for its

LEFT: F-16As from Luke Air Force Base.

BELOW: The YF-16 was converted to become the CCV F-16.

APX-109 advanced 'Identification Friend of Foe' system. These blade antenna were mounted on the nose just ahead of the cockpit. The other giveaway is a bulged horizontal stabiliser base, which housed the rudder actuators – these were moved so the tail could accommodate a new HF radio antenna.

F-16 ADF machines were delivered from 1989 – mainly to Air National Guard units. ADFs are still flown by Jordan and Thailand, although the ANG flew its final ADF mission in 2007.

F-16A/B BLOCK 20

Essentially equivalent to a Block 50/52 F-16C/D, this designation was a purely political one. Ordered by the Taiwanese Air Force, the earlier model designation hints at a less capable machine – which it is not. These aircraft benefit from the later Mid Life Updated (MLU) a cockpit identical to the Block 50 F-16 C/D, the F-100-PW-220 engine and the AN/APG-66 (V) 2 radar suite.

Deliveries began in the mid-1990s, when C/D model production was already in full swing. In 2017 it was announced that 144 Block 20 machines for Taiwan were to be upgraded to F-16V standards with the AN/APG-83 AESA radar and numerous other improvements.

F-16 AM/BM MLU

The USAF and the original four European nations that fielded the F-16A/B variant joined forces in the late 1980s to look at a Mid-Life Update (MLU) for these first versions of Fighting Falcon.

With a projected lifespan until the turn of the millennium it was felt that it would be prudent to give the early F-16 models some form of update to keep them fully combat capable in a modern threat environment.

The MLU programme started in 1989 and what followed was a two-year study programme followed by the development phase which lasted until 1997. First flights were made of MLU aircraft in 1995. Initial go ahead was given in 1991 for the MLU which would effectively give the original A/B model Viper the same sort of capabilities as the C/D model that had made its first flight back in 1984.

By 1992 the USAF had left the programme, but for the Europeans, around 360 MLU packages were ordered in early 1993: 139 for the Dutch, 58 for Norway, 92 for Belgium and 70 for Denmark. One aircraft was produced as a prototype for the USAF, which did order some MLU computer improvements for a number of their F-16C/Ds on fleet.

Before any airframe was allowed to enter the MLU programme the airframe was extensively checked and examined in the Aircraft Structural Integrity Programme or (PACER SLIP) as it was known. It was found that – due to the high stress factors and ever-increasing loadouts – a few airframes needed remedial modification due to hairline stress cracks in some of the airframe's bulkheads.

The MLU featured considerable improvements to the on-board avionics and computer systems on board, as well as changes to cockpit layout/design and weaponry. In the cockpit, two Honeywell liquid-crystal colour displays were used, a wide-angle Head Up Display was fitted along with night-vision goggle friendly cockpit lighting, the ability to use a helmet-mounted

***RIGHT:* The F-16/79 used the older General Electric J-79 motor. It performed well enough but politics overtook it and it received no orders.**

***BELOW:* Edwards Air Force Base runs a number of F-16 models in its attractive colours.**

General Dynamics F-16A Block 10

1. Pilot tube
2. Glassfibre radome
3. Planar radar scanner
4. ILS glidescope aerial
5. Scanner drive units
6. Radar mounting bulkhead
7. ADF aerial
8. Forward electronics equipment bay
9. Westinghouse AN/APG-66 digital pulse doppler radar electronics
10. Forward identification light, Danish and Norwegian aircraft only
11. Radar warning antenna
12. Cockpit front pressure bulkhead
13. Instrument panel shroud
14. Weapons systems fire control electronics
15. Fuselage forebody strake fairing
16. Marconi-Elliot wide-angle raster-video head-up-display (WARHUD)
17. Side stick controller (fly-by-wire control system)
18. Cockpit floor
19. Frameless bubble canopy
20. Canopy fairings
21. McDonnell-Douglas ACES II zero-zero ejection seat
22. Pilot's safety harness
23. Engine throttle
24. Side console panel
25. Cockpit frame construction
26. Rear pressure bulkhead
27. Ejection seat headrest
28. Seat arming safety lever
29. Cockpit sealing frame
30. Canopy hinge point
31. Ejection seat launch rails
32. Rear electronics equipment bay (growth area)
33. Boundary layer splitter plate
34. Fixed geometry engine air intake
35. Lower UHF/IFF aerial
36. Aft retracting nosewheel
37. Shock absorber scissor links
38. Retraction strut
39. Nosewheel door
40. Forward position light
41. Intake trunking
42. Cooling air louvres
43. Gun gas suppression nozzle
44. Air conditioning system piping
45. Forward fuselage fuel tank, total system capacity 1,072 5 US gal (4058 litres)
46. Canopy aft glazing
47. Starboard 370 US gal external fuel tank (1400 litres)
48. Forebody blended wing root
49. Upper position light and flight refueling floodlight
50. Fuel tank bay access panel
51. Rotary cannon barrels
52. Forebody frame construction
53. M-61 Vulcan, 20-mm rotary cannon
54. Ammunition feed and link return chutes
55. Ammunition drum, 500-rounds
56. Ammunition drum flexible drive shaft
57. Hydraulic gun drive motor
58. Leading-edge flap control shaft
59. Hydraulic equipment service bay
60. Primary system hydraulic reservoir
61. Leading-edge manoeuvre flap drive motor
62. TACAN aerial
63. No 2 hydraulic system reservoir
64. Leading-edge flap control shaft
65. Inboard pylon
66. Pylon fixing
67. Wing centre pylon
68. Triple ejector bomb rack
69. MK 82 500-lb (227-kg) bombs
70. Oldeft Orpheus reconnaissance pod, Netherlands aircraft only
71. Infra-red linescan
72. Camera ports
73. Reconnaissance pod pylon adaptor, centre line fixing
74. SUU-25E/A flare launcher
75. AN/ASQ aircraft instrumentation system data link transmitter
76. Outboard wing pylon
77. Missile launch shoe
78. AIM-9L Sidewinder air-to-air missile
79. Advanced medium range air-to-air missile (AMRAAM)
80. Aluminium honeycomb leading-edge flap construction
81. Starboard navigation light
82. Static dischargers
83. Fixed trailing edge section
84. Multi-spar wing construction
89. Centre fuel tank bay access panel
90. Intake ducting
91. Wing mounting bulkheads
92. Universal air refuelling receptacle (UARSSI)
93. Engine compressor face
94. Pratt & Whitney F100-PW-100 (3) afterburning turbofan engine
95. Jet fuel starter
96. Engine accessory gearbox, airframe mounted
97. Gearbox drive shaft
98. Ground pressure refuelling receptacle
99. Flaperon servo actuator
100. Rear fuselage frame construction
101. Rear integral fuel tank
102. Main engine mounting suspension link
103. Upper UHF/IFF aerial
104. Fuselage skin plating
105. Starboard side-body fairing
106. Fin root fillet
107. Flight control system hydraulic accumulators
108. Anti-collision light power supply unit
109. Starboard tailplane (increased area "big tail")
110. Tailplane surfaces interchangeable port and starboard
111. Graphite-epoxy skin panels
112. Fin construction
113. Aluminium honeycomb leading-edge panel
114. Steel leading-edge strip
115. VHF communications aerial
116. Anti-collision light
117. Tail radar warning antennae
118. Aluminium honeycomb rudder construction
119. Rudder servo actuator
120. Radar warning power supply
121. Brake parachute housing, Norwegian aircraft only
122. Tail navigation light
123. Electronics countermeasures aerials, port and starboard (ECM)
124. Fully variable exhaust nozzle
125. Nozzle flaps
126. Split trailing edge airbrake, upper and lower airbrake
127. Airbrake hydraulic jack
128. Port tailplane (increased area "big tail")
129. Static dischargers
130. Graphite-epoxy tailplane skin panels
131. Corrugated aluminium sub-structure
132. Hinge pivot fixing
133. Tailplane servo actuator
134. Nozzle sealing fairing
135. Fueldraulic nozzle actuators
136. Afterburner tailpipe
137. Rear fuselage bulkheads
138. Rear engine mounting
139. Aft position light
140. Port side-body fairing
141. Runway arrester hook
142. Ventral fin, port and starboard
143. Port flaperon
144. Flaperon hinges
145. Aluminium honeycomb flaperon construction
146. Static dischargers
147. Fixed trailing edge section
148. Port AIM-9L Sidewinder air-to-air missiles
149. Missile launcher shoe
150. Wing tip launcher fixing
151. Port navigation light
152. Outboard pylon fixing rib
153. Multi-spar wing construction
154. Centre pylon attachment rib
155. Wing centre pylon
156. MK84 2,000-lb (908-kg) low-drag bomb
157. Leading-edge manoeuvre flap
158. Leading-edge flap rotary actuators
159. Integral wing fuel tank
160. Inboard pylon fixing
161. Wing attachment fishplates
162. Landing/taxying lamp
163. Main undercarriage shock absorber strut
164. Mainwheel leg strut
165. Retraction strut
166. Mainwheel door
167. Forward retracting mainwheel
168. Port underwing fuel tank, 370 US gal (1700 litres)
169. Centre line external fuel tank, 300 US gal (1378 litres)
170. Electro-optical forward looking infra-red pod (EO-FLIR)
171. Laser target designator pod (LAST)
172. LAU-3/A rocket launcher, 19x2.75-in (6.98-cm) ground attack rockets
173. Westinghouse AN/ALQ119-1 electronic supression system radar jamming pod (ESM)
174. Snakeye, 500-lb (227-kg) retarded bomb
175. GBU-10C/B 2000-lb (908-kg) laser guided bomb

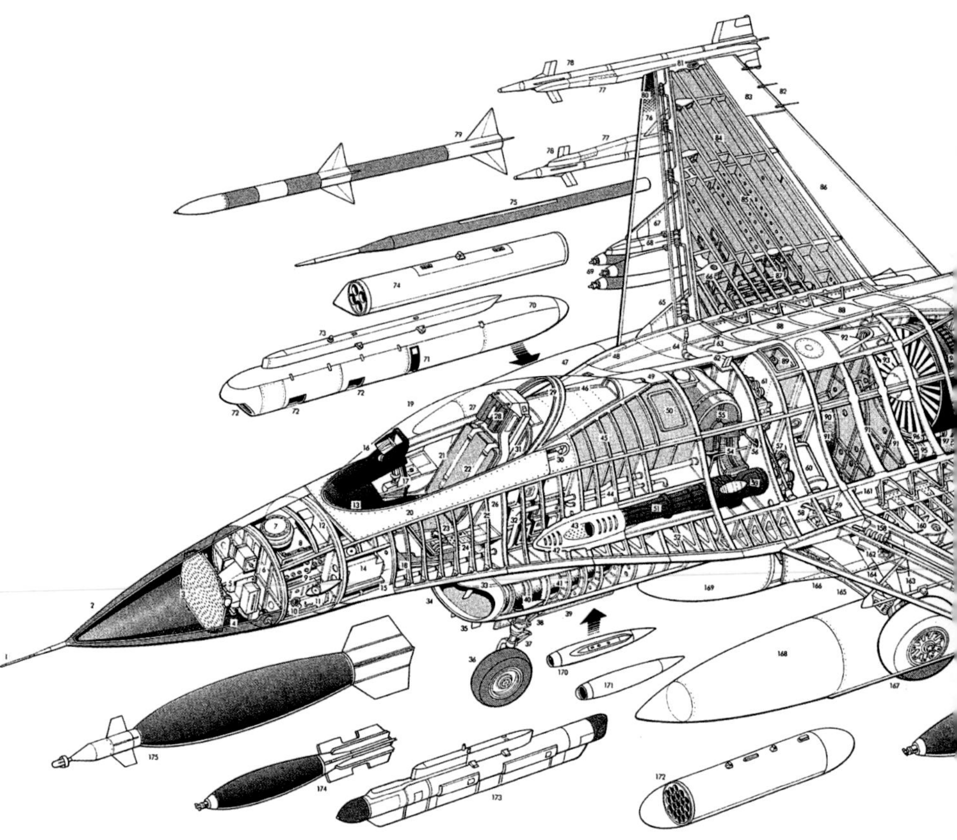

The MATV F-16 flanked by the Grumman X-31 and the NASA thrust-vectoring F/A-18 Hornet.

display system (later upgraded to a Helmet Mounted Cueing System) and updated and more modern GPS navigation system.

The radar was upgraded to AN/APG-66 (V) 2A capability, improved mission computers and EW (electronic warfare) management system was installed and an 'Advanced Identification Friend or Foe' (AIFF) system was introduced, as on the F-16 ADF. The ability to carry the 'cheek' mounted LANTIRN (Low Altitude Navigation and Targeting Infra-Red, Night) pod system was also provided for as well as a Digital Terrain System for improved low-level flight safety. Provision/interface for reconnaissance pods was now simpler and provision was also made for a Microwave Landing System: another welcome safety feature. The Pratt & Whitney engines were also upgraded to F-100-PW-220 level.

As well as the original four European nations a number of other customers upgraded with the MLU. Portugal upgraded 20 of its 45 A/B F-16s to MLU standard in 2001 and a number of Jordan's F-16 ADFs received the MLU, with the first jet being re-delivered in 2007. In 2010 Pakistan also upgraded 35 of its Block 15 machines to MLU standard while Taiwan's 150 F-16A/Bs (Block 30 airframes but built to a retrospective Block 20 level/designation) are almost identical to MLU-spec aircraft.

Successive upgrades has seen the MLU F-16 fleet able to use progressively more modern weaponry including later versions of the AIM-9 family (and IRIS-T short-range AAM) medium-range AIM-120D AMRAAM (with a significant off-boresight capability and increased range) and High Speed Anti-Radiation missile (AGM-HARM) integration, as well as increasingly more sophisticated air-to-ground ordnance, including GPS-directed weapons such as Joint Direct Attack Munition (JDAM, GBU-30/32), AGM-154 Joint Stand-Off Weapon, Small Diameter Bombs (GBU-39) and other families of air-to-ground weapons including the Laser JDAM GBU-54.

F-16 C/D BLOCK 25

The C/D models of the Viper are effectively the second-generation of F-16 machine, ushering in a new era of capability and beginning with Block 25, albeit in an airframe that looks largely identical. If you want to 'spot the difference' from a Block 25 C or D model compared to an earlier A or B, the only external difference is the introduction of an enlarged triangular base on the rear fuselage on which sits the vertical stabiliser, which has a small blade antenna sticking upwards on it. It was

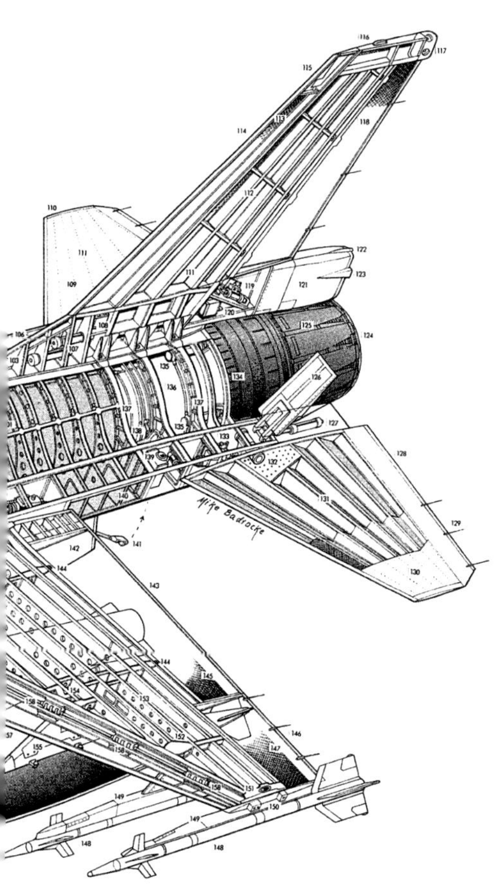

***TOP:* Early development F-16s came in this attractive camouflage pattern.**

***ABOVE:* This F-16A with inert bombs on the pylons was seen in 1985.**

originally supposed to house a Westinghouse ALQ0165 Airborne Self-Protection Jammer (ASPJ), but this was never fitted.

The modifications to the F-16 made it a far more effective multi-role fighter – especially in adverse weather and (in the fighter role) in any beyond visual range (BVR) engagements.

As seen with the early designations of F-16, confusion often reigns with the various Block numbers, Operational Capability Upgrades (OCUs) and Multi-national Staged Improvement Programme (MSIPs), so production of the F-16C/D began with 'Block 25' or MSIP Stage II. The first F-16C flew on June 19, 1984, and was introduced onto the production line in December of that year. Block 25 enabled the F-16 to carry Advanced Medium Range Air-to-Air Missile (AMRAAM) and AIM-7F Sparrow radar-guided missile as well as bringing in a new era of precision ground-attack capabilities to the F-16 community, which included the use of the AIM-65D Maverick air-to-ground missile. An improved fire control computer, stores management system and an inertial navigation system were added along with multifunction displays, new data transfer unit, radar altimeter, and UHF radio system, which was more resistant to jamming.

The biggest avionics update related to the radar, which was the improved Westinghouse (from 1996 Northrop Grumman) AN/APG-68 radar. This new radar set offered better range, new operating modes, was more resistant to jamming and offered improved resolution of targets. The APG-68 was a big step up in capability for the F-16 pilot. Many air-to-air modes were now added, including up-look and velocity search, single-target track, raid-cluster resolution, range-while-search and track-while-scan for up to 10 targets and of course the ability for continuous-wave (CW) illumination for the guidance of the Sparrow semi-active radar guided missile. For air-to-ground work modes included maritime – which included sea search, fixed target track and ground moving target indication – and updated modes for fixed and moving ground targets.

All Block 25s were originally powered by the Pratt & Whitney F-100-PW-200, but the engines have since been upgraded to the -220E configuration. Maximum take-off weight was now in the region of 19,640kg (43,300lb). Block 25 F-16C/Ds have only been operated by the USAF.

F-16C/D BLOCK 30/32: NEW MOTIVE MUSCLE

The Block 30/32 version of the F-16C/D (sometimes called the MSIP Stage III) was produced from 1986 through to 1989 and more than 730 were built. The first Block 30/32 C-model flew on June 12, 1986, and the biggest change was the switch to an alternative engine to the Pratt & Whitney F-100.

Any subsequent model of the F-16 with a two (2) retains a version of the Pratt & Whitney F-100 engine, but the use of a common engine bay saw the Block 30 variant powered by the General Electric F-110 motor. Since the introduction of this block, any subsequent model with a zero (0) ending to the block number has since been powered by the General Electric engine.

So why introduce a new engine into the F-16's development? Well, the Americans are nothing if not sticklers for getting the best deal they can and the monopoly that Pratt & Whitney had with

An F-16A of the 308th Tactical Fighter Squadron of the 31st Tactical Fighter Wing in 1986.

©Berry Vissers

***ABOVE:* An F-16D out of Edwards Air Force Base carrying AMRAAMs and training Maverick rounds.**

***ABOVE RIGHT:* Always colourful, the F-16Cs used by the Aggressors are now some of the oldest in the USAF inventory.**

***RIGHT:* One of the strangest mooted F-16s was this: SFW or Swing Forward Wing. It was never built.**

the F100-powered F-15s and F-16s (as well as the teething troubles with the early engines) led the US government and military to look for a back-up plan.

The Alternative Fighter Engine (AFE) programme – also known by the protagonists as 'The Great Engine War' – meant that two engines were now in the running to power this latest block of F-16 model. The two engines were the latest Pratt & Whitney F-100 variant, the F-100-PW-220 and a derivative of the engine that flew in the YF-17, the General Electric F-101-DFE, now called the General Electric F-110.

Fighter Wings that received the General Electric-powered version of the F-16C/D were largely those that served outside the continental USA (but not exclusively, as we shall see) and also no differently-powered machines served in the same units, to ensure commonality. In February 1984 it was announced that 75% of the F-16C/D order for the following year would be powered by the GE F-110 engine – this would be the Block 30, with the other aircraft being powered by the P&W F-110-PW-220E – the Block 32 aircraft.

Despite the term 'common engine bay' it was a little more complicated than that to ensure the smoothest grafting of the GE F-110 into the assembly lines. Similar engine mounts were used, but modification kits were needed to change the different engines between one aircraft, meaning that the process was – effectively – impractical. Also, the later adoption of a larger 'Modular Common Intake Duct' (MCID) was needed for the GE engine, although (again, despite that word 'common') some early F-100-powered aircraft used the earlier, smaller intake duct as the engine cannot handle the extra air being ingested.

In fact the only 'big mouth' F-100-powered F-16 was the Variable Inflight Stability Test Aircraft (VISTA/F-16) which used the larger air intake to feed the updated P&W F-100-PW-229 motor. Whether 'big mouth' or 'standard inlet', the F-16 was always a target with a sizable radar cross section (RCS) and some of this was down to the large intake which served as an excellent reflector of radar energy. In a bid to trim down the F-16C and D's RCS, the inlets of both versions was specially treated with Radar Absorbent Materials or RAMs which has drastically reduced the aircraft's RCS.

These 'Big Mouth' Block 30 F-16C/Ds benefited from the F-110's extra 5000lb (2273kg) of thrust over the F-100-powered machines, but the Block 32 also benefitted from improvements to the Pratt & Whitney F-100-PW-220. Ironically, due to its maturity in service in the early days of F-16C/D operations the F-100 machines had the edge over the GE F-110-powered machines when it came to reliability and stalling characteristics. In cold comparison, the P&W F-100-PW-220 had 14,590lb (6632kg) of static dry thrust and 23,770lb (10,805kg) with afterburner. The General Electric F-110-GE-100 turbofan was rated at 17,155lb dry (7798kg) and 28,984lb (13,175kg) with afterburner/re-heat. It should be noted that pre 'Big Mouth' General Electric-powered machines were at first limited by air-flow to 25,735lb (11,698kg) in afterburner.

Offensively, the Block 30/32 F-16 can carry AGM-88A High-Speed Anti-Radiation missiles (HARMs) (as well as the older AGM-45 Shrike Anti-Radiation Missile (ARM) while full 'multi-target' facility for the AIM-120 AMRAAM was added during 1987. Defensively the avionics and decoy measures stored aboard the aircraft were 'beefed up'.

This included the carriage of twice the previous number of chaff/flare dispensers for self-protection in the Block 30D models and the forward-looking radar warning receiver antennas – known as 'beer cans' for obvious reasons – moved to the leading edge flap and were later retrofitted to the F-16C/D fleet. Other upgrades included a new flight data recorder and upgrades to the multi-function displays in the cockpit.

All-told, 733 Block 30/32 aircraft were manufactured, the first being delivered in July 1987 and the two-year production run ended in 1989. Aircraft from this Block served with the USAF, US Navy, Turkey, Greece, Israel, Egypt and South Korea.

F-16N: NAVY AGGRESSOR

This was a Block 30 variant developed for the United States Navy to serve

What could have been… a number of A-16s or 'F/A-16s' were mooted as a successor to the A-10 Warthog.

F-16Cs replaced F-16Ns when the latter were found to have small fractures in bulkheads following 11 years of hard, high-G use.

solely as an aggressor/Dissimilar Air Combat Training (DACT) aircraft.

The aircraft was powered by the General Electric F-110-GE-100 engine but had the 'small inlet' associated with early Block 30 machines. The F-16N carried the APG-66 radar from the early F-16A models, were strengthened for air combat manoeuvring (ACM) and the M-61 20mm cannon was removed from the airframe, saving at least 250lb (114kg) with the deletion of the gun, let alone the associated ammo/feed systems. A total of 22 F-16Ns and four TF-16Ns two-seaters were built from 1987 to 1988 and used until 1998 by three US Navy Adversary Squadrons when they were found to be suffering with fatigue – probably due to the excessive strain of high-G ACM missions.

These machines – and the subsequent 2002/2003 replacement F-16A/B Block 15 machines, originally destined for Pakistan – are among the most colourful F-16 variants, coming in a weird and wonderful array of faux Eastern Bloc and 'Red-Air' camouflage schemes.

F-16 SWING FORWARD WING (SFW)

Perhaps one of the strangest versions of the F-16 – albeit never to fly – was the F-16 SFW. In 1976, DARPA (Defence Advanced Research Projects Agency) gave a number of manufacturers – including General Dynamics – an invitation to join its Forward-Swept Wing Programme.

An FSW version of the F-16 was thought to offer low-drag and improved low-speed handling characteristics. The wing itself was to be made from advanced composite materials to keep the structure strong and light. General Dynamics' designers looked at several designs, including one with canards and an aft-mounted wing. The final design submitted to DARPA had a slightly lengthened and strengthened fuselage to allow the forward-swept wing to be attached, since the new wing was

FALCON FACTS

The Viper was linked with a buy from Saudi Arabia in the late 1990s - which never materialised.

slightly larger than the traditional wing.

The SFW/F-16 was rejected by DARPA in January of 1981 in favour of the Grumman X-29A, which was based on Northrop's F-5 family of aircraft, although it did use around 15% of F-16 components including the aircraft's Fly-By Wire system.

F-16 J79

The F-16/79 was an ultimately unfruitful attempt to make a downgraded version of the standard F-16A for the export market.

Born during Jimmy Carter's presidency, the FX Export Fighter Program was to offer for export an aircraft with capabilities and a cost bridging that of the Northrop F-5E (already by the mid-1970s a sales success) and the F-16A. It was to be a multi-role design but it would be optimised for the air-to-air defensive role and payload and range specifications had to be inferior to US fighters then available.

The FX Programme saw the F-5G/F-20 Tigershark take on a downgraded version of the F-16A, powered with the legendary General Electric J-79 single-shaft turbojet that was used in aircraft such as the Lockheed F-104, McDonnell Douglas F-4 and the B-58 Hustler.

The F-16/79 first flew on October 29, 1980. Even when fitted with the 'Combat Plus' system, then being developed for the J-79 and the USAF's Phantom fleet, where performance can be enhanced for a short time, the performance of the F-16/79 was inferior to the F-16A. In comparison, the Combat Plus J-79 produced 20,840lb (9473kg) of thrust in afterburner at height compared to the 23,830lb (10,832kg) of the Pratt & Whitney F-100 powered F-16A. The biggest drawback was the increased fuel consumption of the J-79 powered F-16.

The rear of the F-16/79 was longer than the F-16A and much modification was needed to get the engine to fit. Two factors led the F-16/79's demise. Firstly, many potential operators did not want a less-effective (and heavier) version of a current front-line fighter (even if the flyaway cost compared to an F-16A was thought to be $1 million less) and secondly during the development of the aircraft Republican President Ronald Reagan came to power and the policy of selling a downgraded weapon system to allies/customers was reversed.

Around 20 countries expressed an interest in the F-16/79 before the project was shelved, most notably Venezuela who had already ordered the F-16A and was being persuaded to go for the downgraded aircraft. Other air forces included Austria, Malaysia and Thailand.

F-16N (VOUGHT 1600-1602)

The original navalised F-16 mooted for the US Navy. Modifications included a strengthened airframe with arresting hook for use on US carriers, carriage of AIM-7 Sparrows on the engine inlet. The US Navy instead opted for a navalised version of the YF-17, which became the F/A-18 Hornet.

F-16/101 DERIVATIVE FIGHTER ENGINE (DFE)

When the Rockwell B-1A Lancer swing-wing strategic bomber was cancelled, General Electric urgently began looking around for a home for its GE F-101 turbofan engine. At the same time both the USAF and US Navy were looking at alternative engines for the P&W F-100 and TF-30 found in the F-16, F-15 and F-14 aircraft.

Using some components from the F-404 powerplant which had been selected for the-then developing Northrop/McDonnell Douglas F-18 Hornet, testing began at the end of 1979. By the autumn of 1980 ground testing ended and the first aircraft fitted with the DFE or 'Derivative Fighter Engine' flew on December 19, 1980. By the time flight testing ended in May of 1981 only one major issue had been encountered, forcing an engine-out landing, thanks to a fuel leak.

The F-101 was not adopted for the F-16 fleet, but – with development – the engine became the F-110 which would power the lion's share of later F-16C/D models.

MAIN:* *A colourful F-16AM of the Dutch 312 Squadron.

A New Jersey F-16D. AMRAAMs are now de rigueur on most late-model Viper wingtips. The rumour is they help with 'flutter' too.

A-16 AND F/A-16 CLOSE AIR SUPPORT (CAS)

A fair few years before the Fairchild A-10 Thunderbolt II (or Warthog) had proven itself in the Gulf, many in positions of power in the USAF and US Army had doubts as to whether a slow-moving, heavily-armoured CAS-focused aircraft could survive in a modern threat environment.

With this in mind, a close-support version of the F-16 was considered. This was to be a Block 60 designated machine, called the A-16. Aircraft were modified to A-16 standard, armament was to include a 30mm cannon in place of the 20mm item and Kevlar-laminate armour to make the A-16 more survivable over the battlefield. It was also to have an

BELOW: The F-16XL's wing shape compared to a standard F-16A.

ABOVE: A close-up view of the business end of a Viper. Note the IFF aerials ahead of the canopy.

integrated targeting system called Falcon Eye, which included some conformal sensors as well as twin Forward Looking Infra-Red sensors up front. It's said that a number of training sorties were carried out by General Dynamics test pilots, including Joe Bill Dryden, using the system which were successful.

Political problems over who controlled the aircraft and whether the A-16s could do the job led to the decision at the end of 1990 to retaining the A-10 into that decade. It would be a wise move considering the wars to come.

With that decision made, it was thought that it would instead be cost-effective for some F-16s (or F/A-16s) to be refitted for the CAS role. Plans were drawn up to give around 400 F-16C/Ds (Block 30/32s) the ability to carry a number of systems such as a Digital Terrain System, GPS, updated mission computers and an Automatic Target Hand-off System (ATHS) which shared information on ground targets between allied systems in the air and on the ground. A Block 30 was modified in this way for the CAS/BAI (Battlefield Air Interdiction) roles and was going to – like the F/A-18 Hornet – use the 'Fighter/Attack' F/A acronym. Eventually in late 1992, this model was also scrapped in favour of the simpler option of using LANTIRN-carrying Block 40/42 F-16C/Ds.

Other attempts to supplant the A-10 included the use of a podded version of the A-10's lethal General Electric GAU-8/A Avenger cannon as well as the Pave Penny designator system used on the A-10. The Avenger is a 30mm calibre, seven-barrelled hydraulically-driven 'Gatling' gun which utilises depleted uranium bullets.

A four-barrelled, pneumatically-powered version – the GAU-13/A – was used in the GPU-5/A Pave Claw gun pod, which was designed for aircraft including the F-15 and F-16 aircraft and was fitted to the F-16A Block 10s of the 174th Tactical Fighter Wing of the New York Air National Guard in 1988. They saw service in the first Gulf War with the 174th TFW, but the outcome wasn't positive with pilots complaining that aiming was difficult with the podded weapon (rather than being rigidly/internally mounted), that the appropriate aiming/cuing systems were not on the aircraft and that the F-16's speed was a disadvantage when employing it.

Another issue was that the pod – even if it carried the same hard-hitting depleted uranium shells – could only carry 353 rounds compared to the A-10's 1174, so even with the Pave Claw having a firing rate half that of the A-10's (2400 rounds per minute with the podded weapon) there was only enough ammunition available for a few seconds of use.

F-16 CCV

The prototype YF-16 was reconfigured in late 1975 to become the CCV – Control Configured Vehicle – demonstrator. It first flew in March 1976.

Fitted with twin vertical canards underneath the air intake, CCV aircraft have independently actuated or de-coupled flight control surfaces, which make it possible to travel in one plane without movement in another – for example, turning without having to bank in that direction: handy for not telegraphing your tactics in a dog fight and for agility.

The CCV used a full triple redundant FBW system with the ability to transfer fuel from ➤

one tank to another to adjust the centre of gravity of the aircraft and the flaperons could move in conjunction with other control surfaces to allow the CCV F-16 to perform amazing feats of agility. The CCV's last sortie took place in the spring of 1977 with the information gathered being utilised in the F-16/AFTI programme.

F-16 AFTI

Following on from the CCV programme, March 1980 saw the handing over of the sixth full-scale development F-16A which had been converted into the Advanced Fighter Technology Integration (AFTI) demonstrator for that programme.

Again the aircraft used the canards mounted under the air intake, a bulged spine which housed additional electronics and a full digital flight control system. The aircraft was also to evaluate unconventional control systems acting on an aircraft in flight. One interesting thing of note with the programme was the use of a Voice-Controlled Interactive Device (VCID), which was a voice recognition system which went from simple commands from the pilot through to complex phrase recognition – all very Craig Thomas and Firefox – although issues were found with the recognition of a pilot's voice when he was subjected to extreme Gs. A helmet-mounted designation sight (HMTDS) was also integrated with the aircraft.

Following delivery, the aircraft first flew in July 1982 and served for a number of years, also undertaking work in the use of the F-16 as a CAS aircraft. The aircraft was upgraded with a Block 25 wing from an F-16C and inherited other, later features such as an updated radar and LANTIRN as well as researching collision and ground proximity systems. The AFTI F-16 programme ended in 1997.

F-16 VISTA / MATV / NF-16D

This was a version of the F-16 equipped with a 'Multi-Axis Thrust Vectoring' motor. Aimed at introducing a thrust-vectoring version of the F-16 into service, the programme was a collaborative effort initially between General Electric, General Dynamics and the Israeli Air Force. The IAF left the programme in 1992 and the USAF took over.

VISTA stood for 'Variable Stability In-flight Simulator Test Aircraft' and in 1988 General Dynamics was awarded a contract to launch a programme to look into variable stability flights. Initially there wasn't a connection between the use of thrust-vectoring and the VISTA programme but the aircraft did adopt a centre-stick, which was removable due to certain ejection envelope issues.

The VISTA F-16D was re-christened the NF-16D, which effectively meant the machine could not be re-configured to standard. With its 'variable stability' performance, this made the VISTA NF-16D a useful 'flying simulator' with a series of computers altering the control inputs to help simulate aircraft in various performance envelopes. The aircraft flew in VISTA NF-16D configuration from 1988 until 1992.

From July 1993 the aircraft was reconfigured as the MATV demonstrator, with the machine researching the use of thrust-vectoring and high-alpha (high angle of attack) agility at medium to high altitudes. The core of the MATV is the Axisymmetric Vectoring Exhaust Nozzle (AVEN) which is equipped by the GE F-110-100 engine. In the AVEN system the nozzle can be deflected in any direction through an angle of up to 17-degrees.

The research ended in 1994 but a similar system was later installed in the NF-16D – this time with the Pratt & Whitney F-100-PW-229 powerplant. This axisymmetric nozzle system featured full 360-degree thrust vectoring at a maximum deflection angle of twenty degrees. The programme was due to go ahead in 1997 with a nozzle ready to be retro-fitted to customer aircraft before the turn of the millennium but instead it was cancelled.

> *Perhaps the most visually striking versions of the F-16 that made it into the air were the F-16XL or SCAMP versions of the airframe*

F-16XL SCAMP

Perhaps the most visually striking versions of the F-16 that made it into the air were the F-16XL or SCAMP versions of the airframe.

The programme began in 1977 as the SCAMP (Supersonic Cruise and Maneuver Prototype or Supersonic Cruise and Manoeuvring Program) which used wing technology first proposed for supersonic airliners. The cranked-arrow delta wing had more than double the surface area of a standard F-16A wing, generating a lot of lift and being able to hold a lot of fuel and weapons stations.

The purpose of the research was to explore the innovative wing planform and camber shapes to provide efficient supersonic cruise performance (super-cruise) while providing fighter-like transonic and supersonic turn agility. The design was intended to offer low drag at high speeds without compromising low-speed manoeuvrability: effectively many of the design issues had by big delta fighters such as the Mirage III and V were negated by the use of the F-16's modern flight control system.

The programme initially came from the manufacturer, but by 1980 the USAF was on board and two full-scale development F-16As became SCAMP or by now 'F-16XL' prototypes. The fuselage was lengthened to allow the wing to be fitted, the XL had a longer engine inlet, no ventral fins near the jet nozzle (the XL displayed superior stability characteristics to the standard F-16A) and the cranked-arrow wing was 120% larger than that of the baseline F-16A model.

Carbon composites were used in the wing's construction to save weight and give strength and – with the wing acting almost as a large fuel tank – fuel capacity was up by 82% over the standard F-16A. With such a large wing, up to 27 external stores stations could be carried on the F-16XL. The final configuration of the F-16XL saw a 25% improvement in maximum lift-to-drag ratio in the supersonic flight regime and 11% at subsonic speeds. Handling at high-speed and low level gave a very smooth ride compared to the baseline F-16A. Both XLs were powered by the Pratt & Whitney F-100-PW-200.

The desirable characteristics shown by the XL led it to be submitted in the USAF's

A curious asymmetric load-out on this F-16.

The NF-16D VISTA as seen in 2014.

Advanced Tactical Fighter Program. General Dynamics was up against a modified F-15B Eagle, which was configured with conformal fuel tanks called 'FAST' (Fuel And Sensor Tactical) packs scabbed under each wing. Despite the fact that the F-16XL could carry double the payload of the standard F-16A over a distance 40% greater a number of tactical issues came to light over which weapons stations could be used with external fuel tanks. Even in light of these issues, many in the 'know' felt that the overall performance of the F-16XL was superior in the role of strike aircraft than the McDonnell Douglas product, but in February of 1984 the F-15E Strike Eagle was announced as the winner of the competition.

In late 1988 the two F-16XLs were turned over to NASA to evaluate wing design and aerodynamics and was fitted with a number of hybrid wing shapes and profiles. The NASA programme ended in 1999 and despite rumours of the airframes being brought back to flight status in the mid-2000s, both F-16XLs have been in storage at Edwards Air Force Base since 2009.

The DB-110 recce pod is carried by this F-16.

A Danish Viper makes a quick getaway.

F-16 AF

The F-16 AF or 'Agile Falcon' came about in the mid-1980s when the Soviet RAM series of fighters, including the MiG-29 and Su-27 came to light.

To counter this new Eastern Bloc threat of highly-agile and potent warplanes a number of mooted improvements were to be married to the basic F-16 airframe along with a wing with a 25% larger area as well as a higher-powered version of either the GE F-110 or P&W F-100.

The F-16AF was also suggested as a replacement to then-current NATO fighters in-theatre during the late 1980s/early 1990s (effectively as low-cost alternatives to the likes of the Eurofighter and SAAB Gripen then in development.) The F-16AF was also suggested as a low-cost, low-risk alternative to the F-22/F-23 Advanced Tactical Fighters that were then being developed. A version using the fuselage design of the F-16XL but with a trapezoidal wing, similar to those found on the F-22 and F-23 was also suggested – as the F-16 AT or 'Falcon 21' but nothing came of it.

RF-16

Considering the prolific nature of the basic General Dynamics/Lockheed Martin F-16 design, it made perfect sense that a reconnaissance version of the basic airframe be developed.

The USAF – the major customer for the F-16 series – had a fleet of ageing McDonnell Douglas RF-4Cs that required replacing and an RF-16 would seem the safest bet. With the scaling-down of modern recce systems in the 1970s to the 1990s it was found that any future 'RF-16' aircraft could carry cameras and sensors in a pod, rather than have them mounted internally in the aircraft.

In the late 1980s, it was decided to replace the ageing RF-4Cs with an RF-16, using the ATARS centreline pod. Standing for 'Advanced Tactical Air Reconnaissance System', this electro-optical set-up allowed for images to be transmitted in 'real time' via a secure digital datalink to any 'friendly' ground station.

Bizarrely the USAF cancelled ATARS, but the US Navy equipped a portion of its McDonnell Douglas F/A-18D fleet with it, where the force welcomed the huge advance it offered over the out-going Navy and Marine RF-4B/C Phantoms.

A number of other pods to be used by standard F-16 aircraft have been developed over the years to help the standard airframe fulfil the recce role.

Of the original European nations to buy F-16s, the Dutch needed to replace their F-104G Starfighters which were used in the reconnaissance role and therefore used modified Orpheus camera pods, salvaged from F-104Gs and these received the F-16A(R) designation. In the mid-1990s a number of Belgian F-16s were also modified to carry the Orpheus pod and studies were made to integrate the ATARS pod.

A number of other podded systems have been developed with the large worldwide F-16 fleet in mind, including the Red Baron Recce pod, the LMTAS Multi-Mission Sensor and Avionics pod (MMSA), the TARS (Theatre Airborne Reconnaissance System pod, and the Goodrich DB-110 reconnaissance pod, which is similar to the RAF's RAPTOR (Reconnaissance Airborne Pod for Tornado) pod.

Over the last 40 years many special F-16 schemes have commemorated anniversaries of some kind or another but few are as striking as this Dutch F-16AM's.

Watching an F-16 go through a display is a breathtaking event. Still, more than 40 years after the aircraft first showed us what it could do, little has bettered it. Even the onset of the fifth-generation of fighter aircraft such as the F-22 Raptor and the F-35 Lightning II hasn't fully overshadowed the display of raw power and outright agility that is the hallmark of the singleton F-16 Fighting Falcon show.

From the mid-1970s, General Dynamics knew it had a winner and it had to get on the road to show it off. On June 7, 1975, the YF-16 put on a superb display above the crowds at the Paris Air Salon – it was the very day that the General Dynamics F-16 won the competition to be the future air-combat fighter of choice for four European nations as each nation signed a Memorandum of Understanding (MOU) to sign up for 348 aircraft.

The display itself that day was the icing on the cake for the hard work done to seal the deal, but do not underestimate the draw of the air show routine. It is devised to show the aircraft off at its very best. The machine itself is often flown in 'clean' form – that is without fuel tanks or even wing pylons or wingtip air-to-air missiles – although since the 1990s the F-16 demo aircraft of most nations have been equipped with smoke

DISPLAY DIVA, *celluloid star*

From its very first display as the YF-16, the Fighting Falcon took airshow routine flying to another level.

> ***It there were ever any challengers to the F-16's 'Display Diva' crown, it could only be the likes of the Harrier and Sea Harrier with its unique VSTOL manoeuvres***

F-100 in full afterburner and leading edge leading edge flaps clawing at the sky for grip.

dispensers on the wingtips, to accentuate the beauty of the aircraft's display.

If there were ever any challengers to the F-16's 'Display Diva' crown, it could only be the likes of the Harrier and Sea Harrier with its unique VSTOL (Vertical/ Short Take-off and Landing) manoeuvres – including the crowd pleasing 'bow' and (possibly) the advent of the high-alpha routines and high angle-of-attack 'Cobra' move which came along with the likes of Soviet/Russian MiG-29 – first displayed in Finland in 1986, then the Farnborough Air Show in September 1988 – and later the Sukhoi Su-27 series of aircraft.

Any F-16 display is always impressive: making a short take-off, the lightly-loaded jet streaks down the runway in full-afterburner, the Pratt & Whitney F-100 or General Electric F-110 making an intense cacophony that rattles your fillings and internal organs.

Suddenly, aloft, the pilot makes a quick move, either vertical or a climbing turn, sitting atop 29,000lb of thrust as they both quickly gain height. The fast fly-by is a dazzle of noise and disbelief as the F-16 approaches the speed of sound at low-level, before trading all that speed for height: reefing the aircraft round in a hard turn, vortices streaming off the cobra-like Leading Edge Root Extensions and – on moist days – leading to a bow-wave of vapour boiling over the wing's leading edge. Then there are the knife-edge passes, the slow-rolls, the hesitation rolls, and – just as exciting – the low-speed, high-alpha pass – showing just what control the pilot has over this amazing machine at all speeds and in all regimes.

There's no real way to translate a singleton F-16 demo display into words, it's best to watch one. But the men and women behind each display effort show you the teamwork required for each short display.

PACIFIC AIR FORCES DEMO TEAM

Misawa Air Force Base in Japan has reverberated to the sound of the F-16 for many years, but in recent times it's also been the home of the Pacific Air Forces (PACAF) F-16 Demonstration Team.

Former PACAF display pilot Major

Reefing round in a tight turn...

Tiger Meet markings are also popular, where aircraft with ts as part of their squadron badges meet up, often with lly-marked aircraft.

Too heavily armed for an air show, but this F-16AM sure looks pretty, kitty: Belgian Air Force 31 Sqn.

It's always the Europeans who do the best air show schemes, it seems!

T-BIRD EJECTION!

Captain Chris Stricklin escapes his F-16C a second before impact in 2003.

When displaying an aircraft, the worst thing is for anything to happen to your aircraft and it crashes into any spectator areas. It just doesn't bear thinking about.

The second to worst, is having to get out of the plane yourself. This happened in September 2003 to Captain Chris Stricklin of the Thunderbirds. Stricklin was flying Thunderbird Number 6 on September 14 at Mountain Home Air Force Base in Idaho, when he performed a Split-S manoeuvre. This was something he had done successfully as a Thunderbird pilot and F-16 driver hundreds of times, but something had gone wrong.

Stricklin needed 2500ft to complete the manoeuvre, but with Mountain AFB being 1100ft (509m) higher than his home base back at Nellis his instruments weren't set for the local area and he had insufficient altitude to complete the move.

He managed to guide the F-16C aircraft down the runway away from the spectators and ejected less than one second before impact. He survived with only minor injuries and no one on the ground was injured, although the $25 million F-16C was destroyed.

It could have happened to anyone – and as a result – procedure for Split-S manoeuvres was changed for the team. The USAF and airshow ground controllers both now work in elevations that are 'above-MSL' or 'mean sea level' as opposed to ground-control working in AGL or 'Above Ground Level'. This led to two sets of numbers that had to be taken into consideration before the manoeuvre, rather than just one.

As a buffer, Thunderbird pilots since 2003 have put on an extra 1000ft on any Split-S manoeuver – just to make sure.

FALCON FACTS

Pakistan is so far the only air-force to use the Vulcan 20mm cannon air-to-air successfully.

Conformal fuel tanks do not hinder ZEUS!

Austin Brown says: "The purpose of the demonstration team is to display the combat capabilities of the USAF and the F-16 as well as to foster a productive relationship between the United States and our allies. We primarily performed in Japan, but we also travel around the Pacific, displaying the F-16."

The team itself is two pilots, a demonstration pilot, a safety observer and eight aircraft maintainers. All are the best in their respective fields. All of these personnel have to uphold the image of the USAF and PACAF. Brown adds: "All of the airmen on this team have to project the outstanding image of the USA. We are often the first US military personnel foreign populations see and our first interaction is showing them this awesome display of airpower."

As well as being a very visible part of the air display start-up routine, the airmen also carry out their primary duties to ensure that their display jet is up and ready to go. It's said that in many ways, working on a demo team helps sharpen these skills: just as it does for the pilot.

To make it as a demo pilot, any potential recruit has to complete a gruelling training programme of up to 20 flights, along with instructors in a two-seater F-16D, before flying solo and being given certification by the

ABOVE: Wingtip smoke generators add pizazz to the proceedings.

BELOW LEFT: PACAF display is go!

RIGHT: It's a truly team effort.

BELOW RIGHT: It's not just the pilots that are at the top of their game.

The F-84F Thunderstreak was used by the team in 1955.

RIGHT: The evening light accentuates the curves on this BAF demo bird.

wing commander. Then, the team also has to perform in front of the 5th Air Force and PACAF commanders before the onset of the display season.

Captain Richard Smeeding was the PACAF F-16 demonstration pilot for 2016. He explains that his job was mainly showing just what his aircraft could do in combat. "Most of the other demonstration teams out there are used for recruiting purposes," he says. "But we are also showcasing all the combat capabilities of the F-16. I show everything from flying slow, slightly above the ground to almost hitting supersonic over the field, showcasing all aspects of what this aircraft can do."

Smeeding adds: "Flying this routine is absolutely brutal for my body; it is very physically demanding. But, it is comparable to interval training for squadron flying. I am pulling the most constant G-force in my life, which makes it easier to fly tactically when needed."

For the demo team, a full schedule of up to 25 events a season, over the course of up to nine months means that professionalism needs to be always at 100%. Major Austin Brown adds: "Being a part of the demonstration team has been the highlight of my career. During my two years, we have performed for more than two million spectators. That's a real good feeling to have."

THE THUNDERBIRDS

Perhaps the ultimate expression of the F-16 as an aerial performer comes at the hands of The Thunderbirds, or 'America's Ambassadors in Blue'.

Formed in May 1953 and originally known as the 3600th Air Demonstration Unit, the unit's name was taken from where they were based – Luke Air Force Base in Arizona – where the native American culture looks to the 'Thunderbird' as a supernatural being of power, strength and speed.

The mount for this new unit was the Republic F-84G Thunderjet. This machine – perhaps the definitive model of F-84 – was a machine with most of the 'early jet' bugs ironed out and it entered service in 1951.

With the name of the new unit set as well as the aircraft, a new cadre of pilots were welcomed by team leader Major Richard 'Dick' Catledge and this curiously included twins Cuthbert 'Bill' and Charles ➤

The original Thunderbirds team line-up from 1953.

LEFT: The Thunderbirds patch.

BELOW: As ambassadors for the USAF, they're second to none.

It takes more than 20 days just to do the paint!

Wing-tip vortices stream of these T-birds.

FALCON FACTS

The Italian Air Force operated the F-16 for a short time (2001-2012) as a stop-gap before the arrival of the Eurofighter Typhoon.

VIPER ON CELLULOID - IRON EAGLE

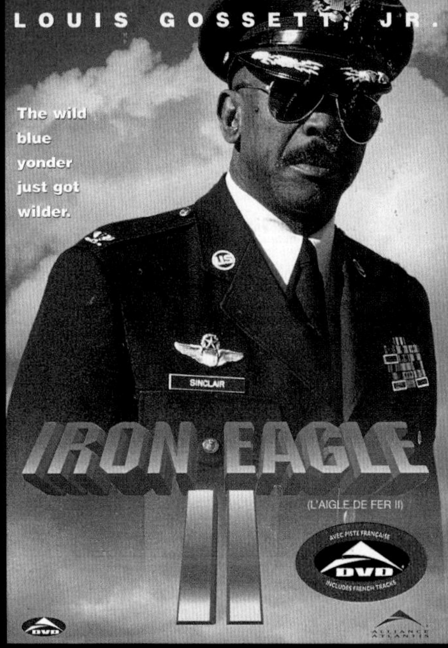

While TOPGUN showed off the F-14 Tomcat to its advantage, the F-16 Fighting Falcon had the very questionable Iron Eagle series to show off the machine's agility to cinema goers.

The 1986 first film saw Doug Masters (Jason Gedrick) rescue his father Colonel Ted Masters (Tim Thomerson) from the heart of an evil stereotypical Middle Eastern regime after Masters Senior had been shot down. What follows is a laughable plot where Doug and his teenage friends manage to get intelligence on the prison where they are holding his father in the fictional Arab state of Bilya and manage to get two fuelled-up and bombed-up F-16s ready for Doug and Colonel Charles 'Chappy' Sinclair (Louis Gossett Junior) to stage the rescue attempt.

In the film the snarling bad guy Colonel Akir Nakesh is played by British actor David Suchet, who also is the main opponent in the dogfight at the end, where his 'MiG-23' is destroyed by Masters and the whole thing ends happily.

While the film is a bandwagon exercise following from the much more polished TOPGUN, it does have its moments. Writer/director Sidney J Fury was forced to turn to the Israeli Air Force to help make the film when the USAF refused. This means that the action scenes feature some very cool aerial footage by Jim Gavin (of Blue Thunder fame) of Vipers tangling with 'MiG-23s' played by IAI Kfirs.

In the second film, imaginatively titled 'Iron Eagle II' Doug Masters is shot down in the opening sequence by Russian 'MiG-29s' after straying into prohibited airspace. The plot that follows is a mix land/air force action involving Russians and Americans attacking a rogue state's nuclear facility. In traditional fashion, what starts as a mission which could never succeed thanks to the warring, over competitive nature between the two nations' pilots and soldiers is transformed by the end of the film as we see both groups working together to get the job done. In the second 1988 film, the MiGs were played by the IAF's F-4E Phantom II Kurnass aircraft from 69 Squadron (complete with blacked-out rear cockpits) so – again – there is some good air-to-air film of these two great aircraft in action together and in battle with the 'bad guys' played once more by IAI Kfirs.

Like the first film, Iron Eagle II was filmed on location in Israel at various locations including at the Israeli Air Force base near Haifa and various desert locations and mountainous areas where much of the final, exciting air-to-air sequences were shot. IAF pilots were used throughout filming and they were always on alert during filming in case of any threats from their Arab neighbours.

Aces: Iron Eagle III followed, but this saw 'Chappie' James in a travelling mock air-combat warbird show and was dire to say the least. The formula went even more crazy with the final instalment Iron Eagle IV – On the Attack, where Doug Masters returns (he'd been lazing in a Soviet prison camp, it seems) and is enlisted to help Chappie turn a bunch of idle kids into pilots when they stumble on a chemical warfare plant. Again F-16s are used (this time in combat with T6 Harvards flown by teenagers of all things) but the series really by this time had lacked what made the original a modest success.

LEFT: The second film saw F-16s and F-4E Kurnass aircraft mix-it.

BELOW: It's another day at the office for Doug Masters in IRON EAGLE!

The 2017 F-16C Block 52 of The Thunderbirds.

Low-speed handling of this F-16C is accentuated with the use of smoke generators on the wingtips.

ABOVE: The Thunderbirds are GO!

BELOW: Best job in the world? He thinks so.

'Buck' Pattillo who flew left and right wing in the formation. With their three years of experience flying for the 3600th, they were natural choices and Bill also had time as a NATO demo pilot called 'The Skyblazers'. 'Slot' between both wingmen and behind the leader was taken by Captain Bob Kanaga, with the spare being flown by Captain Bob McCormick.

The straight-wing F-84G would put up a spirited display in their hands, totalling some 15 minutes and – as that first season progressed – they would soon incorporate some solo displays with a spare aircraft.

The Thunderbirds went from strength to strength, adopting the swept-wing F-84F Thunderstreak in 1955 then the North American F-100C Super Sabre in 1956, allowing some 'supersonic' fly-bys as part of the routine, until they were banned. By this time the unit had moved to Nellis Air Force Base in Nevada. A disastrous change to the Republic F-105 Thunderchief in April/May 1964 (it lasted for just six shows) saw a return to the F-100 before changing to the mighty F-4E Phantom II in the Spring of 1969.

The Rhino became a victim of the fuel crisis of 1974, seeing the team revert to a training (rather than front-line) aircraft in the shape of the Northrop T-38 Talon. This supersonic trainer did a sterling job, holding the line until the first F-16A was taken on charge at Nellis AFB on June 22, 1982. Conversion to the new, agile fighter took a whole season under the close eye of Major Jim Latham and no shows were flown that season as the team 'worked up' on the new fighter aircraft. The first show with the F-16A took place in 1983, reuniting the team with a 'front-line' fighter at last.

The Thunderbirds have been an F-16 unit since then... flying the F-16A until 1992 when the F-16C Block 32 took over and then the Block 52 aircraft with its Pratt & Whitney F-100-PW-229 engine which gave a useful 3600lb of dry thrust increase over the previous P&W motor.

So what goes into a T-bird? Each Block 52 airframe back in 2009 received the Falcon Structural Augmentation Roadmap programme, also known as Falcon STAR. This programme replaces or repairs the known life-limited structures to avoid the onset of widespread fatigue damage in order to maintain flight safety, enhance aircraft availability and extend the life of affected components.

Then, all weapons systems are removed from the aircraft and replaced with The Thunderbirds' trademark smoke-generating system. The F-16C Block 52s also get the full red, white and blue Thunderbirds paint scheme, which on its own takes 25 days per aircraft to complete. Like the UK's Red Arrows, the aircraft remain in the domain of the defence of their country. Lieutenant Elbert Mose explains: "If these aircraft were needed in a combat situation, they can be reverted back to combat-ready in three days. We have never had a situation where that has happened, but in 72 hours we could put the guns system back into a plane and they'd be completely ready."

"The change to Block 52 means that the pilots will be able to accelerate quicker and climb steeper," said Thunderbird pilot Major Tyrone Douglas, back in 2009. "The Block 52, overall, is just a much nicer jet. It's like going from a Corvette to a Ferrari." We're not sure what American car fans think of that, but, well...

Following the terrorist attack on September 11, 2001, The Thunderbirds curtailed their foreign shows, but came back to Europe in 2007, putting on shows in Poland, Bulgaria, Romania, France, Italy, the UK and (for the first time) Ireland.

Despite The Thunderbirds consistently showing the professionalism and pride in the USAF, in 2013 the team flew only two demonstrations, following a number of budgetary cuts. But now they're currently back in the air and entertaining the crowds.

A flawless four-ship.

Viper variants & building

FALCON FACTS

Romania became one of the latest users of the F-16 late in 2016.

ABOVE: *The F-16IQ for Iraq is still trickling along and keeping the F-16 production line open – at time of writing.*

blocks

:PART 2

RIGHT: The modern and updated incarnations of F-16 are as relevant as ever – perhaps more so in today's austere times.

As the F-16 family headed into the 1990s and then the new millennium, the rugged airframe was continually improved before being put out to pasture as a target drone. But even in 2017 there's life in the F-16 yet, thanks to the latest version – the F-16V Block 70: V for Viper.

F-16C/D BLOCK 40/42: NIGHT FALCON

Originally mooted as an 'F-16G' in the late 1980s, politics once more prevailed over common sense and the idea of a more modern 'sounding' F-16 variant was changed so that it was not deemed a threat to the likes of the F-22 Raptor. Instead, the F-16 CG/DG family was a night/adverse weather precision attack variant which gained huge capabilities and improvements across the board. Again, the 'common engine bay' could take either a Pratt & Whitney or General Electric powerplant.

The first MSIP III Block 40/42 F-16 left Forth Worth in December 1988, with production lasting until 1995, but then restarting with the Egyptian order of Block 40 aircraft under the Peace Vector V and VI orders which ended in 2002 and an order for ten F-16C Block 40s for Bahrain delivered between 1999 and 2000. A total of 615 Block 40 airframes were built.

Big changes under the hood included the inclusion of digital flight controls over the old analogue system, more efficient APG-68V (5) radar, along with a new, holographic Head Up Display which worked with the Martin-Marietta LANTIRN (Low Altitude Navigation and Targeting Infra-Red, Night) targeting pods (AAQ-13 navigation pod on the left intake pylon, the AAQ-14 targeting pod on the right) upon which the pod's infra-red image could be displayed for targeting and navigation.

The use of LANTIRN meant that the undercarriage legs had to be extended slightly for ground clearance issues and the landing gear had bigger wheels and tyres retracting behind bulged landing gear doors. Landing lights as a result moved from the main gear doors to the nose-gear door. The avionics also now had automatic terrain following (courtesy of LANTIRN), a new GPS navigation receiver and new decoy launchers. With another increase in all-up weight (maximum take-off weight – MTO – was now in the region of 42,300lb or 19,187kg) the airframe was further beefed-up, raising the 9g rating from 26,900lb (12,227kg) to 28,500lb (12,955kg).

Weaponry evolved with the various systems used on the CG/DG family, including the Paveway family of guided munitions, such as the GBU-10, GBU-12, and GBU-24 Paveway family of laser-guided bombs and the GBU-15 glide bomb. To employ these weapons at night, ➤

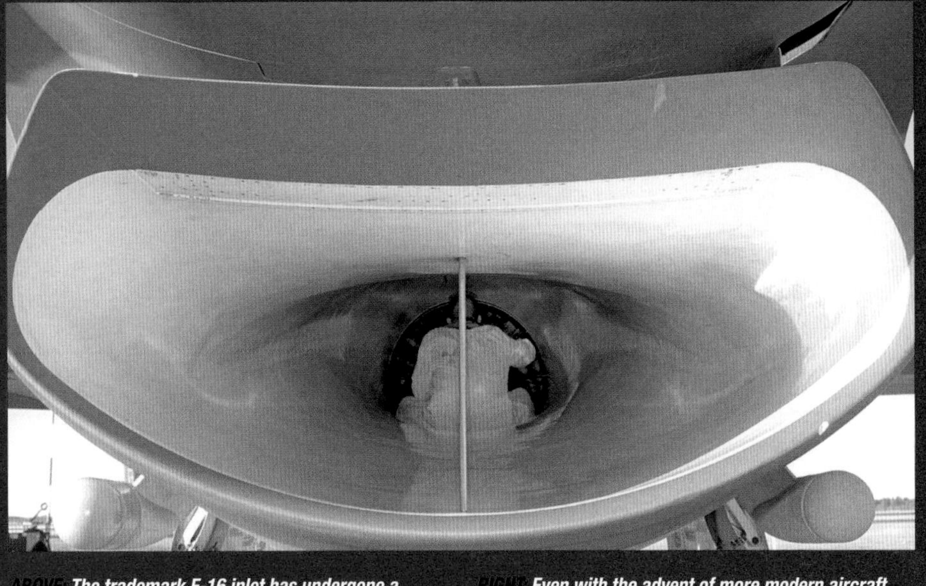

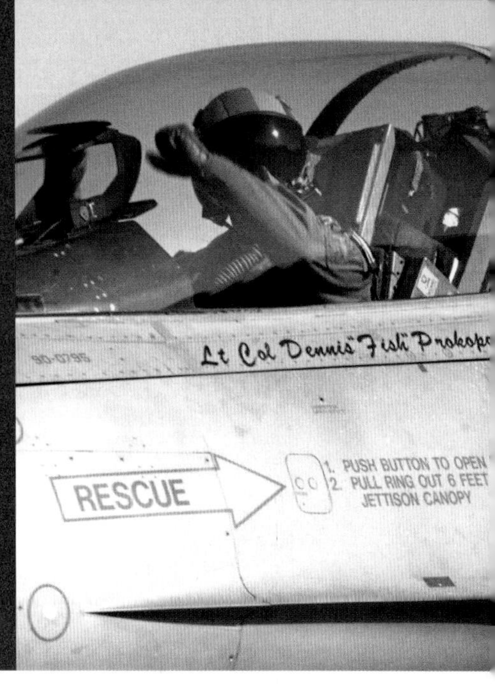

ABOVE: The trademark F-16 inlet has undergone a number of subtle design changes over the years, but largely looks the same.

RIGHT: Even with the advent of more modern aircraft around the world, a seat in an F-16 is much sought-after and morale is always high.

following the 'Sure Strike' upgrade, the Block 40 could utilise Night Vision Goggles (NVG) and use a data-link system where any Forward Air Controller (FAC) could upload information to the aircraft's weapons system computer so it shows up as a waypoint in the new holographic HUD.

With efforts being made with the Block 30 family to reduce the F-16's sizable Radar Cross Section (RCS) the Block 40 family introduced the Have Glass technology. Have Glass was a series of measures to make the F-16 a little more 'stealthy'. The measures included a gold-tinted 'indium tin oxide' (ITO) cockpit canopy – which would reflect any radar energy – as well as the use of RAM (Radar Absorbent Material) in a number of areas. It was thought that the overall RCS of the F-16 was reduced by up to 15% as a result and was the first in a number of Have Glass measures, as we will see.

Another addition to the Block 40/42 family was an important one, coming under the Combat Edge upgrade. During the F-16's service career, its phenomenal agility has led to the boundaries of human endurance being pushed to their very edge. We're talking about how a human body can absorb the force of gravity.

With the F-16 being able to pull 9g – or nine-times the force of gravity – this means that you (literally) weight nine times your normal weight. With that amount of force acting on the body, in certain positive G situations the blood will not be able to be pumped to organs in the upper part of the body. 'Speed Jeans' or a G-Suit consisting of external trousers that inflate under high-G loads can help, as does Anti-G Straining Manoeuvres (AGSM) where you continually strain your core torso muscles to stop the blood pooling in the lower extremities, but the onset of high-G can be hard to counter.

Loads of just 4 to 6 sustained G are enough to endanger a pilot and each individual handles G-tolerance differently. These loads can cause 'blackout' (where a lack of blood to the eyeballs literally makes you go 'blind' while still being able to otherwise function) or the full G-LOC, meaning 'G-induced Lack of Consciousness. Between 1993 and 2009 the G-LOC incident rate in the USAF's F-16 community was 1.32 per 100,000 flying hours so any improvements to save aircraft an aircrew needed to be made.

Thankfully, often the pilot who experienced G-LOC would come round before a disaster, but sometimes he or she did not. The Combat Edge system came about thanks to advances in flight medicine which found that if oxygen was pumped into a pilot's lungs under pressure then the O2 content in the blood was higher and therefore the brain and other extremities could stay active for longer. Allied with a newly-designed face mask and counter-pressure vest, pilots soon noticed the improvement in their G-resistance.

F-16C/D BLOCK 50/52 WILD WEASEL

Delivery of the Block 50/52 F-16C/D (originally known as CJ/DJ but now CM/DM) started in December 1991 following first flight in October.

In the nose the Northrop Grumman AN/APG-68 V(5) radar is once more fitted. This offers longer range detection against air targets and further improved reliability. As time has progressed the radars have gone through to V(9) levels with yet more reliability and small detail improvements. Avionics included on the 50/52 family of F-16s include the Honeywell H-423 Ring Laser Gyro Inertial Navigation System (RLG INS) for quicker in-flight alignment, a new GPS receiver, AN/ALR-56M advanced Radar Warning Receivers (RWR), a Tracor AN/ALE-47 counter-measure system and – from 1997-on – Block 50/52 machines also had further improved colour cockpit displays, advanced IFF interrogator and most importantly the ability to use and carry the

Greece has been a member of the F-16 club for the last 30 years, including recent orders of advanced Block 52 Plus aircraft. Rumours abound as to whether they have actually met Turkish F-16s in combat…

LEFT: Captain Chad Greer checks his forms before taking on the 'bad guys' at Red Flag in 2004.

BELOW: This F-16C seen in 2014 has received the Have Glass V colour scheme which links radar absorbent material and paint to reduce the F-16's radar cross section.

ASQ-213 HARM Targeting System (HTS).

The Block 40/42 and 50/52 variants were a step above the Block 30 F-16C/Ds and were developed to complement each other. For the 50/52, this meant a mission profile that traditionally was one of the most dangerous of them all: Wild Weasel.

For a long time since both the Vietnam and Yom Kippur wars in the 1960s and 1970s modern air forces have looked at the SEAD mission – or the Suppression of Enemy Air Defences – where missile or bomb-laden aircraft would actively seek out enemy surface-to-air missile (SAM) sites or Anti-Aircraft Artillery (AAA) and destroy them. To 'ferret out' the enemy in their den was the original task, which soon changed to 'Wild Weasel' and even led to the wing later running 'WW' tail codes on their F-4Gs.

For the USAF, a series of aircraft were used, from North American F-100 Super Sabre two-seaters, Republic F-105Fs through to the ultimate aircraft – the McDonnell Douglas F-4G. From Wild Weasel I through to the F-4 – which was Wild Weasel V – tactics and technology had progressed quickly so that both SAM and AAA defences could be dealt with.

In the 1980s up to Operation Desert Storm the F-4G had performed admirably and – during The Cold War in Europe – been paired-up in 'hunter-killer' teams with F-4E and later F-16 fighter bombers. The tactics were that the specialist F-4Gs would sniff out the emitters and engage with suitable Shrike or HARM (High Speed Anti-Radiation Missiles) while the 'killer' element would clean up the target with dumb bombs or Maverick missiles.

In the 1991 Desert Storm campaign both the electronic warfare assets such as the General Dynamics EF-111 Aardvarks and Grumman EA-6B Prowler as well as the Wild Weasel F-4Gs were highly prized and the F-4Gs flew a total of 3942 sorties, fired more than 1000 missiles and destroyed around 200 SAM sites. But while the Prowler was consistently upgraded and the USAF's 'Spark Vark' retired, when the F-4G Advanced Wild Weasel was retired in 1995, no aircraft was ready to fill the role.

Successors were mooted as a Follow On Wild Weasel (FOWW) – including a model-specific version of the McDonnell Douglas F-15 and even a US-version of the Panavia Tornado was suggested – but instead the (by now) venerable F-16C/D airframe came up with the goods thanks to a 'Weasel in a can' system. This was the ASQ-213 HARM Targeting System or HTS and Texas Instruments (now Raytheon) and General Dynamics began work on the system from April 1991. Effectively it was some of the goodies from the F-4G Wild Weasel V, neatly packaged in a pod and delivered to the USAF and their Block 50/52 machines in 1993-1994. The system was situated on the left intake hard-point, opposite LANTIRN. Initially, the primary function of the HTS pod was to give the F-16 the ability to fire the HARM in 'range-known' mode, where the pod will triangulate the range to where ➤

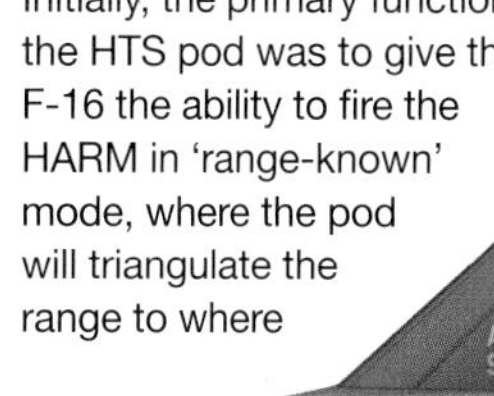

MOTIVE POWER

In broad terms the power and reliability behind the F-16 airframe has increased dramatically to keep up with increasing empty and all-up weights of the various F-16 models.

The original F-16A was powered by a Pratt & Whitney F-100-PW-200 turbofan rated at 12,240lb (5563kg) in dry thrust 14,670lb in full military thrust (6668kg) and 23,830lb (19,832kg) in full afterburner. Empty weight of the F-16A was 16,285lb (7387kg) empty, 25,281lb (11,467kg) in combat configuration and 37,500lb (17,009kg) as a maximum take-off weight. As the weight of the F-16's successive variants has increased, so has motive power, which all helps keep the thrust-to-weight ratio up at combat loads as well as maximum speed in the Mach 2 class – even if such speeds are really only useful as 'Top Trumps' facts.

The latest F-16E/F is powered by the General Electric F-110-GE-132 turbofan, which rates at 19,000lb (8636kg) in static 'dry' thrust 32,500lb (14,773kg) in full afterburner. Compared to the F-16A, weights range from 22,000lb (10,000kg) empty, 29,000lb in air-to-air fit (13,182kg) and a maximum take-off (MTO) weight of 46,000lb (20,909kg).

But it's not just about outright performance, how the engine handles and its ease of maintenance is also valued.

The Pratt & Whitney F-100s used in early F-16s required anything from six to eight seconds to spool up from idle power to full afterburner. Since then, digital electronic engine controls have replaced hydro-mechanical systems and these changes allow the current powerplants to spool up from idle to full afterburner in two seconds. Modern digital engine controls also ensure the engine is giving optimum performance in all areas of the flight envelope and in all conditions. Add into the fact that the later versions of both the P&W F-100 and the GE F-110 can deliver up to 10 years of operational service between major inspections and you can see how technology, avionics and engine development have married with the intrinsic growth potential in the airframe to ensure good value and service for another 20 years at least.

The use of two competing engine powerplants for the F-16 has served the USAF well, with Pratt & Whitney and General Electric raising the bar with every engine model and development.

On the most common variant – the F-16C/D family – of the 1446 ordered by the USAF, 556 were fitted with the F-100 series engine from Pratt & Whitney with around 890 delivered with the General Electric F-110. For various foreign customers the choice often comes down to commonality with other aircraft in service – such as the Israeli Air Force choosing the P&W F-100-229 to power its F-16I Sufas as the engine is shared with the Boeing F-15I Ra'am.

Lockheed Martin F-16E Block 60

1. Pilot tube
2. Glassfibre radome
3. Planar radar scanner
4. ILS glidescope aerial
5. Scanner drive units
6. Radar mounting bulkhead
7. ADF aerial
8. Forward electronics equipment bay
9. Westinghouse AN/APG-66 digital pulse doppler radar electronics
10. Forward identification light, Danish and Norwegian aircraft only
11. Radar warning antenna
12. Cockpit front pressure bulkhead
13. Instrument panel shroud
14. Weapons systems fire control electronics
15. Fuselage forebody strake fairing
16. Marconi-Elliot wide-angle raster-video head-up-display (WARHUD)
17. Side stick controller (fly-by-wire control system)
18. Cockpit floor
19. Frameless bubble canopy
20. Canopy fairings
21. McDonnell-Douglas ACES II zero-zero ejection seat
22. Pilot's safety harness
23. Engine throttle
24. Side console panel
25. Cockpit frame construction
26. Rear pressure bulkhead
27. Ejection seat headrest
28. Seat arming safety lever
29. Cockpit sealing frame
30. Canopy hinge point
31. Ejection seat launch rails
32. Rear electronics equipment bay (growth area)
33. Boundary layer splitter plate
34. Fixed geometry engine air intake
35. Lower UHF/IFF aerial
36. Aft retracting nosewheel
37. Shock absorber scissor links
38. Retraction strut
39. Nosewheel door
40. Forward position light
41. Intake trunking
42. Cooling air louvres
43. Gun gas suppression nozzle
44. Air conditioning system piping
45. Forward fuselage fuel tank, total system capacity 1,072 5 US gal (4058 litres)
46. Canopy aft glazing
47. Starboard 370 US gal external fuel tank (1400 litres)
48. Forebody blended wing root
49. Upper position light and flight refueling floodlight
50. Fuel tank bay access panel
51. Rotary cannon barrels
52. Forebody frame construction
53. M-61 Vulcan, 20-mm rotary cannon
54. Ammunition feed and link return chutes
55. Ammunition drum, 500-rounds
56. Ammunition drum flexible drive shaft
57. Hydraulic gun drive motor
58. Leading-edge flap control shaft
59. Hydraulic equipment service bay
60. Primary system hydraulic reservoir
61. Leading-edge manoeuvre flap drive motor
62. TACAN aerial
63. No 2 hydraulic system reservoir
64. Leading-edge flap control shaft
65. Inboard pylon
66. Pylon fixing
67. Wing centre pylon
68. Triple ejector bomb rack
69. MK 82 500-lb (227-kg) bombs
70. Oldeft Orpheus reconnaissance pod, Netherlands aircraft only
71. Infra-red linescan
72. Camera ports
73. Reconnaissance pod pylon adaptor, centre line fixing
74. SUU-25E/A flare launcher
75. AN/ASQ aircraft instrumentation system data link transmitter
76. Outboard wing pylon
77. Missile launch shoe
78. AIM-9L Sidewinder air-to-air missile
79. Advanced medium range air-to-air missile (AMRAAM)
80. Aluminium honeycomb leading-edge flap construction
81. Starboard navigation light
82. Static dischargers
83. Fixed trailing edge section
84. Multi-spar wing construction
89. Centre fuel tank bay access panel
90. Intake ducting
91. Wing mounting bulkheads
92. Universal air refuelling receptacle (UARSSI)
93. Engine compressor face
94. Pratt & Whitney F100-PW-100 (3) afterburning turbofan engine
95. Jet fuel starter
96. Engine accessory gearbox, airframe mounted
97. Gearbox drive shaft
98. Ground pressure refuelling receptacle
99. Flaperon servo actuator
100. Rear fuselage frame construction
101. Rear integral fuel tank
102. Main engine mounting suspension link
103. Upper UHF/IFF aerial
104. Fuselage skin plating
105. Starboard side-body fairing
106. Fin root fillet
107. Flight control system hydraulic accumulators
108. Anti-collision light power supply unit
109. Starboard tailplane (increased area "big tail")
110. Tailplane surfaces interchangeable port and starboard
111. Graphite-epoxy skin panels
112. Fin construction
113. Aluminium honeycomb leading-edge panel
114. Steel leading-edge strip
115. VHF communications aerial
116. Anti-collision light
117. Tail radar warning antennae
118. Aluminium honeycomb rudder construction
119. Rudder servo actuator
120. Radar warning power supply
121. Brake parachute housing, Norwegian aircraft only
122. Tail navigation light
123. Electronics countermeasures aerials, port and starboard (ECM)
124. Fully variable exhaust nozzle
125. Nozzle flaps
126. Split trailing edge airbrake, upper and lower airbrake
127. Airbrake hydraulic jack
128. Port tailplane (increased area "big tail")
129. Static dischargers
130. Graphite-epoxy tailplane skin panels
131. Corrugated aluminium sub-structure
132. Hinge pivot fixing
133. Tailplane servo actuator
134. Nozzle sealing fairing
135. Fueldraulic nozzle actuators
136. Afterburner tailpipe
137. Rear fuselage bulkheads
138. Rear engine mounting
139. Aft position light
140. Port side-body fairing
141. Runway arrester hook
142. Ventral fin, port and starboard
143. Port flaperon
144. Flaperon hinges
145. Aluminium honeycomb flaperon construction
146. Static dischargers
147. Fixed trailing edge section
148. Port AIM-9L Sidewinder air-to-air missiles
149. Missile launcher shoe
150. Wing tip launcher fixing
151. Port navigation light
152. Outboard pylon fixing rib
153. Multi-spar wing construction
154. Centre pylon attachment rib
155. Wing centre pylon

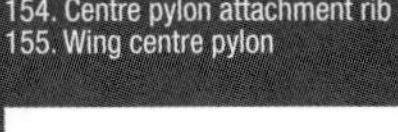

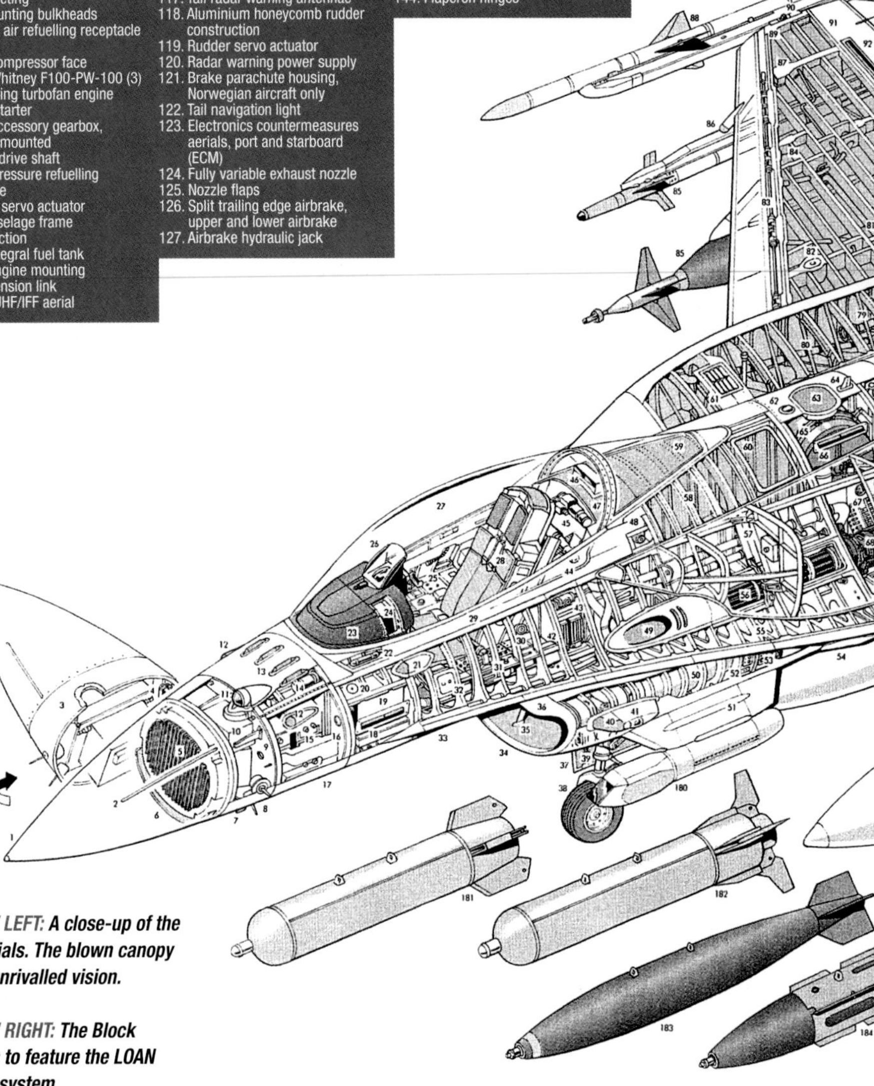

the SAM emitter is located. Many improvements have come since the initial HTS delivery.

Block 50s had the ability to employ all previous weapons in the F-16 arsenal, along with the AGM-154A/B Joint Stand-off Weapon (JSOW) and it was the first F-16 version to integrate the AGM-84 Harpoon anti-ship missile.

The Block 50/52 is powered by Increased Performance Engines (IPE) the General Electric F-110-GE-129 (for Block 50) and the Pratt & Whitney F-100-PW-229 (Block 52): each rated to deliver over 29,000lb thrust (13,182kg) in afterburner and a number of Block 50/52 airframes have been brought up to the latest standard.

The Have Glass project moved through a number of generations through to the most recent – Have Glass V. This is where the Wild Weasel Block 50-series aircraft are given the most technological up-to-date 'Radar Absorbent Material' and paint to help them deal with this most difficult role.

Similar to that used on the F-35 Lightning II, the 'Have Glass 5th Generation' is a two-tone grey colour scheme which consists of special radar absorbent paint. This was originally applied to the F-16CM/CJ Block 50s tasked with SEAD or Supression of Enemy Air Defences. Some form of stealth is seen as vitally important in the SEAD role (it always has been) hence the F-35 will be taking over the F-16's role in this soon.

BELOW LEFT: ***A close-up of the IFF aerials. The blown canopy gives unrivalled vision.***

BELOW RIGHT: ***The Block 70 was to feature the LOAN nozzle system.***

F-16C/D BLOCK 50/52+ 'PLUS'

Improving on the basic elements of the Block 50 series of Viper, the Plus features the Northrop Grumman AN/APG-68 V(9) radar (increased detection range, +30%, and other improved air-to-air and air-to-ground capabilities) and the ability to employ the Boeing Joint Direct Attack Munition (JDAM) in various capacities. The most visible change to earlier models is the capability for the Block 50/52+ to use the conformal fuel tanks on the top of the F-16's

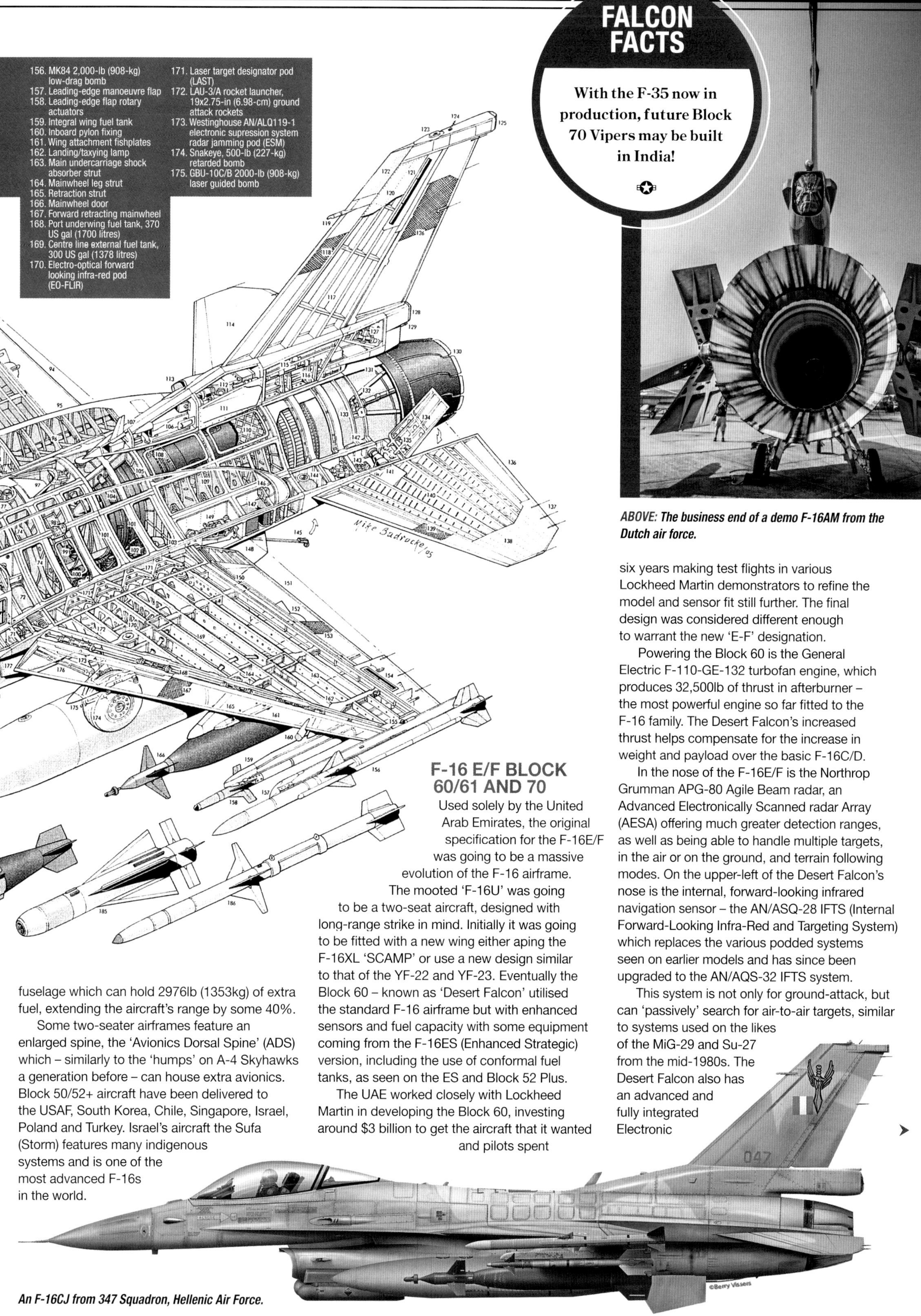

***ABOVE:* The business end of a demo F-16AM from the Dutch air force.**

An F-16CJ from 347 Squadron, Hellenic Air Force.

fuselage which can hold 2976lb (1353kg) of extra fuel, extending the aircraft's range by some 40%.

Some two-seater airframes feature an enlarged spine, the 'Avionics Dorsal Spine' (ADS) which – similarly to the 'humps' on A-4 Skyhawks a generation before – can house extra avionics. Block 50/52+ aircraft have been delivered to the USAF, South Korea, Chile, Singapore, Israel, Poland and Turkey. Israel's aircraft the Sufa (Storm) features many indigenous systems and is one of the most advanced F-16s in the world.

F-16 E/F BLOCK 60/61 AND 70

Used solely by the United Arab Emirates, the original specification for the F-16E/F was going to be a massive evolution of the F-16 airframe. The mooted 'F-16U' was going to be a two-seat aircraft, designed with long-range strike in mind. Initially it was going to be fitted with a new wing either aping the F-16XL 'SCAMP' or use a new design similar to that of the YF-22 and YF-23. Eventually the Block 60 – known as 'Desert Falcon' utilised the standard F-16 airframe but with enhanced sensors and fuel capacity with some equipment coming from the F-16ES (Enhanced Strategic) version, including the use of conformal fuel tanks, as seen on the ES and Block 52 Plus.

The UAE worked closely with Lockheed Martin in developing the Block 60, investing around $3 billion to get the aircraft that it wanted and pilots spent six years making test flights in various Lockheed Martin demonstrators to refine the model and sensor fit still further. The final design was considered different enough to warrant the new 'E-F' designation.

Powering the Block 60 is the General Electric F-110-GE-132 turbofan engine, which produces 32,500lb of thrust in afterburner – the most powerful engine so far fitted to the F-16 family. The Desert Falcon's increased thrust helps compensate for the increase in weight and payload over the basic F-16C/D.

In the nose of the F-16E/F is the Northrop Grumman APG-80 Agile Beam radar, an Advanced Electronically Scanned radar Array (AESA) offering much greater detection ranges, as well as being able to handle multiple targets, in the air or on the ground, and terrain following modes. On the upper-left of the Desert Falcon's nose is the internal, forward-looking infrared navigation sensor – the AN/ASQ-28 IFTS (Internal Forward-Looking Infra-Red and Targeting System) which replaces the various podded systems seen on earlier models and has since been upgraded to the AN/AQS-32 IFTS system.

This system is not only for ground-attack, but can 'passively' search for air-to-air targets, similar to systems used on the likes of the MiG-29 and Su-27 from the mid-1980s. The Desert Falcon also has an advanced and fully integrated Electronic

***RIGHT TOP:* Seen in 2009, the 425FS F-16D is based at Luke AFB for training purposes.**

***RIGHT MIDDLE:* Block 50/52+ have been delivered to a number of nations, including Greece, Poland, Turkey, Chile, Singapore, Israel and the USAF.**

***RIGHT BOTTOM:* AIM-120 AMRAAMs have often replaced wingtip Sidewinders on the F-16C/D series from the 1990s. It scored the F-16's first kill in USAF hands in 1992 over a MiG-25.**

Warfare (EW) system called 'Falcon Edge' which comprises threat warning, emitter location and a number of other advanced modes which work in concert with the integral chaff/flare decoy dispensers. The ALQ-165 Electronic Countermeasures system, known as the Airborne Self-Protection Jammer or ASPJ, is at the heart of the system giving the pilot information on the various threats encountered.

That's not all: other automated modes for the Desert Falcon include an automatic recovery system where if the pilot senses he's lost situational awareness the aircraft will recover to level flight at the touch of a button. The aircraft also takes full advantage of the advances in computing power that controls the sensor and weapon integration.

In the cockpit, the Block 60 features three advanced 5x7in colour displays and the Desert Falcon is configured for the use of a helmet-mounted targeting system. As well as being able to carry the arsenal used by the previous versions of the F-16, the E/F is also ready to use a wide range of current and project weaponry in both the air-to-air and air-to-ground roles.

The Block 60 faced tough opponents the in fight for selection, including the Eurofighter Typhoon and Dassault Rafale as well as political issues over source codes for the sensitive avionics systems and weaponry. With the 80 aircraft being delivered from around 2004, the UAE's Desert Falcons are considered to be half a generation ahead of the previous model of F-16 and similar models have been offered for sale (unsuccessfully) in Brazil's fighter competition (F-16BR) and India's M-MRCA (Medium Multi-Role Combat Aircraft) fly-off as the F-16IN 'Block 70', which uses the updated Northrop Grumman APG-83 Scalable Agile Beam Radar (SABR) which has some commonality with the advanced radars used in both the F-22 and F-35 fifth generation fighters. The radar is immensely powerful, being able to maintain and track around 20 high and low-flying targets within a +/- 60 degree cone in front of the aircraft. The Block 70 also uses the Auto GCAS (Ground Collision Avoidance System) used on some earlier models of F-16.

Meanwhile, more than a decade after delivery and introduction, small component upgrades to the basic Block 60 airframe had led to designation changes to 'Block 61' and all Block 60s are now at this common equipment level.

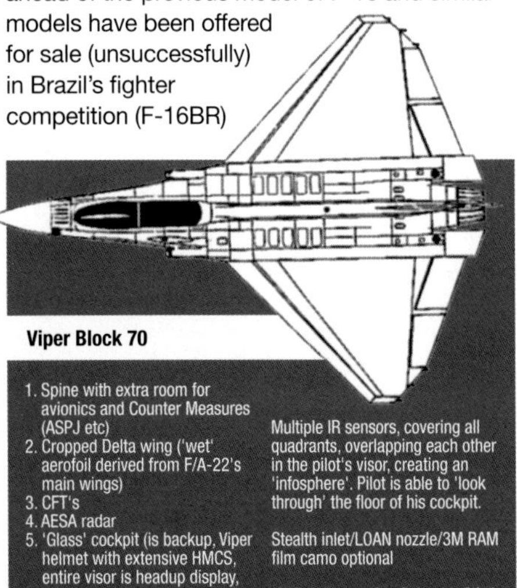

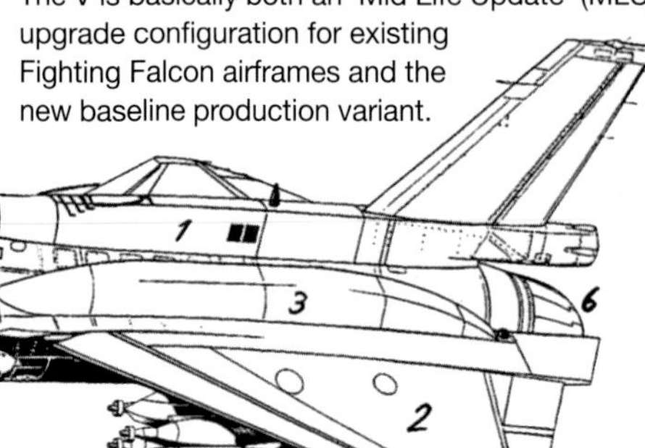

An artist impression of what the Block 70 could have looked like, along with some F-35-type sensors aboard.

F-16V 'VIPER' BLOCK 70

The F-16V is an ambitious programme by Lockheed Martin to keep the F-16 series current in the modern environment – while ensuring it isn't a threat to any potential F-35 Lightning II orders. The V is basically both an 'Mid Life Update' (MLU) upgrade configuration for existing Fighting Falcon airframes and the new baseline production variant.

At its heart is again the Northrop Grumman APG-83 Scalable Agile Beam Radar (SABR), the developed cockpit from the Block 60, including the latest colour displays and the large centre 'pedestal' display between the pilot's knees. With the upgraded radar, avionics, secure data-link system and electronic warfare systems, Lockheed Martin see the F-16V variant as a perfect link with and stepping stone to the likes of its own F-22 and F-35 fifth generation fighters as the V is designed with interoperability with such assets in mind.

QF-16

With more than 2300 F-16s having been delivered to the United States alone, it was no surprise to hear that the F-16 was going to be the target of choice for the drone programme.

Historically, ageing fighters as they near retirement have been used by the USAF as target drones and this began in the 1960s with the use of Lockheed F-104 Starfighters that were surplus to requirements. Over the years other aircraft have been used, including the North American F-100, Convair F-102 and F-106 Delta Dagger/Delta Dart and more recently with retired F-4 airframes. Each has been given the 'QF' designation.

The QF-4 programme began in 1997 and came to an end in 2014 after 238 airframes had been converted and with its upgrade in performance – and the sheer number of available airframes – a 'QF-16' was the most feasible solution. The work began in 2010 before the final QF-4s had been retired. Boeing won the contract for the work, which includes the use of Block 15/25 and 30 F-16s. Parts such as the F-16s General Electric Vulcan cannon and radar are removed and changes are made to the flight control system to allow for both manned and un-manned NULLO (Not Under Live Local Operation) flights. A self-destruct system is also fitted to the aircraft and various telemetry systems including one that can assess the accuracy of air-to-air missiles and systems.

The first QF-16 NULLO flight took place in September 2013.

LATER EXPERIMENTAL/ MOOTED F-16S

F-16ES (ENHANCED STRATEGIC)

The F-16ES was developed to take on the F-15I Strike Eagle in a competition for a strike fighter for the Israeli Air Force. The F-16ES used an internal Forward Looking Infra-Red system (similar to that found on the F-16E/F) and conformal fuel tanks.

Despite having a comparable range to the F-15E/I of more than 1000 miles without air-to-air refuelling the aircraft lost out to the Boeing type, some say due to the fact that the smaller aircraft was single-engined. A demonstrator F-16ES first flew in November 1994 and completed flight testing by January 1995.

F-16 GCAS

Later models of the F-16 have featured various GCAS or 'Ground Collision Avoidance Systems'.

The USAF from the 1990s found they were losing around five aircraft per year to Controlled Flight Into Terrain (CFIT), where pilots were either unaware they were flying into the terrain through loss of situational awareness or through G-LOC – G-induced lack of consciousness.

In the late 1990s the USAF teamed up with the Swedish Air Force who had similar concerns with a CFIT rate twice that of the US. From 1998 the F-16 GCAS demonstrator was built, using an upgraded Block 25 F-16D. Over the course of 29 flights the aircraft demonstrated the validity of the technology. More than 350 test manoeuvres were completed over a wide envelope of flight regimes, such as diving at the ground, or approaching the side of mountains.

The results were that an automatic GCAS system could reduce the CFIT rate and systems have been on USAF F-16s since 2014. By the end of 2016 it was thought that at least four F-16s – and the aircrew – were saved by Auto-GCAS.

F-16 LOAN

In 1996 a modified USAF F-16C was fitted with a LOAN or 'Low-Observable Asymmetric Nozzle' on its Pratt & Whitney F-100-PW-200 engine. This came from the Joint Strike Fighter programme. The LOAN offers lower infrared heat signature, radar cross section (RCS) and lower maintenance costs. Plans to retrofit such nozzles on the existing F-16 fleet failed to materialise.

F-16X

Another attempt to make a next-generation combat aircraft from the basic F-16 airframe in the early 1990s, the F-16X Falcon 2000, mated a lengthened F-16C/D with a wing similar in shape to that seen on the F-22 Raptor. The aircraft would also not feature a vertical tail fin but instead utilise thrust-vectoring technology.

The increase in size and wing area would give the F-16X 80% more internal fuel and allow conformal carriage of AIM-120 AMRAAM medium range missiles.

UCAV

Similar to the use of the F-16 as a target drone, a number of ideas have been developed in the last 30 years for the use of old 'war-weary' or even 'new-build' F-16 variants as some form of Unmanned Combat Aerial Vehicle (UCAV.)

The success of pilotless drones in use in both the Vietnam air-war and the Middle East – especially by the Israelis – along with increasing threat from anti-aircraft defences against manned strike aircraft led many to consider the use of some form of 'stopgap' UCAV strike aircraft.

From the mid-1990s it was thought that older F-16 airframes from the Davis-Monthan 'Boneyard' could be cheaply configured into some sort of armed UCAV strike aircraft. Since then dedicated UCAVs have been built and are used with a high degree of success, but the use of the F-16 in this role has continued. The Have Raider concept showed as recently as April 2017 how an unmanned F-16 could undertake strike missions either working autonomously or as a 'drone' with control coming from other, manned, aircraft. ✪

ACAT stands for Automatic Collision Avoidance Technology. The F-16 is still earning its corn as a test ship.

Both the Pratt & Whitney F-100 (seen here) and the General Electric F-110 have served the F-16 well.

***RIGHT:* South Korea became the fifth country to have an F-16 production line. Known locally as KF-16s, this C-model is seen in 2010 from the 123rd Fighter Squadron, RoKAF.**

COMBAT IN THE GULF AND BEYOND...

Three F-16Cs hauling Mk.20 Rockeye cluster munitions during Operation Desert Storm. The two nearest the camera are from the 363rd TFW and the furthest from the 50th TFW.

With the F-16 blooded by the Israelis in the early 1980s, it took until 1991 and Desert Storm for the US F-16s to see combat. The Viper has been in battle on and off ever since, up to the present day.

ABOVE: *Tankers were much-needed in Desert Storm and in the build-up – Desert Shield.*

In the early morning of August 2, 1990, Iraq – which fielded the world's fourth largest army at the time and the biggest in the Middle East – invaded its much smaller neighbour Kuwait.

Behind the attack was Saddam Hussein's Iraqi regime claiming that both Kuwait and the United Arab Emirates were tapping into its oil reserves and that Kuwait's increased oil production was reducing oil prices and affecting the Iraqi economy. Iraq was already financially broken following its long war with Iran and Saddam's regime began massing forces near the border and demanding reparations as well as telling the Kuwaitis to write-off his loans taken on during the Iran-Iraq War.

Emboldened by what he saw as a lack of backing from the USA and despite widespread condemnation, he went ahead with the invasion, pouring more than 120,000 troops and 300 tanks into Kuwait, against the defending nation's 20,000 troops and 165 elderly Chieftain tanks. The main aim was to deliver a quick knockout punch to its smaller neighbour, secure Kuwaiti oil fields and consolidate the position with fortifications near the Saudi Arabian border as soon as possible, so any immediate counter-attack could be repelled.

The Kuwaitis put up a brave resistance. The Kuwait Air Force could field some four fighter-bomber squadrons, two armed with McDonnell Douglas A-4KUs and the other two with Dassault Mirage F1s. Despite a brave defence where the KAF was even forced to operate from bomb-cratered runways, it was a foregone conclusion and by the end of August 3 Saddam Hussein declared that Kuwait had become Iraq's '19th province'. His armed forces began to dig in, while foreign nationals were shepherded together at potential targets as 'human shields'. Saddam, it seemed, was there to stay.

Contrary to what Iraq initially thought, the international outcry was intense and the response immediate. The UN Security Council passed Resolution 660 which called for immediate Iraqi withdrawal, which didn't come. What followed would be Operation Desert Shield, a six-month operation where the US and its allies would transport men and materiel into the potential warzone.

Come January 1991, the Allies could field 2400 aircraft from nine coalition nations as well as 1400 helicopters. Almost a million allied soldiers faced 700,000 Iraqis. November 1990's Resolution 678 had given the Iraq regime until January 15 to withdraw from Kuwait. The clock was ticking.

The air war was planned to go ahead in phases. Phase 1 was to be a strategic attack on Iraq, it's leadership, command and control, air defences, munitions sites, power stations, logistical targets as well as production facilities for purported NBC (nuclear, biological and chemical) warfare sites. Phase 2 would destroy Iraq's air-defences in the Kuwait Theatre of Operations (KTO) and Phase 3 would destroy the Republican Guard's ability to fight. Phase 4 would support the ground units as they liberated Kuwait. By January 1991, it was felt that stages 1-3 could take place simultaneously, such was the force assembled in the theatre.

THE F-16'S AIR WAR

The F-16 Fighting Falcon was the most numerous aircraft fielded by the coalition in the area: 249 aircraft in total and a real mix of blocks, variants and capabilities. Five hastily-provisioned

***ABOVE:* Total F-16 losses for the campaign were five in total and a further two in accidents.**

> ***The F-16 Fighting Falcon was the most numerous aircraft fielded by the coalition in the area: 249 aircraft in total and a real mix of Blocks, variants and capabilities.***

F-16 wings would take the fight to Saddam Hussein's invading forces.

The 4th Tactical Fighter Wing (Provisional) comprised of the 138th Tactical Fighter Squadron (New York Air National Guard – now flying the MQ-9 Reaper drone) from the 174th Tactical Fighter Wing. During combat, they would have the GPU-5 'Pave Claw' gun pod (otherwise known as the GEPOD30) at their disposal, but not for long as they were found to be unsuitable for combat. The other squadron was the 157th TFS (South Carolina Air National Guard), from the 169th TFG, otherwise known as 'The Swamp Foxes'. Both units would fly the F-16A from Al Kharj Air Force Base in Saudi Arabia.

The 363rd Tactical Fighter Wing (Provisional) would comprise of the 10th TFS from USAFE, normally based at Hahn AFB in Germany and the 17th TFS from the 33rd TFW normally based at Shaw AFB in South Carolina. Flying the F-16C Block 25, these aircraft would be based in Al Dhafra Air Base in the United Arab Emirates.

Also based in the UAE, but at Al Minhad AFB, was the 388th TFW (Provisional). This comprised the 4th and 421st Tactical Fighter Squadrons from the 388th TFW normally based at Hill AFB, Utah, along with the 69th TFS from the 347th TFW out of Moody AFB, Georgia. This composite wing would fly the Block 40 F-16C.

Qatar would provide a home for 401st Tactical Fighter Wing, comprised as it was of 614th TFS from USAFE, normally based at Torrejon Air Force Base in Spain. They flew the Block 30 F-16C.

Far to the north in Turkey, would be the 7740th Composite Wing. They would field F-16C Block 30s, based at Incirlik. They would be formed from Detachment 1 of the 401st TFW from (USAFE) also normally based at Torrejon, they were joined by the 23rd TFS from the 52nd TFW (USAFE) normally based at Spangdahlem, in Germany – these were the 'killer' element F-16s, teamed up with the specialist 'hunter' F-4G 'Wild Weasels', of which there were 12 working alongside them although other F-4Gs were based in Bahrain.

Overall, Desert Storm was the war that pushed the case for precision and stand-off weapons over traditional 'old-school' weapons. Dumb bombs had their place,

MIG-25 KILLER

The F-16 may not have scored any kills in Desert Storm, but it did take a notable scalp after the conflict and make a notable 'first'.

On December 27, 1992, Lieutenant Colonel Gary North, commander of the 33rd TFS was policing the 'No Fly Zone' over Iraq known as 'Southern Watch' when he engaged a fast-moving target. AWACS had told North and his wingman that the two aircraft were at least 14 miles below the 32nd parallel.

The aircraft he was flying was an F-16D Block 42 tail code 90-0778 and it wasn't necessarily the best machine out on the line. Crew Chief Roy Murray recalls: "I launched 'Benji 41' for a combat mission from Dhahran, Saudi Arabia. The only reason for it flying the four-hour long combat mission that day was to take flying hours off the airframe so it could go in for a phase inspection. Most of its flight time during Operation Southern Watch was familiarisation rides for incoming pilots and VIPs as it was the only D model we had! The canopy was so bad and scratched that North said 'it was like landing with a paper bag on your head'."

But it got the job done: when given the okay to fire, North fired an AIM-120A AMRAAM which destroyed the MiG-25. This was the first kill for the F-16 in USAF colours and the first kill for the USAF's new medium-range air-to-air missile. The very missile used in the kill had been returned from the flight-line as being defective just a day before the historic victory.

Murray adds: "The family bus still got the job done that day! I remember a reporter asking Lieutenant Colonel North why he did not use the cheaper missile, his comeback was great. He said that if you were in a fight and had a knife and a gun, which one would you use? We painted the star and a blue tail on the aircraft while it was in phase, because it was on loan from the 19th TFS at the time, then it became a 33rd TFS aircraft. I stayed as the Crew Chief of 778 when we returned to Shaw, AFB and then transferred out with it to Luke AFB in Arizona. I took my retirement flight in 90-0778 and launched General North one more time when he came through Luke. I do miss those days!"

The MiG-25 kill marking was placed on the left side just below the canopy frame to mark that kill. AMRAAM gained a second victory in January 1993 when an Iraqi MiG-23 was shot down by a USAF F-16C.

CIRCLE: ***The kill marking on F-16D Block 42 tail code 90-0778.***

The MiG-25 is capable of speeds up to Mach 3.2 but found itself outclassed by the USAF's new AMRAAM missile in 1992.

50th TFW F-16s hauling Mk.84s during Desert Storm: more sorties came from the F-16 than any other in-theatre.

> ***The Iraqi gunners know exactly where I am and they have me locked. My mind is task saturated, but If I get shot down, then so be it. I am not going to miss this time.***

but the ability to be many miles away from your target as you release your weapons was a wise one – especially if the weapon could be guided to its target without over-flying it.

The sheer numbers of anti-aircraft guns and missiles made each target in Iraq and Iraqi target in Kuwait a dangerous place to loiter around. For years the likes of the RAF and Luftwaffe Tornados had planned and practised the use of JP233 and MW-1 by flying low and at high-speed over an airfield – but just days into the war, this was seen to not be a viable tactic for the RAF crews following such losses.

For the F-16 contingent – like all allied aircraft – it was a case of the 'haves' and the 'have nots'. Having a smart weapon capability and the ability to find the target (at night or in bad weather) was a 'have' capability. Otherwise the 'have nots' had to make do with using older tactics with dumb bombs, which – in a high-threat environment – was always risky.

The more advanced versions of the F-16 in theatre were equipped with LANTIRN (Low Altitude Navigation and Targeting Infra-red for Night) pods but only 72 were capable – most went to the new F-15E Strike Eagles. So how good was LANTIRN? The job of this pod was to turn night into day for the pilot, allowing him or her to navigate to and deliver their weapons with accuracy and then navigate home. Colonel Dave Martin (retired) was an early test pilot on the LANTIRN programme and – after a while learning to trust the equipment – found it to be invaluable. He recalled: "You'd be going down lower and lower, down to 200ft, zooming along at 575mph in an airplane, at night. It was the first time I imagined doing something like that in a military jet but after practice it became second nature."

One of the best records of the air war is Vipers in the Storm by Keith Rosenkranz. 'Rosey' was an F-16 pilot with the 421st TFS 'The Black Widows' and he was one of the few LANTIRN-qualified pilots in theatre. In his book he says: "LANTIRN was developed for one reason only – so a pilot flying at night could navigate and deliver weapons as if he were flying during the day. The pod

uses a forward looking infrared sensor that displays the infrared picture of the terrain ahead either directly onto the HUD or one of the multi-function screens."

PACKAGE Q PROBLEMS

The 'Package Q Airstrike' took place on January 19 and it was the largest combined strike of the war and employed the largest numbers of F-16s ever in such an operation. It was also the operation that made the coalition realise that big unwieldy formations weren't as good as stealthy, precision strikes.

The large force sent against Al Tuwaitha was aimed at dealing a knockout blow to the Iraqi defences, but a series of problems instead led to an unsuccessful outcome and two aircraft being lost. A total of 56 F-16s were used in the raid, coming from the 388th TFW and 401st TFW along with McDonnell Douglas F-4G 'Wild Weasel' aircraft and top cover provided by F-15C Eagles.

The issues began with some orders for the strike coming late, the day before the strike, while overnight on the 18th/19th other targets – this time in downtown Baghdad – were added. This meant that after hitting Al Tuwaitha and the Osirak nuclear reactor, the whole force had to fly through concentrated (and by now very alert) SAM belts and triple-A units. Adding to these issues were the fact that the F-16s were heavily laden – bombs, two fuel tanks and two AIM-9 Sidewinders, while the F-4Gs were only carrying two High Speed Anti-Radiation Missiles and fuel tanks.

Even before the mission, things were getting complicated, thanks to bad weather and issues with the air-to-air refuelling – tankers were throttling back to avoid having to turn back early and this meant a number of F-16s were so far behind the main force after they tanked, they had to be sent back to base.

On the way in to the target all aircraft were subjected to triple-A and SAMs and under this barrage communication between the various groups in the ➤

BELOW: *Seen here in Europe just before Desert Shield, a pairing of McDonnell F-4G Wild Weasel and F-16C prepare for a mission.*

The desert would bring a whole new set of challenges compared to traditional Northern European weather.

BOTTOM: *Behind the scenes men and women worked tirelessly to keep the F-16s capability rate higher even than peacetime.*

Desert Storm was the USAF F-16 and the F-15's baptism of fire. Both performed superbly.

FALCON FACTS

Rumoured/failed F-16 orders over the years included Argentina, Austria, Canada, Iran, New Zealand, South Africa and Spain.

AIR COMBAT ART

F-16s seen in Desert Storm often came with morale-boosting 'nose art' which revived the practice first begun during the Second World War.

Some of the most famous Desert Storm nose arts were made by Technical Sergeant Warren Trask, who is now retired from the USAF. He recalls: "I wanted to do some paintings, but there weren't any canvases available. I asked if I could do a drawing on one of the F-16s, something that might boost morale like the nose art of the Second World War. My commander said I could, but only if it could be washed off!"

Once completed, his commander had to approve the work before the aircraft was allowed onto the flight line. With the fact that it had to be 'temporary only', Warren decided to do a test piece and use grease pencils. He was told that – following a test flight – if the artwork didn't smear then Warren could do more works of art on other aircraft in the squadron. Warren says: "In my free time, I'd make rough sketches of possible nose art pieces. Once I came up with a promising design, I'd ask the aircraft crew chiefs if I could draw it on their aircraft.

"Some of them had their own ideas, so I'd incorporate those into my drawings. Once I got their approval, I'd grab a maintenance stand, a few grease pencils, and begin work. I would do a rough sketch in white to start with then fill the other colours in later. Blending the colours was just like with oil paints, but instead of a using a paint brush, I smeared the colours around with the side of my right thumb!"

With such high temperatures in the desert, Warren would draw during the later afternoon or early evening when it wasn't too hot and the grease pencils were softer and therefore easier to apply. Most of the more complicated nose art pieces took two or three days to complete and would often need to be 'touched up' every 30 days.

"I really think it boosted morale," says Warren. "It helped people feel like the belonged and gave many of us a sense of pride. It's also a tradition that I think should carry on. I think my favourite piece was the '363 TFW – Desert Shield' piece. I did that one for then Colonel Ralph 'Ed' Eberhart when we found out that he was being promoted to brigadier general. We were all very proud of him and wanted to give him something to express our thanks for his leadership and for all the things he did for us as our commander."

strike package began to suffer. The Wild Weasel F-4Gs did engage some of the threats, but not all of them were over the target nor did they shoot all their HARMs and – to make matters worse – they had to leave before all of the F-16 strikers were over the target area itself.

Cloud cover also obscured the target, making things yet worse.

This was Rosenkranz's 'mission from hell'. In his book he recalls: "The flak is thicker than soup. Within seconds my RWR (Radar Warning Receiver) scope fills up again. The Iraqi gunners know exactly where I am and they have me locked. The launch indications are continuous: it finally reaches a point where I can no longer hear them. My mind is task saturated. I do hear radio calls and tones from my RWR but I don't have time to discern their meaning: nor could I – not with all my energy focused on hitting the target. If I get shot down, then so be it. I am not going to miss this time." Despite the facility being obscured by smoke, Rosenkranz hit the target and made it back to base, two others would not be so lucky.

Other problems saw the strike package get strung out – differences in the performance of the various F-16s and the different engines saw to that. By the time the F-4G Wild Weasels had egressed, the F-16s were on their own and – while previously many missiles had been launched 'unguided' – these were now slaved to their targets. And there were many targets for them to choose from...

Many F-16s hit their targets, either primary or secondary ones, but many others were forced to jettison both bombs and tanks before hitting the target itself. It was foolish to do anything else with the number of SAMs in the air.

Some pilots said as many as 20 to 30 SAMs had been fired, as they tried to hit the target and then get the hell out of there. Many aircraft

RIGHT: ***'Hot Cock' shows a rooster on a beach being cooled by babes in bikinis.***

BELOW: ***Warren and his favourite piece of artwork 'Desert Shield'.***

BELOW RIGHT: ***One of Warren's classics: 'Feel Lucky?' shows a Sidewinder-toting troll looking for a target. Bizarrely the F-16 never scored a kill in Desert Storm.***

were lost – both pilots surviving the war as prisoners of war. And still the pain went on... this time the Iraqi Air Force began to shadow the strike force as it left the target area. Eight MiG-29s closed on the rear of the F-16 formation as they struggled to get the heck out of Dodge. To add insult to injury, the F-15C top-cover had already left with the F-4Gs...

Safe in the knowledge that they could best anyone in air-combat, some of the F-16s turned around to face their attackers and the MiG-29s turned tail and fled. This meant that – by the time they crossed the border – some of the F-16s were perilously low on fuel. It's said more than one tanker crew disobeyed orders and crossed the border to top up the tanks of a few thirsty Vipers.

These difficulties led to the US adopting different tactics – and swiftly. It's to their credit that they didn't blindly send another large strike package into a heavily defended area. Instead high-risk targets in heavily-defended areas like Baghdad and Al Tuwaitha would receive the attentions of the F-117A Nighthawk stealth fighter-bomber.

DESERT STORM AIR-TO-AIR

The strangest thing about Desert Storm was the total of enemy aircraft (rotary or fixed wing) that had been claimed by the F-16 in theatre. It was zero, zilch, nothing. Everything from the F-15C, down to the lowly A-10 Warthog scored victories (a helicopter with its 30mm cannon) and only one aircraft (an F/A-18) was shot down by the Iraqis and this by a MiG-25.

This was largely down to the structure of the sorties themselves. The F-15 Eagle drivers were the ones doing the Combat Air Patrols and in charge of the defence of the attackers: it was their job. The US Navy's F-14 (which only managed to nab a single helicopter in combat) was widely feared by the Iraqis as it had faced Iranian Tomcats in their previous war and when one appeared on any Iraqi radar warning gear with their AWG-9/APG-71 radar they fled. F/A-18 Hornets would self-escort and escort US Navy strike packages so had their own opportunities, while the F-16 was mainly used as a bomb truck – even ➤

THE F-16 IN THE BALKANS

NATO was forced to intervene in the armed conflict which took place in The Balkans during the early 1990s.

Reports of alleged war crimes and atrocities in the Bosnian War led to United Nations intervention and Operation Deny Flight which took place between April 1993 and December 1995.

Twelve NATO countries contributed to the operation and the USAF – and the F-16 – was at the sharp end, patrolling the skies and supporting the UN ground troops with air-strikes.

On February 28, 1994, the 526th Tactical Fighter Squadron, 'The Black Knights' were operating out of Aviano, Italy, as part of the provisional 401st Operations Group, supporting Operation Deny Flight.

Early that morning, two F-16Cs were in the air on a close air support training mission near Sarajevo, Bosnia, when they were vectored onto six unidentified radar contacts travelling east in the no fly zone. At first, it was hard to pick out the contacts in such mountainous terrain, but eventually NATO AWACS aircraft picked up six Soko J-21 Jastrebs and two J-22 Oraos on radar, bombing a military target at Novi Travnik. What happened next became known as the 'Banja Luka incident' following from the location where the air combat happened.

Warnings were issued as per the NATO ROE (Rules of Engagement) but despite being told to exit the no fly zone or land, they did not and the aircraft bombed their target. Reports say that the two J-22 Oraos then headed towards Croatia, leaving the four J-21s to their fate. Only one clearance call was needed for the F-16s to engage and that was made at 6.45am.

The Bosnian-Serb J-21 Jastrebs then headed north back to their base at Udbina and the F-16s moved to intercept them. The first Jastreb was struck by an AIM-120A AMRAAM, fired by Captain Robert Wright. This aircraft was flying at an altitude of around 5000ft and when this J-21 went down, the remaining three dropped to very low level, of maybe just a few hundred feet, desperately trying to mask themselves against the mountainous terrain.

Wright wasn't finished yet. Closing to within range of his AIM-9M Sidewinder infrared homing short-range missile, he took down another two Jastrebs with these missiles, before handing over to Captain Scott O'Grady, his wingman. O'Grady locked on his own Sidewinder on one of the remaining Jastrebs, and fired. It wasn't clear whether the missile impacted or not, although it was locked-up and was fired well within the AIM-9M's launch parameters.

With Black Flight on 'bingo' fuel, they had to go hook up with a tanker before their flight back to Aviano. It was 6.50am and another 'Black Flight' had been sent to the area to support Wright and O'Grady.

It was now Captain Steve Allen's turn. He descended to get onto the tail of the jinking Jastreb, which was still flying at low level. Again, the Sidewinder was the weapon of choice and Allen locked his AIM-9 onto the J-21, fired and destroyed it.

Flying wing for Allen that day was Colonel John Meyer and he locked his radar onto another aircraft which was heading for Udbina at tree-top height, but after a few minutes contact was lost and the pair went back to their combat air patrol. That remaining J-21 made it home.

Three kills were credited to Wright and one to Allen, but the Serbs claimed that five of their number were shot down – perhaps O'Grady's missile did the job? They claimed that three pilots died – one following a low level ejection – while another

Desert Storm showed that while dumb bombs – like these Mk.84 2000-pounders – had their place, precision, stand-off bombing was the future for the F-16.

two survived ejecting and another pilot made it back to Udbina with a damaged aircraft.

Other UN-backed campaigns included Operation Deliberate Force during 1995 and Operation Allied Force in 1999. Again F-16s were used and in May 1999 an F-16C was shot down by an SA-3 SAM, with the pilot being picked up after a successful ejection, while in the same month a Yugoslav MiG-29 was destroyed by an AMRAAM when it was intercepted by a pair of USAF F-16Cs from the 78th Tactical Fighter Squadron.

Scott O'Grady has already been mentioned here, for his part in the actions which took place on February 28, 1994, but on June 2, 1995, O'Grady made the headlines when he was shot down by an SA-6 Gainful, surface-to-air missile. Again Rob Wright was flying with him.

The Serbs had laid a trap for NATO aircraft and were cagey about when they were switching their radars on – often doing it when the aircraft were just overhead, making things difficult for the NATO planes to do anything about it.

On that day in June, the Serbs adopted this tactic at Mrkonji Grad and had a series of mobile SAM batteries in the location. Overflying the site, O'Grady knew he was being painted by a Serbian radar site and then he knew a missile had been launched, but as he was flying through cloud, he couldn't see it to evade it. This first missile exploded between him and wingman Wright but a second was in the air and this hit O'Grady's F-16C in the belly and the horrified Wright did not see O'Grady get out of his stricken aircraft.

Landing in what was (effectively) enemy territory O'Grady took the survival bag from under his ejection seat and ran. This survival kit would save his life. In it was a survival radio (with spare battery) a first-aid kit, a mirror, a signal kit, personnel distress flares, a compass, a whistle and a strobe light with flash guard and infrared filter. He also had a small raft, some raft repair plugs, a 5in knife, a container with matches, water, a blanket, a packet of sea dye, a survival pamphlet, drinking water storage bag, a beacon and his pistol. This would add up to almost 30lb (13.5kg). In his survival vest was a Global Positioning System (GPS) receiver; distress signals and a tourniquet.

Bosnian-Serb forces were out looking for him – it would be a remarkable coup for them to have a captured pilot to parade in front of the TV cameras. Thankfully he was undiscovered, despite the soldiers coming within just a few feet of his hiding place and two civilians walking straight past his hiding place. He would later say that he also heard gunfire and thanked his luck that no dogs were used in his pursuit.

O'Grady used all of the tricks learned during his Survival, Evasion, Resistance and Escape (SERE) training. He dirtied his face and slept during the day – covering himself in a camouflage net – and moved only during darkness. Over the next six days he survived as best he could, soaking up rainwater and keeping it in plastic bags. His survival notes also told him what insects he could eat – and that he should remove the legs first…

Tactically, he knew that many downed pilots are captured soon after ejection as they call for help on their emergency radio too soon – so on his fourth day on the run he risked it… He signalled his location using his radio's dwindling battery power and these were picked up by US forces. Very early on June 8, he was on the radio and was being quizzed by a fellow F-16 pilot so they could verify it was him, it was only then that the order to rescue O'Grady was made.

Two CH-53 Sea Stallions with 51 Marines on board lifted off from the USS *Kearsarge* to begin the rescue attempt. It was quite an armada. Also involved were two Marine AV-8B Harrier IIs, two AH-1W Bell Super Cobras as well as back up aircraft including two US Navy EA-6B Prowler electronic warfare aircraft, a similarly-tasked EF-111 Raven, as well as two A-10 Thunderbolts and a pair of F/A-18 Hornets.

Around 6.30 that morning, the two Sea Stallions approached the pine forest where O'Grady's beacon had been picked up. One CH-53 landed and 20 marines formed a defensive perimeter and – as the second landed – out from the trees came O'Grady, pistol in hand. He boarded one of the helicopters, the marines embarked upon the other and they took off. The rescue had taken just minutes to execute, but they weren't home yet…

As they flew back to the USS *Kearsarge*, they were illuminated by a Serbian SAM position, but they did not fire – but two portable SAM missiles were fired at the helicopters but thankfully missed. The helicopters also took some small arms fire and the door gunners returned fire. At 7.30am both helicopters made it back aboard the USS *Kearsarge*.

BELOW: After taking part in the Banja Luka incident in 1994, Scott O'Grady was shot-down and part of a successful rescue attempt in 1995.

A USAF F-16C bares its teeth.

Once again for the F-16 it was in support of the ground war where the aircraft was most employed.

Shot from a KC-135 tanker, by the time Operation Iraqi Freedom came around the F-16 fleet was much more advanced with sensors and smart weapons.

Wingtip AMRAAMs were the popular fit and flare and chaff decoys were used extensively.

An F-16C rolls in on its target.

BACK TO IRAQ

F-16s went back to Iraq for 2003's Operation Iraqi Freedom.

This time there was no UN backing, just the desire of President George W Bush for regime change in Iraq, which meant a full invasion – no holding back at the border.

Following the first Gulf War, Saddam Hussein's regime was effectively isolated, with coalition allies enforcing no fly zones and keeping a close watch on his every move. When Bush Junior was elected, foreign policy changed and – with a small number of allies, most notably the United Kingdom – the rush towards ousting Hussein began.

Under the shadow of inferred Iraqi involvement in 9/11 and 'sexed up' dossiers describing Iraq's huge arsenal of Weapons of Mass Destruction (WMDs) and the short time it could take for an attack to come from Iraq, a 'coalition of the willing' was put together and by early 2003 it seemed as if the only road this coalition was on led to war and invasion.

F-16s would once more be at the sharp end for the invasion of Iraq. The invasion would take less than a month and a half to complete and – once more – the onus was on ground-to-air operations, especially SEAD – or the Supression of Enemy Air Defences.

One interesting incident occurred on March 25, when a US Patriot Missile system was hit by an AGM-88 HARM fired from an F-16CJ which was on patrol in Southern Iraq. When the pilot was painted by the Patriot system it came up on his warning gear as a Russian-made SA-2. What the USAF had said they needed all along were Army Ground Liaison Officers (GLOs) to tell them precisely where any army surface to air units were during the swift advances.

A US Army Patriot missile had already destroyed an RAF Tornado on March 22, killing the two men on board, so when the SA-2 warning came up in his cockpit, Major Douglas Blouser reacted instantly and fired a HARM towards the emitter. Thankfully no-one was hurt. Speaking after the conflict, F-16 pilot Major 'Bear' McAtee explained: "It didn't take a brain surgeon to work out that if we knew where the army was, they would have air defence assets around them.

"We had no idea where the Patriot missile systems were and they were locking us up on a regular basis. No-one was hurt when the Patriot got hit, but at least from our perspective they were down one radar. So that's one radar they couldn't target us with anymore." On April 2 the Patriot system also shot down an FA/18 from the USS *Kitty Hawk*, killing its pilot.

For the F-16 only one loss occurred during Operation Iraqi Freedom when an F-16CG from the 421st TFS crashed near Baghdad after running out of fuel.

The following 'War on Terror' has seen the F-16 take part in operations over Afghanistan, Libya and Syria and against ISIS with a number of losses.

In the 'War on Terror' it wasn't just the USAF's F-16s that held the line in Iraq, Afghanistan and Libya. F-16s from other nations – like this Danish F-16BM were also employed, most recently against ISIS forces.

FALCON FACTS

Israel is the second biggest user of the F-16 after the USA.

One USAF F-16CJ actually destroyed a Patriot missile radar system that had 'locked up' on it during Iraqi Freedom. This was days after the system had shot down an RAF Tornado, killing its crew.

if it still carried wingtip air-to-air missiles. But with any USAF/Allied package being looked after by the F-15 Eagles, little came their way. Although when one finally did in 1992, it would be a 'big catch'.

Desert Storm showed that radar missiles could work. After the heat-break of hundreds of Sparrow shots in the Vietnam War, modern versions of the missile did their job in The Gulf War: 29 of the confirmed or probable 44 air-to-air kills were made with the AIM-7, doubtless due to upgraded versions of the missile and training which saw crews launch them within the appropriate parameters and without the constraints of ridiculous rules of engagement (ROE).

But the Viper did one hell of a job. It attacked targets at day and at night in good and bad weather, it attacked SCUD sites, it hit important production sites and chemical weapon facilities. All-in-all around 13,500 sorties were generated – around 300-400 a day – the highest sortie total for any aircraft in-theatre and 25% of the whole coalition effort. The pilots may have had their frustrations and their problems concerning weapons fit and kit (every aircraft in-theatre did) but they put up a 95.2% mission capable rate, which was around 5% more than the force had shown in peacetime. Those equipped with LANTIRN hit a 98% rate. This was a team effort and air and ground staff from the F-16 force did the USAF proud.

Of course all of this was not without paying the ultimate price and five F-16s were lost during the course of hostilities with a further two during training for the campaign.

CLOSE COUSINS

Not only has the General Dynamics airframe found itself to be able to grow in capability over the decades, it has also helped inspire a number of other designs: some with the help of GD/Lockheed Martin and others without.

ISRAEL'S 'F-16'

The Israel Defence Force/Air Force originally relied on some very clandestine means to secure its aircraft.

Following the formation of Israel on May 14, 1948, the country's leaders knew that they were surrounded by enemies and that they needed to have the airborne means with which to defend themselves and also be on the offensive. In late 1947, the Haganah Sherut-Avir, or Air Service, was formed under Aharon Remez, a former RAF fighter pilot from the Second World War and from this would come the IDF/AF.

Initially the force would be equipped with small, light observation machines such as Austers, Tiger Moths and Zlins but soon more potent aircraft were sought. Czechoslovakia needed foreign currency and they were approached by Jewish representatives to sell arms to the nascent state, following this a deal was struck to supply 10 Avia S199 aircraft to the Haganah.

These machines were based on the old Messerschmitt Bf 109 fighters from the war, but featured 1350hp Jumo 211F engines instead of the normal Daimler-Benz DB 605 powerplant. The Jumo engine's high torque made handling tricky and led to the Czech pilots calling it the 'Mezc' ➤

FALCON FACTS

Lawn Dart was the unflattering nickname given after early-year issues with the F-16!

The KAI T-50 Golden Eagle is clearly a close relative of the F-16, albeit an 80% scaled down one.

or Mule – but by May 29, 1948, these unsuitable machines were given to the 101st Fighter Squadron to be based near Tel Aviv and they were soon in action against Egyptian Spitfires.

In the years following more suitable aircraft became available, such as the Supermarine Spitfire Mk.IX, again sourced from the Czechs (although their first Spitfire in service was a crash-damaged Egyptian machine) and then North American P-51 Mustangs from the USA. As the IAF went into the jet age in 1953 a relaxation in trade embargoes saw the Jewish state field aircraft from the UK, such as the Gloster Meteor and the De Havilland Vampire. The first swept-wing fighter in service was the Dassault Mystere IVA which arrived in 1956 and this heralded a decade of relying on French-built aircraft.

Much of the image of the much-vaunted Dassault Mirage IIIC and E came from the skilful handling of these delta-winged jets by the Israelis in the 1960s and 1970s, so much so that the IAF pushed the need for a specific model of Mirage. This would be something simpler, lacking a radar but with the ability to carry more ordnance for a wide-range of roles from air-to-air to air-to-ground missions. This aircraft became the Mirage V and an order for 50 was swiftly placed. The delivery was going to be expanded to 100 machines, but it was never delivered, thanks to

The IAI Kfir (Lion Cub) was the marriage of an unlicensed Mirage V copy mated to the US General Electric J-79 turbojet.

CLOCKWISE FROM ABOVE: *Israeli Aircraft Industries did well with export versions of the Kfir and its predecessors during the 1980s. This is a Falklands War veteran with Argentina. / Although the wing plan is radically different, there are many similarities between the Lavi (Young Lion) and the F-16. / The two-seater in flight. One wonders what the Lavi would have been developed into? / Little survives of the Lavi programme today.*

French president Charles de Gaulle's decision to impose an arms embargo on Israel in 1969 following the previous year's raid Israeli raid on Lebanon.

This left Israel in a precarious state as it relied on quality to counter any quantity advantage its neighbours may have. As well as not delivering the agreed Mirage Vs, it also meant that support was cut off for the-then fleet of Mirage III CJs. The cunning Israelis countered this in two ways.

Firstly, since the early 1960s Israel had tried to buy American combat aircraft so as to not rely on the French. Defensive systems such as Hawk surface-to-air missiles and other equipment were forthcoming, but not aircraft. Eventually in 1965 48 A-4 Skyhawk light-attack aircraft were ordered, but orders for F-4 Phantoms and A-6 Intruders were refused. It took until 1968 when the US Government agreed to supply Israel with 50 F-4Es following increased Soviet involvement in the equipping of Israel's Arab neighbours. These aircraft began to arrive in 1969.

The second way they planned to combat the frozen Mirage deliveries was through unlicensed production. Since 1953 the Israeli Aerospace Industries (IAI) company had been born and had been state-owned. Originally looking at civilian applications, it was only a matter of time before IAI started producing military aircraft. ➤

THE MITSUBISHI F-2 VIPER ZERO

Japanese aviation history is a rich and diverse one showing innovation in their own clean-sheet designs as well as an acceptance to utilise and adapt existing designs for their own unique needs.

Following the Second World War, a mixed approach saw Japan's military aviation industry use its own indigenous designs, such as the Fuji T-1, T-5, the Kawasaki T-4 and Mitsubishi F-1/T-2 as well as adopt foreign-designed aircraft – although often produced under licence by Japan's impressive home-grown defence contractors. These include the likes of the licence-produced F-86 Sabre, F-104 Starfighter, F-4 Phantom and F-15 Eagles.

Today, recently in-service aircraft like Kawasaki's C-2 transport and the P-1 maritime patrol aircraft show just how accomplished the Japanese are at designing aircraft that meet their own stringent and unique needs.

Due to its geography, for most of the Cold War, the Japan Air Self-Defence Force (JASDF) followed a strategy of foiling any armed amphibious attack on the Japanese home islands. The onus was on the use of aircraft to break up any such attack far out to sea with a range of air-to-surface missiles and weapons. The indigenous Mitsubishi F-1 was one of the aircraft tasked for this mission. Developed from the T-2 trainer, at first glance the F-1/T-2 family looked similar to the SEPECAT Jaguar and used a licence-built version of the Rolls-Royce Turbomeca Adour as well as a radar fit similar to that of the RAF's McDonnell Douglas F-4 fleet. It was equipped with a range of air-to-ground weapons including the ASM-1 and ASM-2 anti-ship missile. Around 77 were built from 1975 through to 1987 and they were phased out in 2006.

The F-1's replacement would be the Mitsubishi Heavy Industries F-2, also called by some 'Viper Zero'. This requirement came about in the early 1980s to give the JASDF a follow-on multi-role fighter from the successful F-1 itself. Japan did look at an 'off-the-shelf' aircraft, but the FS-X (soon called F-2) that was selected in 1987 moved to what was effectively a hybrid machine, based largely on the General Dynamics Block 40 F-16C/D Fighting Falcon. Mitsubishi would be prime contractor in a 60:40 split with the USA.

The design – being based on the Lockheed Martin product – was very much recognisable as an 'F-16' even if it was very different under the skin.

Both the main wings and tail-planes are 25% larger than those on the F-16. While a larger wing area can boost the ability to carry payload and increase agility – this has to be offset against weight. To this end, the F-2 became the first production multirole fighter to use a fully composite carbon-fibre wing (the Harrier AV-8B's is not fully composite). This wing design was based on that developed for the F-16XL Agile Falcon which never saw production. The F-2 family also employs a drogue chute system, similar to that in use by a number of F-16 customers, but not the USAF.

The easiest way to tell the F-16 and F-2 apart is the canopy: the F-2A has a three-piece canopy compared to the F-16's two-piece unit. Engines for the F-2 were selected to be the General Electric F-110-GE-129, similar to the majority of the late-build F-16C/D, in the 17,000lb thrust class (7728kg) and 29,000lb (13,182kg) in afterburner, giving it nominal Mach 2 capability, although it breathed through a larger intake than on the F-16C. In the nose of the F-2 was the world's first operational Active Electronically Scanned Array (AESA) radar, the J/APG-1, while the cockpit aped the latest fighters in using three colour multi-function displays along with a Japanese-designed head-up display (HUD.)

Along with the radar, the Japanese-designed electronic warfare equipment is integrated into the aircraft. Armament includes the venerable General Electric M61-A1 20mm Vulcan 'Gatling' cannon and 13 weapons stations which can carry a wide variety of munitions. Air-to-air weapons include the Japanese-built AAM-3 short-range missile, the ubiquitous AIM-9 Sidewinder family, as well as Sparrow and AMRAAM medium-range missiles.

In the important air-to-ship role, the F-2 employs either the ASM-1 or ASM-2 anti-ship missiles which were originally developed in the 1980s/90s and offer similar performance to both the French Exocet, British Sea Eagle and American Harpoon missiles. The ASM-1 offers a range of around 30 miles while the newer ASM-2 – which entered service in 1993 and is both electro-optically and infrared guided – has a ➤

range of around 100 miles. The F-2 can also carry an array of air-to-ground bombs and missiles, including iron bombs and JDAMs.

The aircraft's development wasn't always a smooth one. Like in European collaborative efforts with the likes of the Eurofighter Typhoon and the Panavia Tornado, technological issues and politics both served to place delays and cost rises in the way of the programme. The partnership between Japan and the USA was also not always a harmonious one. Delays included two-years where the Japanese had to develop their own fly-by-wire system on the earlier Mitsubishi T-1 Control Configured Vehicle, when the US refused to release the vital source code for the F-16's FBW system. Technological issues included the use of the carbon-composite wing when cracks were found in the structures due to the large payloads being tested on the F-2. This delayed the initial in-service date of 1999 by a further year.

Development of the variants (F-2A single-seater and F-2B two-seater) saw the use of six prototypes: four flying and two for static tests. The F-2 first flew in 1995 with the first machine entering production in 1998 and the first joining the JASDF in 2000.

Although it was initially thought that the JASDF needed 140 aircraft this was subsequently reduced and when production stopped in 2011 the totals were the four flying prototypes and 94 production aircraft. The aircraft made its first overseas deployment in 2007 in Exercise Cope North in Guam.

Despite the huge price tag of the F-2 (unit cost was rumoured to be around $100 million dollars per aircraft, compared to a unit cost of around $20-$30 million for a late-model F-16C/D variant) and the eventual dropping off of the Soviet sea-borne threat, the F-2 series is serving Japan well and will probably serve until 2030 when the next-generation of indigenous Japanese 'stealth' fighter enters service.

With the Japanese being unable to tout the F-2 to any foreign power, it was left to the JASDF to be the customer for potential improved versions. These included an F-2 Super Kai, with advances similar to that of the Block 50/52+ and Block 60 F-16s. That meant advanced targeting/navigation pods, conformal fuel tanks and a helmet-mounted sight as well as the potential for a 'big spine' dorsal avionics hump. Another version mooted featured an F-2 with a higher-powered version of the F-110 engine.

Neither upgrades were forthcoming, but what is happening with the current fleet of F-2s are upgrades to the aircraft's air-to-air role. These include data-link upgrades, a new radar variant – the J/APG-2 – use of advanced air-to-air missiles such as the AAM-4 (similar to the US AMRAAM but the first AAM to use its own Active Electronically Scanned Array – AESA – radar) and the short-range AAM-5 infrared missile, which uses thrust-vectoring and is therefore highly agile.

Such air-to-air upgrades are useful, as while the sea-borne threat from the Soviets have reduced, Russian Air Force fighters and bombers have once again been pushing the boundaries of Japanese airspace in recent years. F-2s have been used alongside the F-15CJ Eagles to protect Japanese airspace time and again.

ABOVE: ***The Lavi was an ambitious – but ultimately extremely costly programme.***

RIGHT: ***The Lavi would have flown operationally with largely Israeli developed systems.***

A licence-production version of the Fouga Magister was the first such product, but the issue with the undelivered Mirages prompted IAI into action. Using espionage, Israel obtained plans for the Mirage V and its Atar 9C powerplant from Swiss engineer Alfred Frouenknech. The first Mirage copy – called the IAI Nesher – first flew in September 1969 and the first production machine was delivered to the IAF in May 1971. Production lasted until 1978 when an improved version, powered by the General Electric J-79 engine which powered the F-4 Phantom, entered service. This machine was called the Kfir – or Lion Cub.

By the 1970s Israel knew it could prove costly to rely on any one nation for arms, so it embarked on an ambitious plan to develop its own lightweight fighter, to be called the IAI Lavi – or Young Lion. This would be a fighter-bomber to directly replace the Kfir and older F-4E and A-4 airframes in IAF service. Former Israeli defence minister Moshe Arens, who was also a vice president of IAI explained the primary reason for the need for an indigenous fighter aircraft. He said: "This would be a machine exclusive to Israel's inventory, unlike advanced US aircraft, which are found in other Middle Eastern air forces." Israel estimated that development costs would be $750 million and that each Lavi would cost $7 million to manufacture.

The announcement came in 1979 that the Lavi programme would go ahead with the launch in February 1980. By that time the Israeli Air Force had the most

The Mitsubishi F-1 served Japan well until 2006.

combat experience of any air-arm – it had after all been fighting for its very survival since 1948 – so the aerospace industries of the world were intrigued to see what sort of machine Israel would develop. Of course, by now the General Dynamics F-16 Fighting Falcon had entered service with the USAF and a number of European air forces and the IAF had also received its first Falcons in 1980, so it was going to be interesting to compare the two aircraft.

Initially the Lavi was intended as a close air support and battlefield interdiction machine, with a secondary role of air-to-air. Coming in single and two seat variants, the two-seater was going to be a conversion trainer and be fully combat capable. In the light attack role the Lavi was intended to replace the existing IAI Kfirs, the ageing McDonnell-Douglas A-4 versions used in the IAF and the F-4E – which itself was going to be subject of an upgrade as the Kurnass 2000.

The Lavi was initially going to be powered by the General Electric F-404 turbofan, which was just coming into service with the F/A-18 Hornet and (in its licence-produced Volvo RM12 guise) the later SAAB Gripen. This engine was developed from the F-17's YJ-101 and in its F-404 form had a maximum thrust of 11,000lb in military power and 17,700lb in afterburner as well as all the carefree handling that a modern engine provided. The engine seemed a good choice, but was considered to not have as much future growth potential as the more powerful Pratt & Whitney PW-1120. Ironic looking back, as future versions of the F-404 power both the Gripen and the Super Hornet.

This two-seat F-2B shows the very similar shape to the Lockheed Martin F-16.

Not only was the F-16 constantly developed over more than four decades, it also spawned a number of similar designs: some made with the help of Lockheed Martin and some without.

The PW-1120 was a development of the F-100 which was in service with both the F-15 Eagle and the original F-16 A and B Fighting Falcons. Following its adoption in the Lavi project in June 1980, much of the PW-1120 was straight from the F-100 – it offered 70% commonality with the earlier engine. Unique PW-1120 components included a wide chord low pressure compressor, single-stage uncooled low pressure turbine, simplified single stream augmentor and a light-weight engine nozzle. Testing began in 1982 with flight-testing beginning in 1984. Plans were in hand to licence-build the engine in Israel itself. The PW-1120 was tested in a Phantom airframe, not just for Lavi development but because the PW-1120 was also slated for use in the Super Phantom or Kurnass 2000 project, where elderly F-4Es were to be improved with modern avionics and systems and a new powerplant to replace the smoky GE J-79s. For its use in the Lavi, the PW-1120 produced around 14,000lb of thrust in military power and 20,500lb in full afterburner.

In 1982 the whole concept of the aircraft changed considerably. Yitzhak Rabin, then Israeli Defence Minister said: "The aircraft was changed to a high performance fighter-bomber capable both ➤

The anti-ship mission was a key part of the F-2's development.

of close support and of air defence and air superiority missions." Apparently he was behind the change, demanding a machine that was more capable. He said to IAI: "If you want to develop this aircraft, make it better than what we have now." Moshe Arens apparently agreed, stating that: "The original concept of an A-4 replacement was an unusual one and not very good. It would have had to be cancelled sooner because it would not have been a survivable aircraft."

To become more capable meant that the Lavi began putting on weight and became more of a rival to the IAF's own F-16 fleet and the McDonnell-Douglas F-18, something the Americans who were selling them wouldn't really like. In October 1982 maximum take-off weight of the Lavi was supposedly 37,400lb (17,000kg), but soon this crept up.

RIGHT: The F-2 used the first ever fully carbon composite wing – which was larger than the F-16's.

BELOW: Developing the F-2A/B has led to unit cost being many times that of the F-16.

FALCON FACTS

F-16 Fighting Falcon it may be, but around the world it is also: Netz, Barak, Sufa, KF-16 and Jastrzab (Hawk) in Poland!

A full-scale mock-up of the Lavi was shown in 1985 with the first Lavi (B-01) flying at the end of December 1986, by IAI chief test pilot Menachem Schmul, who described the handling of the Lavi as excellent. The second machine flew in March 1987 – both these first machines were two-seaters. More than 80 flights were made with the two prototypes and it had flown at speeds in excess of Mach 1 and at angles of attack up to 23°. The third, fourth and fifth Lavi prototypes would be fitted with the definitive wing, the mission avionics and other production items. But by the end of August 1987 the Lavi programme was cancelled when the Israeli cabinet voted 12 to 11 – with one abstention in favour of ceasing development of the aircraft.

So why was the Lavi programme cancelled? As usual it was a mixture of high cost and politics. The United States initially supported the project and was willing to allow Israel to use its foreign military sales (FMS) credits to buy US components for the Lavi – of which there were many. Apparently more than $2 billion of US aid and technology transfer went into the Lavi project, with the US covering a huge percentage of the Lavi's development costs anything upwards of 40% of the programme, depending on what figures you read.

By 1983 these costs had rocketed up from $750 million in development and $7 million per aircraft to $1.5 billion and $15.5 million per Lavi – by the time the programme was cancelled the cost per aircraft was estimated to be in the region of $20 million. Both in the US and in Israel questions were being asked as to why so much money was being spent. In the USA it seemed as if the government was happier to spend money on a foreign plane than a US-built one. Meanwhile, in November 1986 Northrop cancelled the promising F-20 Tigershark development of the F-5E Tiger lightweight fighter thanks to a lack of orders from the USAF or US

The Mitsubishi F-2 will serve in strike and air defence roles until replaced by the F-35 and Japan's own fifth-generation fighter.

The Japanese are rightly proud of having their own fourth-generation fighter aircraft.

The F-2 gives Japan a capable fourth-generation jet fighter which will stay in service until replaced by the F-35 and the country's own fifth-generation combat plane

Navy. More than a billion dollars was lost as well as 2000 American jobs.

In Israel itself, critics of the programme were defence chiefs who simply saw chunks of their precious defence budget being eaten away by an aircraft that wouldn't even be in service for the best part of a decade, this and an economic depression in 1985 didn't help matters in Israel. The truth was that Israel couldn't make the Lavi without US financial help and when US Congress withdrew that funding the writing was on the wall for the entire Lavi programme.

The legacy of the Lavi can still be felt today. Moshe Arens said of the cessation of the Lavi programme that it: "Sentenced IAI to remain a medium sized player in the global aerospace industry rather than fulfilling its potential of becoming a rival to Boeing, Lockheed, Grumman or General Dynamics." Certainly it had a seismic effect on those laid off at IAI when the project was terminated. Truth-be- ➤

SIMILAR SHAPES

With the F-2 being the nearest shape to the F-16 in the sky, what about other military machines that seem to have been inspired by Harry Hillaker's genius?

The AIDC F-CK-1 Ching-kuo is a mouthful and thankfully better known as the Indigenous Defence Fighter or 'IDF'. Designed initially as a response to the USA's refusal to sell either F-16s or F-20 Tigersharks to Taiwan's Air Force, the IDF made its first flight in 1989 and entered service in 1997.

The IDF was seen as a replacement for the fleet of Northrop F-5 and Lockheed F-104s and began development in 1982. Some co-operation and design consultation did come on the airframe from General Dynamics and this can clearly be seen on the IDF. The aircraft itself is a strange blend of F-20 Tigershark (nose) F-5 (small, twin engines, in this case the TFE 1042 based on a 'civilian' engine with around 9460lb of thrust each) and F-16 (blended wing/body, single tail) and cheek intakes almost reminiscent of Dassault's later Rafale fighter. The IDF was designed as an inherently unstable aircraft with a full fly-by-wire system.

The radar in that F-20-esque nose was in fact based heavily on the APG-66/67/68 units seen in the F-16/F-20 family, albeit using a larger antenna that that seen on the F-20 Tigershark. Performance-wise the IDF is a bit of a mystery although it is clearly superior to both the F-5 and F-104 it largely replaced. Upgrades have included a digital cockpit with large multi-function screens, more powerful flight control computers and updated countermeasures as well as increased internal fuel capacity.

Politics has hampered the IDF's own sales at home. Initially 250 were to be ordered, but Taiwan and the USA finally reached an agreement in 1992 over the sale of 150 F-16A/Bs to the country. Added to this was the purchase by Taiwan of 60 French Mirage 2000-5s. This meant just 130 production IDFs were built, the last being delivered in early 2000. Around half of these received the upgrades which were complete by around 2012.

Another, smaller 'F-16 shape' is the KAI FA-50 Golden Eagle from the Republic of Korea.

Samsung Aerospace had been licence-building the F-16 for years and needed a modern, combat-capable lead-in-trainer to replace a number of types in the Republic of Korea's Air Force. In 1992 work began on a supersonic, tandem-seat design alongside Lockheed/GD, and Samsung Aerospace had joined with other South Korean aerospace companies to form Korea Aerospace Industries or KAI. Full-scale development began in 1997 after the Republic of Korea's government gave the go-ahead. The first flight took place in 2002.

The basic design of the resulting T-50 is so clearly a child of the F-16's airframe, albeit an 80% scale model of one and with touches from the F/A-18 Hornet (LERX or Leading Edge Root Extensions) and side/cheek mounted engine inlets. Versions include an Advanced Trainer and a Lead-in fighter/Light Attack version.

A number of air forces use the T/TA-50, including Indonesia, the Royal Thai Air Force and the Iraqi Air Force while a version has been put forward for the USAF's T-X programme, which would see the replacement of the aging Northrop T-38 Talon fleet.

The F-2 uses an extended-tail braking parachute system akin to some F-16 models.

***ABOVE:** The closest F-2A is configured for the anti-ship mission, the other air-to-air.*

***RIGHT:** Licence production of the F-16 means KAI learnt many techniques and design methods.*

told, while it would be hard to see such a small nation being able to manufacture such an advanced warplane, the fact that Israel already had produced machines of the potency of the Kfir and that Sweden is in the modern fighter arena with the Gripen, shows what could have been.

The production run of the Lavi was supposed to be around 300 airframes, to be delivered from 1990 with a full in-service operational date of around 1992. Twelve aircraft a month would come off the IAI lines and the Lavi was going to be the backbone of the IAF in that decade and possibly beyond, when one considers airframe updates and weapon upgrades. Instead of the Lavi, extra F-16 and F-15s were ordered, ironically in the forms that were initially refused by the US government.

Today the Lavi would still be in service in some form or other. Perhaps the current Lockheed Martin F-16I Sufa gives some clue as to what shape the Lavi would have today? Certainly the Israelis and IAI have learned much in the development of the Lavi which has filtered through in some way to today's F-16 fleet in the IAF.

LAVI VERSUS F-16

It's always going to be the way that the Lavi was compared to the F-16 as there were some similar design traits. In essence though, the Lavi was smaller and lighter than the General Dynamics F-16, with initially a less powerful powerplant, meaning the resultant thrust-to-weight ratio was slightly lower. Unlike the F-16 with its traditional tail section, the Lavi's configuration was that of a tailless canard delta, although the wing was unusual in having shallow sweep on the trailing edge. The wingtips – like that of the F-16 – were fitted with missile rails to aid combat persistence.

The wing area was 38.50 square metres, 38% greater than the wing area of the F-16, giving an almost exactly proportionally lower wing loading, while the control system was relaxed static stability and quadruplex fly-by-wire (FBW), with no mechanical backup. The Lavi was a very unstable aircraft – even compared to an F-16 – so like the Viper the computers were what kept the Lavi in the air.

One very similar design feature was the engine intake, which was a plain chin type scoop, similar to that of the F-16, which was known to be satisfactory at high angles of attack. The sharply swept vertical tail, effective at high angles of attack due to interaction with the vortices shed by the canards, was mounted on a spine on top of the rear fuselage, and supplemented by the two steeply canted ventral strakes, mounted on the ends of the wing root fillets.

Normally jet fighters are designed as

single-seaters first and then a two-seater – with the second seat taking away either avionics or fuel. IAI designed the two-holer first, allowing the spare room to allow for any future avionics fit – they did after all use the 'camel hump' models of the McDonnell-Douglas A-4. IAI learned lessons well. Internal fuel capacity was 3330 litres around 16% less than the F-16 although figures show that this was offset by the Lavi's lower drag and the better fuel consumption of the PW-1120.

Like the F-16 the Lavi had a blown, wraparound bubble canopy. The cockpit itself dispensed with the F-16's sidestick controller, as IAI wanted a more traditional, centrally mounted one. It's thought that feedback from pilots in combat led to a worry about what would happen to a Lavi or F-16 pilot if their right arm or hand was injured. With a right-hand-side sidestick controller fitted, the left hand could not easily take control and fly the aircraft back to base.

A sidestick controller also meant less console space on the right-hand console. The Lavi also had an upright seat, rather than the raked F-16's ejection seat, due to IAF pilots often complaining of neck strain while scanning the sky in an F-16. Otherwise the Lavi cockpit was of the time – benefitting from HOTAS or 'hands on throttle and stick' controls, a Hughes wide-angle HUD or head-up-display and colour and black and white head-down displays.

In the nose of the Lavi would be the Elta EL/M-2035 multi-mode pulse Doppler radar. Developed from that in the Kfir-C2, it was an advanced set for the day, which could track several targets at once with boresight, look-up and track while scan modes. It had two air-to-ground modes and ground mapping and terrain avoidance. Also as part of a standard fit was the Elta/Elistra Electronic Warning System which could work in both passive and active modes. Carried internally, this could be backed up with podded electronic counter measure pods and jammers.

The weapons to be carried on the Lavi were standard for the IAF of the time. As well as underwing fuel tanks, the internal cannon was from the trusted DEFA company of 30mm calibre, capable of up to 1500 rounds per minute and housed in the right wing-root. Israeli pilots had come to trust the DEFA cannons from the Dassault Mystere of the 1950s, through to the Mirage and even had them fitted on American A-4 Skyhawks rather than the 20mm Colt Mk.12s. Air-to-air armament was to be the Rafael Python 3 infrared homing short-range dogfight missile. Air-to-ground weapons would include the dumb Mk.80-series freefall bombs, the Hughes AGM-65 Maverick family of missiles, the IAI Gabriel anti-ship missile and the IAI Popeye air-to-ground missile.

Some experts feel that the performance of the IAI Lavi would be broadly comparable to today's F-16C/D in most departments and maybe even superior in some. Like the canard foreplanes fitted to the likes of the Eurofighter Typhoon and the SAAB Gripen, control authority of unstable aircraft is better than that of a conventional tailed machine, meaning that the Lavi would supposedly be quicker into a turn than an F-16. Those that flew the Lavi heaped praise on its agility and power.

Today the Lavi is almost a memory. Prototypes B-01, 04 and 05 were sold for scrap. B-02 is on display at the IAF Museum in Hatzerim. B-03 was flying into the 1990s as a demonstrator in support of IAI's advanced fighter aircraft and cockpit technology programmes. There were also rumours that one aircraft was delivered to South Africa in the early 1990s or that design cues were used on the Chinese Chengdu J-10 after technology was sold by Israel to China. This has been denied by both countries.

ABOVE: ***The T-50 is a flexible airframe, handling training duties and lead-in fighter training with ease.***

BELOW: ***Thailand, Iraq and Indonesia have ordered the T-50.***

The Viper today

So long and successful has the F-16 story become that some former 'enemies' such as former Warsaw Pact nation Poland have since become F-16 customers. This would never have been conceivable when the F-16 first flew in the 1970s.

With more than 4500 built over the last 43 years and still in service with 26 users, the F-16 is - nevertheless - entering the twilight of its career.

The General Dynamics/Lockheed Martin F-16 Fighting Falcon – the 'Viper' to most has been one of the greatest aviation successes of all time.

As it stands in 2017, the F-16 is the second most numerous military aircraft flying in the world today, after the Sikorsky S-70/UH-60 Blackhawk helicopter. With around 4573 built since 1974 and with more than 2700 still flying operationally today, the F-16 is the true successor to the McDonnell Douglas F-4 Phantom II family as the 'defender of the free world'.

The venerable F-4 was built in even more numbers (5195 is the accepted total) and is still in service with the air-forces of Iran, Japan, South Korea and Turkey – albeit in dwindling numbers – but with a few hundred airframes still in service as it approaches its 60th birthday, this points the way forward for the F-16 as it approaches its 45th anniversary.

Not only has the F-4 now been replaced by the F-16 in the QF target role in the USA, but around the world the elderly Rhino has been updated with more modern systems, been adapted to carry updated, fourth-generation weapons and has even been engaging the enemy in the fight against ISIS. Not bad for an old girl.

It also shows that in an uncertain world not many air forces will be able to meet the high costs of the next-generation of air combat fighters or may think they do not need the capabilities they offer. And while the F-35 Lightning II programme is as mature as it's ever ➤

FALCON FACTS

The gold-tint on the canopy on some F-16s helps reduce the aircraft's radar cross-section.

The currently offered F-16V 'Viper' Block 70 can be either a new-build aircraft or come in the form of an upgrade kit direct from Lockheed Martin

been and is finally entering service with the USA – after many ongoing and still 'current' issues – the prospects for continued use of the F-16 along with future upgrades look bright, even if it may be a case of Lockheed Martin hedging its bets.

The currently offered F-16V 'Viper' Block 70 can be either a new-build aircraft or come in the form of an upgrade kit direct from Lockheed Martin. Also likely would be future upgrades coming from the Israeli connection. With the second highest total of F-16s ordered and in service (after the USA) the Israeli Air Force has – from deliveries of the first F-16 Netz aircraft in 1980 – been looking at ways of adapting its own avionics and systems that have been born from its own combat experience with the aircraft. Israel's ➤

FROM ENEMY TO ALLY

It's the ultimate irony in a way that as it stands in mid-2017, the orders currently keeping the Lockheed Martin F-16 Fighting Falcon production line open come from Iraq.

It was in the skies above Iraq that – for the USAF at least – the F-16 Viper finally won its spurs, but post-Operation Desert Storm, post-Operation Iraqi freedom and – post-Saddam Hussein – the F-16 became the fighter of choice for the Iraqi Air Force.

With decades of French and Russian equipment, it would be the Block 52, Pratt & Whitney F-100-PW-229-powered F-16C/D – called the F-16IQ – that would bridge the technology gap and bring the Iraqi Air Force up to date. Or would it? The order was put in during 2011 for the Lockheed Martin aircraft and the option taken for yet more still, despite initial plans to reverse the order and push the money into much-needed economic reconstruction.

A total of 36 aircraft were eventually ordered: including 12 F-16D two-seaters with the enlarged avionics spine along with all the required support and weaponry, both air-to-air and air-to-ground, along with targeting pods and reconnaissance pods. The first aircraft was formally received on June 5, 2014, at Lockheed Martin's Fort Worth factory in Texas by Iraq's Ambassador to the US, Lukman Faily. Pilot training began in the US two years previously, sadly with one fatality occurring during 2015 when Iraqi Brigadier General Rasid Mohammed Sadiq crashed his F-16C in Arizona, during a night training mission.

While the specification of the airframes themselves is modern, the weaponry provided is a generation or so behind that of the aircraft themselves. Delivery to Iraq was made of Raytheon's AIM-9L/M Sidewinder short-range, infrared 'heat-seeking' air-to-air missiles, and AIM-7 Sparrow medium-range radar-guided air-to-air missiles. When you consider that the AIM-9L in its original form was used to great effect in the Falklands War by Royal Navy Sea Harriers back in 1982 and the Sparrow is more than a generation behind the AIM-120 Advanced Medium Range Air-to-Air Missile (AMRAAM), you begin to wonder whether it's akin to giving a fully-trained soldier a catapult. For air-to-ground, the deal did include the AAQ-33 Sniper targeting pod as well as AGM-65 Maverick missiles, Paveway laser-guided munitions and four Goodrich DB-110 recce pods, but still no up-to-date JDAM munitions.

It seems a typical US ploy, one to take the dollars, smile sweetly and yet supply downgraded equipment or not offer unique software codes for aircraft and equipment operation. In the air-to-air role especially, the AIM-9L/M and Sparrow loadout means that Iraqi pilots will lack the off-boresight capabilities of the AIM-9X or even some of the more modern Russian missiles, while the Sparrow needs constant illumination from the F-16IQ's radar to make a kill compared to the 'fire and forget', multi-target intercept capability of the AMRAAM. It's also thought that there is very tight control over certain areas of the avionics, including the APG-68 (V9) radar and the targeting pods. Conformal fuel tanks which considerably increase the range of the F-16IQs (by around 40%) have curiously been part of the deal, so the range of the F-16IQs has not been hamstrung.

Supplying the newly-rebuilt Iraqi Air Force has (it seems) been a very political statement, allowing it to combat only the threats that the US wants it to: not the likes of Israel, Saudi Arabia, Turkey or Jordan, but the F-16 was still a league above the Sukhoi Su-25 Frogfoots that had survived the previous wars with Iran and the US and its allies. With this in mind, the Iraqi Air Force has already employed its new mounts against the internal threat of ISIS.

In September 2015, Iraq used the F-16IQs against ISIS in a series of 15 air strikes where what was described as 'smart weapons' were employed against a range of targets in the Salaheddin and Kirkuk areas north of Baghdad.

ABOVE: **With the Thunderbirds having used the F-16 since 1982, it's been the best form of advertising.**

BELOW: **A posting to an F-16 cockpit is much sought-after – even today, 35 years since service introduction.**

BEN CABLE - A BRIT ABROAD!

During 2014, Flight Lieutenant Ben Cable from the Royal Air Force got to savour the raw power and performance of the Lockheed Martin F-16 as he engaged on an exchange posting with the USAF's 79th Fighter Squadron.

Growing up near Biggin Hill, in Kent, there was only going to be one thing on his mind: "I lived in a rich military area. During the Second World War, you would have been able to see planes fighting overhead and even aircraft that had been shot down in the field just down the road from where I lived. I loved watching the planes fly by and going to the air shows and was one of the few children who wouldn't cry when planes would fly by because of the noise!"

Following his heart, Cable joined the RAF and found himself in the seat of a Tornado GR4, making four combat deployments to Iraq and Afghanistan. These experiences would give him the experience needed for his exchange posting with the USAF and a coveted seat in the Lockheed Martin F-16CM Fighting Falcon.

Cable says: "I was deployed in combat when I found out I was going to be a part of the exchange programme. My commander walked in and casually said 'How would you like to be flying F-16s next summer?'"

How cool is that? Although cool would be the last thing on his mind. Despite postings abroad and combat in Iraq and Afghanistan, Cable was used to the more temperate climes of the UK bases where the Tornado was based. He took his young family to Luke Air Force Base in Arizona, ready for training on the F-16. "When we first got here we landed at Luke AFB, Arizona; I don't think I have ever been in such warm weather," he says, but soon he was learning to fly and fight in the F-16. "At first it was tough learning the inner workings of the F-16, but I had a lot of help, and I tried my hardest day-in and day-out."

Despite being a QWI (Qualified Weapons Instructor) with the RAF, learning a new aircraft and its associated weapons systems was tough for Cable, but flying between three to seven times a week, along with the associated planning and pre and post flight briefing soon had him up to speed. Along with being partnered with fellow 79th Fighter Squadron pilot Captain Craig Baker, who says: "Learning how to fly a new jet is a daunting task. Combine that with learning how to apply tactics, techniques and procedures to employ new mission sets and there is no doubt it's a steep learning curve. Even though Ben and I are both fighter pilots, the knowledge we have is different. The more we can work together in training, the better our interoperability will be during wartime: therefore, increasing the effectiveness of meeting national objectives."

Through team-work and his own application, Cable became assistant director of operations for the 79th FS before returning back to the RAF Tornado force.

'YOU CAN'T FLY ANY LOWER!'

With the advances that the F-16 brought to military aviation, came problems. One of which was G-LOC.

G-induced Lack of Consciousness became a big problem in a highly-agile fighter aircraft where 9g sustained turns were the order of the day. This and issues such as a loss of situational awareness led to many losses of aircraft.

These pictures show the HUD (head up display) of a USAF Arizona Air National Guard F-16 as its Auto-GCAS (Automatic Ground Collision Avoidance System) saves both the aircraft and pilot from a fatal crash. Recorded in 2016 it was thought that this was the fourth time that Auto-GCAS had saved a life and an aircraft.

The system itself was developed over many years, in conjunction with the Swedish Air Force and was adopted by the Block 40/50 F-16 fleet in 2014 as part of a flight control software update. The Auto-GCAS system was developed with the sole aim to reduce accidents where aircraft were lost during controlled flight into terrain by 90%.

Auto-GCAS continuously compares a predicted flight path of the aircraft and plots this against a terrain profile generated from data gathered from on-board the F-16 itself. If this trajectory touches the terrain profile then two chevrons in the HUD can be seen to come together and the auto-recovery takes over. This auto-recovery comes in the form of rolling the F-16 'right way up' if it's inverted, or banked and it's not a gentle manoeuvre, then a 5g automatic pull up is automatically initiated until the terrain has been cleared.

In these dramatic shots from the HUD video recorder, a student pilot has been engaging in Basic Fighter Manoeuvres but suffers G-LOC with the F-16 hitting 8.3g. With the pilot now just a passenger, the F-16 enters a steep dive in afterburner starting at an altitude of 17,000ft.

After 22 seconds, the F-16 is now travelling at supersonic speeds, nose down with almost 50° of dive. By now the instructor is beginning to shout to his student: "Two recover!" The F-16 now passes through 12,000ft and two seconds later speed is more than 600 knots (690mph) and in a 55° dive as the aircraft passes through 10,800ft. The instructor calls for the student to recover once more. At 26 seconds the instructor calls for recovery again, but this time the Auto-GCAS takes over. At 8760ft and at around 750mph the recovery begins.

Before recovery two chevrons appear in the HUD around five seconds before auto-recovery, warning the pilot that Auto-GCAS is about to take action. If none is taken the points on the chevrons meet in the centre of the HUD and a flashing 'BREAK X' symbol appears in the HUD along with an aural warning 'FLY UP, FLY UP' along with 'FLY UP' in the HUD.

With Auto-GCAS taking over, the student pilot comes round and pulls back on the stick, pushing the G-meter past the recovery level of 5 to 9.1g. By now altitude is around 4370ft with just around 2940 indicated on the radar altimeter. When the Auto-GCAS takes the aircraft above the threatening terrain the system disengages and says to the pilot: "You got it!" The time elapsed from the pilot's G-LOC to recovery has taken under 30 seconds. It saved this aircraft and the pilot.

During the test procedures for Auto-GCAS many different scenarios were tested. So, for example, if a pilot is in a climb to avoid terrain but there is insufficient power on the aircraft the system will also bark: "POWER, POWER" to the pilot.

Development of the Auto-GCAS system came about in the 1990s. During this time the USAF found they were losing around five aircraft per year in Controlled Flight into Terrain (CFIT) incidents, similar to those described above, meanwhile the Swedish Air Force had a rate twice that. Around 29 test flights in a modified F-16D validated the concept and during many of the test manoeuvres, recovery would be made with not too much room to spare, accurately summed up by the programme's Swedish motto: "Du Kan Inte Flyga Lagre", meaning 'You can't fly any lower!"

Since introduction across the USAF F-16 fleet in 2014 it's thought that at least four aircraft and associated aircrew have been saved.

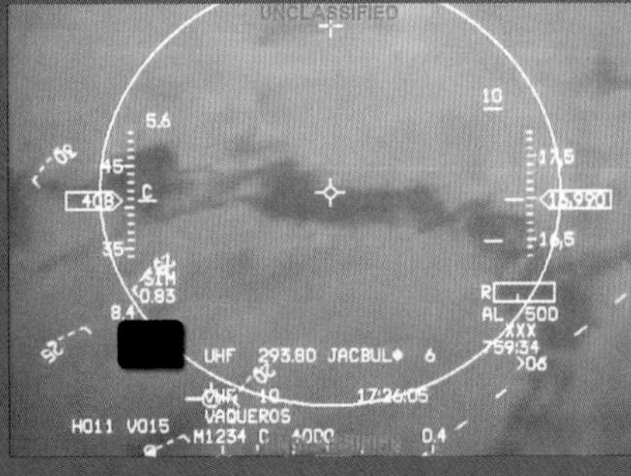

The student pilot has lost consciousness and the F-16 is headed straight down.

Still the F-16 is headed towards the terrain and building speed all the time.

Now the computer takes over – the two chevrons join and an audible and visual warning is shown.

Speed is still high but the AGCAS system begins to take over at just 4600 feet.

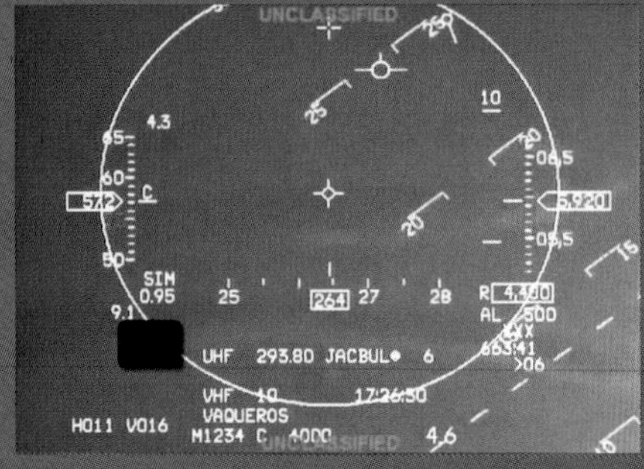

Around this time the pilot comes round and aids the computer's pull up of his aircraft resulting in a steep climb.

Pilot and plane are safe as the aircraft climbs through 10,000ft.

ABOVE: The F-16CM (seen here in 2017) will be the SEAD anti-SAM killer of choice until the F-35 is in widespread service.

BELOW: Chile shows that air forces around the world are still using and choosing the F-16 even when faced with more modern competition.

UCAV - THE FUTURE OF VIPER COMBAT?

Famous TOPGUN graduate and later instructor C J 'Heater' Heatley III was once interviewed for a documentary video which was coming hot on the heels of the success of a certain Paramount film starring Tom Cruise.

He was asked whether unmanned fighters would ever fill the sky in any future war. He shrugged: "Even Star Wars has a man in the cockpit…"

Even when he answered this question in the mid-1980s, unmanned vehicles had shown their worth. For the US, the use of the ubiquitous AQM-34 Ryan Firebee drone during Vietnam had shown the importance that these vehicles could have in the reconnaissance role – especially in a high-threat environment. The battle-hardened Israelis have also been using UAVs (Unmanned Aerial Vehicles) since the 1970s, with their use in the Bekaa Valley during the 1982 Lebanon War being particularly effective. During combat, IAI Mastiff UAV/RPV (Remote Pilotless Drones) using real-time surveillance equipment would relay information back to manned strike aircraft as well as helping to act as radar decoys.

Things have come a long way since the early 1980s and a number of air forces employ UAV/UCAV (Unmanned Combat Aerial Vehicles) not only in recce roles but to employ smart weaponry. Both politically and from a threat perspective it can make sense to employ a drone rather than manned military aircraft and the latest developments could see the use of F-16 airframes in this arena.

In April of 2017 the USAF and Lockheed Martin put on a test which showed the potential of teaming-up both manned and unmanned air assets as part of an integrated attack on a series of ground targets. Known as MUM-T (Manned/Unmanned Teaming) the Have Raider programme uses a QF-16 Fighting Falcon as a surrogate UCAV during strike missions.

Early testing was all about advanced machine control in a low-threat environment, while the April 2017 Have 2 tests at Edwards Air Force Base were two weeks of intensive demonstrations, showing how UCAVs could link in with manned assets and complete missions even when faced by changing threats, targets, route deviations, communications issues and enemy air defence assets trying to bring them down. A Lockheed Martin spokesman said: "During the flight demonstration, an experimental F-16 aircraft acted as a surrogate UCAV autonomously reacting to a dynamic threat environment during an air-to-ground strike mission."

The programme has been impressive and may be seen as the ultimate expression of the F-16 airframe in any future high-threat combat scenario. The plan would be for more-stealthy aircraft such as the Lockheed Martin F-35 to employ UCAV F-16s as 'Loyal Wingmen' to saturate any defences, while the stealthy, lead aircraft avoids contact with the enemy as much as it can. This makes the use of the F-16 as a UCAV a different proposition from the USAF's use of existing drones, like the MQ-1 Predator and MQ-9 Reaper.

aircraft industries have also long been making a good living upgrading aircraft even their own air force has never flown.

In 1987 General Dynamics was building one F-16 a day. This trickled down to just 17 F-16s in the whole of 2014 and just 11 during the whole of 2015. By the end of 2017 it's possible that the final 'new build' F-16 (for the Iraqi Air Force) could be delivered, but that will still leave the slightest chance that other orders could be forthcoming for F-16 variants such as the F-16V Block 70, based on the Block 60 E/F Desert Falcons, with (at time of writing) a number of air forces still looking at new-build F-16s as an answer to their air defence. It could still be that we head towards 2020 with F-16s continuing to roll off a production line somewhere around the world.

What will happen is that – in a similar fashion to the Fairchild Republic A-10 – without a real replacement for the sort of 'down and dirty' work the likes of the F-16 does and does well, the likelihood is that the F-16 will soldier on, possibly until as late as 2050 thanks to a wide-range of upgrades. Think about that: this would mean the F-16 could still be a viable air combat aircraft 76 years since the aircraft's first flight. The SLEP (Service Life Extension Programme) was announced ➤

BELOW: The F-16 may have developed lumps and bumps and changed immeasurably beneath the skin, but the original design is still there.

HIGH-HOUR VIPER PILOT

More than 6000 Viper hours: Mike Brill.

With the long service of the F-16 in the USAF and other air forces, it's little wonder that a number of pilots would become 'high milers' in the Viper community.

The undisputed number one is Lieutenant Colonel Mike Brill, but then he's been breaking records for a while. While other pilots move to desk jobs to move up the career ladder, Mike just wanted to fly. In 1993 he became the first pilot to fly 3000 hours in the F-16, following this up by breaking the 4000 hour barrier in August 1998. By November 2002 he broke the 5000 hour barrier and pushed through the 6000 hour barrier while serving with the 421st Expeditionary Fighter Squadron in 2008.

After breaking through 6000 hours, Brill said: "I was 30 miles north of Baghdad when I hit the 6000 hours but to me it was just another day in the office. I've been lucky, really. You need to have a passion for flying to continue to push yourself over the years, especially with long hours, days, weeks and months of deployments. I've flown the F-15 and the F/A-18 but the F-16 is to me a thoroughbred of them all as it has lots of thrust. The F-15 was always air-to-air, but for me the F-16 is a multirole and jack-of-all-trades so it's been a challenge to do that."

Brill first met the F-16 back in 1980 after graduating from the Air Force Academy in 1979. He went to Hill Air Force Base in Utah and began his training on the 'Electric Jet' and over the years he served across the globe, eventually becoming a full-time reservist. In his time he's taken part in many combat tours – including one 10-hour mission which was one of the first strikes inside Afghanistan following the September 11th attacks on New York which he describes as 'an eye-opener'.

So what have been the big changes in the F-16 community? He says: "The advances in the weapons we carry have had the biggest impact on how we employ. Things like night vision goggles and data link have enhanced our ability to fly in poor weather and at night, but the precision munitions have completely changed how we do business.

"With dumb bombs, we flew at low altitude or in packages of 20-30 aircraft. Now we fly as two-ships at medium altitude. And then there's training. There is now 10 times the amount of pre-mission study and planning we did before. The missions and attack profiles are so complicated that guys will have to do hours of study, where before we only looked at an attack for a couple minutes. We used to fly with one or two pieces of paper that had all our mission data. Now we literally have books of data that we fly with."

Brill knows just what the F-16 is and how it will be remembered. He says: "The F-16 still files the same as it did back in 1980 and will be remembered as one of the best fighters ever produced. It will be in the same class as the P-51 Mustang. I was extremely lucky to be able to fly it for so many years. The 419th was on the leading edge the whole time. We had so many firsts it's impossible to credit it all to luck. The great people we have had and the hard work they put in made us one of the premier wings in the world.

"The fact that I flew more than 6000 hours of incident-free flying is a testament to an amazing machine and our dedicated maintenance support airmen. I've never even blown a tyre on landing. I've had 6000 pretty uneventful hours but then everything we do in the USAF is a team effort. There's just something about me and the airplane. It's almost like when you have a horse and a rider and you stop being two separate bodies and become a single entity. Sometimes I get a sixth sense the airplane would never do anything to hurt me."

Brill would go on to break the 6300 hour barrier – that's the equivalent of spending 263 days in the air. Now, for tanker or cargo pilots – that's nothing – but for a fighter pilot with much shorter missions, that's something very special.

FALCON FACTS

Tests have shown up to 90 years of use could be had from an F-16 airframe: with numerous upgrades, of course...

The UAE's Block 60s could yet pave the way for more orders in the future. Many air forces will not be able to afford fifth-generation fighters and the F-16's adaptable airframe could still adopt modern and future avionics and sensors.

BELOW: Along with Israeli Sufas, the UAE's Block 60s are the most modern and capable F-16s in service. This E-model from 1 Squadron is seen in 2016.

ABOVE: With the QF-16 drones flying for many years (here in NULLO) or 'Not Under Live Local Operation' flight, perhaps fleets of unmanned F-16s will act as wingmen for fifth-generation fighters in future conflicts?

Mike Brill takes off on a combat mission

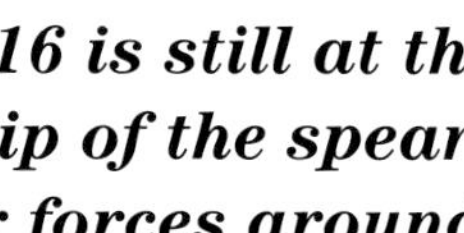

The F-16 is still at the very tip of the spear for air forces around the world. The Viper story goes on...

in mid-2017 and features a range of both structural and avionics upgrades. In a press release the USAF said: "Following F-16 Service Life Extension Program (SLEP) structural modifications, the US Air Force could safely operate F-16C and D Block 40-52 aircraft to 2048 and beyond, extending the each airframe's life by another 4000 hours of use."

This is good news not just for the USAF, which would look at putting around 300 of its F-16s through the SLEP, but for the many foreign operators of the F-16. This, allied to the F-16V upgrades which give it abilities similar to more modern opponents. The F-16 has – after all – beaten '4.5 generation' aircraft such as the Eurofighter Typhoon and the Dassault Rafale in competition and even (allegedly) given the F-35 Lightning II a bloody nose in close-in air combat during exercises.

Modern avionics, trickling down from advanced programmes such as the F-22 and F-35 – not to say about what may come along in the future – will keep the Fighting Falcon as a viable fighter aircraft for some decades to come. That's a helluva testament to how 'right' General Dynamics got the original design.

The story of the Viper may have changed from it being a simple air defence fighter, armed with just two missiles and a cannon and it has slipped from being right at the very cutting edge of technology and fighter design, but the F-16 is still at the very tip of the spear for air forces around the world. The Viper story goes on...

Display F-16 Airframes

BELGIUM
F-16A
- FA-01 – On display at the Royal Museum of the Armed Forces and Military History in Brussels, Belgium.
- FA-55 – On display at the Chateau de Savigny-les-Beaune in Beaune, France. A former Belgian Air Force example.
- FA-113 – On display at Beauvechain Air Base.

GERMANY
F-16A
- 78-0057 – Pylon display at Spangdahlem AB, Germany.

ISRAEL
F-16A
- F-16A Netz 107 – on display at the Israeli Air Force Museum in Hatzerim Airbase, Beer Sheva. This F-16 was credited with 6.5 shot-downs of enemy aircraft and took part in Operation Opera in which the Iraqi nuclear reactor was destroyed.

JAPAN
F-16A
- 78-0053 – Pylon display at Misawa AB, Japan.

PORTUGAL
F-16A
- 15150 – On display at Monte Real Air Base, Portugal.

THE NETHERLANDS
F-16A
- J-215 of the RNLAF on display at the National Military museum at former airbase Soesterberg.

TURKEY
F-16C
- 89-0032 – F-16C Block 40A at Istanbul Aviation Museum.

UNITED STATES
YF-16
- 72-1567 – Virginia Air and Space Centre, Hampton, Virginia.

YF-16B
- 75-0752 – Frontiers of Flight Museum, Dallas, Texas.

F-16A
- 75-0746 – Pylon-mounted gate guard, McEntire Air National Guard Base, South Carolina.
- 75-0748 – Cadet Area Quadrangle, US Air Force Academy, Colorado.
- 75-0750 – On display at the Experimental Aircraft Display Hangar, National Museum of the United States Air Force, Wright-Patterson AFB, Ohio.
- 78-0001 – Langley AFB Memorial Park, Langley AFB, Virginia. First production model F-16A delivered to USAF.
- 78-0005 – 162d Fighter Wing Park, Tucson Air National Guard Base, Arizona.
- 78-0025 – Gate guard, Burlington Air National Guard Base, Vermont.
- 78-0042 – Gate guard, Montgomery Air National Guard Base/ Dannelly Field, Alabama.
- 78-0052 – Eielson AFB Heritage Park, Eielson AFB, Alaska.
- 78-0059 – Selfridge Military Air Museum and Air Park, Selfridge ANGB, Michigan.
- 78-0065 – 388th Fighter Wing and 419th Fighter Wing combined Headquarters, Hill AFB, Utah.
- 78-0066 – On display in Kansas Air National Guard Memorial Park area, McConnell AFB, Kansas.
- 79-0290 – On display at Great Falls Air National Guard Base, Montana.
- 79-0296 – Gate guard, Jacksonville Air National Guard Base, Florida.
- 79-0307 – On display at Cannon AFB Air Park, Cannon AFB, New Mexico.
- 79-0309 – Base park area adjacent to USAFCENT Headquarters, Shaw AFB, South Carolina. Painted as 20th Fighter Wing F-16C 93-0534. Memorial to Major Brison Phillips, 20 FW, killed on March 19, 2000, while flying F-16C 93-0534.
- 79-0312 – On pylon display, 8th Street Park, Douglas, Arizona.
- 79-0326 – Gate guard, Homestead Air Reserve Base, Florida.
- 79-0327 – Pedestal mounted memorial, Luke AFB, Arizona. Painted in 302d Fighter Squadron markings, to include Second World War Tuskegee Airmen 'Red Tails' empennage.
- 79-0334 – USS Alabama Battleship Memorial Park, Mobile, Alabama.
- 79-0337 – Ground-mobile static display aircraft, normally located at Hancock Field Air National Guard Base, New York. Utilized by New York Air National Guard's 174th Attack Wing (former 174th Fighter Wing) at fairs and expositions for Air National Guard recruiting.
- 79-0352 – On static display with 23d Wing at Moody AFB, Georgia.
- 79-0366 – Memorial park static display, Mountain Home AFB, Idaho.
- 79-0373 – On display at Buckley AFB, Colorado. Aircraft painted in markings of Colorado Air National Guard's 140th Fighter Wing based at Buckley AFB.
- 79-0388 – Hill Aerospace Museum, Hill AFB, Utah.
- 79-0402 – Hill Aerospace Museum, Hill AFB, Utah.
- 79-0403 – Intrepid Sea, Air & Space Museum, New York City, New York.
- 80-0481 – Display on Parade Ground, Sheppard AFB, Texas.
- 80-0527 – Former Arizona Air National Guard 162d Fighter Wing aircraft destined for transfer to/ display at the Pima Air and Space Museum, Tucson, Arizona.
- 80-0528 – City park in Pinellas Park, Florida. Painted in markings of 56th Tactical Training Wing-cum-56th Fighter Wing, previously assigned to nearby MacDill AFB in the 1980s and early 1990s.
- 80-0573 – Air Force Armament Museum, Eglin AFB, Florida.
- 80-0612 – Memorial park static display at Puerto Rico National Guard's Camp Santiago, Salinas, Puerto Rico. Former Puerto Rico Air National Guard F-16ADF, painted in markings of PRANG's former 198th Fighter Squadron, but marked as 81612.
- 81-0663 – On display in United States Air Force Thunderbirds markings at the National Museum of the United States Air Force, Wright-Patterson AFB, Dayton, Ohio.
- 81-0676 – Museum of Aviation, Robins AFB, Warner Robins, Georgia.
- 81-0721 – MacDill AFB Memorial Park, MacDill AFB, Florida. Former Florida Air National Guard 125th Fighter Wing F-16ADF repainted in markings of a 56th Fighter Wing F-16A previously assigned to MacDill in the 1980s.
- 81-0807 – On display at Minnesota Air National Guard Museum, Saint Paul, Minnesota.
- 82-0926 – On display at Fargo Air National Guard Base, Fargo, North Dakota.
- 82-0930 – On display at Ellington Field Joint Reserve Base, Houston, Texas.
- On display at Naval Aviation Station Wildwood Museum in Cape May, NJ 08204.

F-16B
- 78-0088 – On display at the Naval Air Station Wildwood Aviation Museum, Cape May County Airport, New Jersey.
- 78-0101 – On display at United States Space Camp / Aviation Challenge, Huntsville, Alabama.
- 78-0107 – On display adjacent to Parade Ground, Lackland AFB, Texas.
- 79-0430 – Stafford Air & Space Museum, Weatherford, Oklahoma.
- 80-0633 – Yanks Air Museum, Chino, California.
- 81-0816 – Pylon display gate guard, Atlantic City Air National Guard Base, New Jersey.
- 81-0817 – Russell Military Museum, Russell, Illinois.

F-16C
- 83-1126 – Pylon display at Hill Memorial Park, Hill AFB, Utah.
- 84-1264 – Air park display, Fort Wayne Air National Guard Station, Indiana. Aircraft retains Air Force Heritage paint scheme honoring 358th Fighter Group during the Second World War.
- 84-1393 – Pylon display at Texas National Guard's Camp Mabry, Austin, Texas. Former Texas Air National Guard 147th Fighter Wing/111th Fighter Squadron aircraft.
- 85-1469 – Static display at Joe Foss Field Air National Guard Station, South Dakota.
- 87-0323 – Preserved as Thunderbird 1 in front of the USAF Air Demonstration Squadron/United States Air Force Thunderbirds hangar, Nellis AFB, Nevada. Assigned to Thunderbirds in the 1992-2008 timeframe. Had number 1 attached on June 11, 1999; number 2 in the 2004 season; number 3 on March 3, 2003, and number 4 on April 1, 2005.

F-16N
- 163269 – San Diego Air & Space Museum, San Diego, California.
- 163271 – Pacific Coast Air Museum, Santa Rosa, California.
- 163277 – Palm Springs Air Museum, Palm Springs, California.
- 163569 – NAS Fort Worth JRB, Fort Worth, Texas. It is painted in USAFR colors of the 457th FS, 301st FW.
- 163572 – National Naval Aviation Museum, Naval Air Station Pensacola, Pensacola, Florida.
- 163576 – Air Power Park, Naval Air Station Fallon, Nevada.